D1756464

University of Edinburgh

30150   025952729

Medieval Romance, Medieval Contexts

Studies in Medieval Romance

ISSN 1479–9308

Series Editors
Corinne Saunders

Editorial Board
Roger Dalrymple
Rhiannon Purdie
Robert Allen Rouse

This series aims to provide a forum for critical studies of the medieval romance, a genre which plays a crucial role in literary history, clearly reveals medieval secular concerns, and raises complex questions regarding social structures, human relationships, and the psyche. Its scope extends from the early Middle Ages into the Renaissance period, and although its main focus is on English literature, comparative studies are welcomed.

Proposals or queries should be sent in the first instance to one of the addresses given below; all submissions will receive prompt and informed consideration.

Professor Corinne Saunders, Department of English, University of Durham, Durham, DH1 3AY

Boydell & Brewer Limited, PO Box 9, Woodbridge, Suffolk, IP12 3DF

Previously published volumes in the series
are listed at the back of this book

Medieval Romance,
Medieval Contexts

Edited by

RHIANNON PURDIE AND MICHAEL CICHON

D. S. BREWER

First published 2011
D. S. Brewer, Cambridge

ISBN 978 1 84384 260 6

D. S. Brewer is an imprint of Boydell & Brewer Ltd
PO Box 9, Woodbridge, Suffolk IP12 3DF, UK
and of Boydell & Brewer Inc.
668 Mount Hope Ave, Rochester, NY 14604, USA
website: www.boydellandbrewer.com

The publisher has no responsibility for the continued existence or accuracy of
URLs for external or third-party internet websites referred to in this book,
and does not guarantee that any content on such websites is,
or will remain, accurate or appropriate.

A CIP catalogue record for this book is available
from the British Library

Papers used by Boydell & Brewer Ltd are natural, recyclable products
made from wood grown in sustainable forests

Printed and bound by the MPG Books Group

Contents

Acknowledgements

This volume developed from a selection of the forty-odd papers presented at the 11th Biennial 'Romance in Medieval Britain' conference hosted by the School of English at the University of St Andrews in March 2008: we extend our warm thanks to the School for its support. We are also very grateful to St Thomas More College in the University of Saskatchewan for their award of financial support towards the publication of this volume. We wish to thank Maha Kumaran for generous help in preparing the Index.

As always, we owe a debt of gratitude to our patient editor Caroline Palmer, the anonymous readers of the press for their input in shaping the volume, and to Boydell & Brewer's superb copy-editing team. We also wish to thank all of our contributors for their good-humoured willingness to align what were in some cases quite different papers with this volume's theme and focus.

Most importantly, we offer our heartfelt thanks to our respective families: Neale, Isaac and Russell; Lisa, Signy and Soren.

Rhiannon Purdie and Michael Cichon
St Andrews, Scotland, and Saskatoon, Canada

Contributors

Marianne Ailes is Senior Lecturer in French in the School of Modern Languages at the University of Bristol.

Nancy Mason Bradbury is Professor and Chair, Department of English Language and Literature, at Smith College in Northampton, Massachusetts.

Siobhain Bly Calkin is Associate Professor in the Department of English at Carleton University, Ottawa.

Michael Cichon is Associate Professor in the Department of English at St Thomas More College, University of Saskatchewan.

Rosalind Field is Emerita Reader in Medieval Literature at Royal Holloway, University of London.

John A. Geck is completing his doctoral thesis in Middle English romance at the Centre for Medieval Studies, University of Toronto.

Phillipa Hardman is Reader in Medieval English Literature in the Department of English Language and Literature at the University of Reading.

Yin Liu is Assistant Professor in the Department of English at the University of Saskatchewan.

Derek Pearsall is Gurney Professor of English, Emeritus, at Harvard University.

Nicholas Perkins is University Lecturer and Tutor in English at St Hugh's College, University of Oxford.

Rhiannon Purdie is Senior Lecturer in Medieval English in the School of English, University of St Andrews.

Robert Rouse is Associate Professor of English Literature at the University of British Columbia, Vancouver.

Judith Weiss is an Emerita Fellow of Robinson College, University of Cambridge.

Emily Wingfield is a Junior Research Fellow at Churchill College, University of Cambridge.

Abbreviations

ANTS	Anglo-Norman Text Society
BL	British Library, London
CUL	Cambridge University Library
EETS	Early English Text Society
	ES Extra Series; OS Original Series; SS Supplementary Series
EUL	Edinburgh University Library
MED	*Middle English Dictionary*, online at quod.lib.umich.edu/m/med/
NAS	National Archives of Scotland, Edinburgh
NIMEV	*A New Index of Middle English Verse*, ed. J. Boffey and A. S. G. Edwards (London, 2005)
NLS	National Library of Scotland, Edinburgh
STC	*A Short-Title Catalogue of Books Printed in England, Scotland, and Ireland, and of English Books Printed Abroad 1475–1640*, eds. A. W. Pollard et al., 2nd edn, 3 vols. (London, 1976–91)
STS	Scottish Text Society
Wing	*A Short-Title Catalogue of Books Printed in England, Scotland, Wales and British America and of English Books Printed in Other Countries 1641–1700*, rev. edn, ed. D. G. Wing (New York, 1972–88): CD-ROM, 1996.

Introduction: Romance and its Medieval Contexts

RHIANNON PURDIE and MICHAEL CICHON

No literature exists in a vacuum. Meaning is generated through context, or rather contexts, since there will always be several that apply at any one point and these will change and multiply over time. This is no less true of medieval romance than of any other genre of literature, and no single study is likely to address all of the relevant contexts for a genre as widespread and popular – in sheer numbers and variety of readers – as medieval romance. The aim of the present collection of essays is to take a selection of English and Scottish romances from the medieval period and explore some *medieval* contexts that might deepen our understanding of them. The contexts explored here include more traditional literary concerns with questions of genre and rhetorical technique or literary-cultural questions of authorship, transmission and readership, but they also extend to such broader intellectual and social contexts as medieval understandings of geography, or the physiology of swooning, or the efficacy of baptism. This is a two-way process: the romances studied here are illuminated by the various contexts in which the volume's contributors set them, but so too are those contexts enriched and altered by romance's interaction with them. The medieval audience for romance was relatively broad and varied: old and young, women and men, clerical and lay, nobility, gentry, merchants and those who could not afford – perhaps could not read – their own manuscript or print copy of a Middle English romance. This socially ubiquitous quality gives romances the potential to collect, encode and sometimes interrogate a similarly broad range of ideas and social concerns, as the following essays demonstrate.

The texts studied range from the very well known (Chaucer's *Troilus and Criseyde*, or *Guy of Warwick*) to those which have received scant critical notice, such as the Middle English fragment known as the *Song of Roland*, the late medieval Scottish romances of *Eger and Grime*, *Rauf Coilyear* and the *Buik of King Alexander the Conquerour*, or the entire field of thirteenth-century Anglo-Norman romance, almost squeezed out of the picture between the exciting birth of the genre in the preceding century, the launch of Middle English romance by the fourteenth century and the greater retrospective prestige of continental French literature generally. This is not a survey volume but an exploration of the arresting potential of reading medieval romances against a variety of medieval contexts.

A framing context for these essays is provided by Derek Pearsall's prefatory essay, 'The Pleasure of Popular Romance'. No student of medieval romance can move far without encountering Pearsall's work, and his 1965 article 'The Development of Middle English Romance' is perhaps the single most quoted article in the field (if not always approvingly these days, as Pearsall wryly observes).[1] His essay here is explicitly presented as a personal 'retraction'. It acknowledges the changes that have taken place in the study of medieval English romance over the past forty-odd years, and in partic-ular the decline in the importance attached to aesthetic evaluation and the correspondingly greater emphasis on historical and social contextualisation, both of the romances and their audiences. Returning finally to the idea of aesthetic evaluation, Pearsall calls for a new, more romance-relevant analysis of narrative structure and poetic form, with more attention to the function of standardised episodic form and formulaically repetitive style in relation to a listening audience: 'repetition of motifs, a common stock of language and metaphor and incident, fast pace, predictable outcome, are what is to be enjoyed in medieval popular romance – anathema to any form of post-medieval aesthetic.... All that needs to be done to release the energies of romance is to put these features at the centre rather than at the margins of our attention.'[2]

Nancy Mason Bradbury's essay begins the exploration of medieval contexts with a study of the literary expression of peasant identity in *Rauf Coilyear*, an unexpected thing to find in a genre normally defined by its near-exclusive focus on the opposite end of the social scale. The socially governed aspects of Rauf's use of language in his encounters with Charle-magne are thrown into relief by comparison with the Middle English prose *Dialogue of Solomon and Marcolf*. This comparison leads to a recognition of *Rauf Coilyear*'s exploitation of two literary subgenres, the proverb and the popular complaint or 'poem of social protest'. Bradbury demonstrates the surprising extent to which 'their represented speech makes use of recognis-able verbal genres, as opposed to ordinary, unstructured "talk"'[3] to construct this peasant identity.

The study of specific medieval literary contexts continues through the next three essays. Bradbury's focus on medieval conceptions of peasant identity and its relation to proverbial literature is complemented by Michael Cichon's study of proverbs in *Eger and Grime*. As Cichon notes, 'proverbs have tended to escape serious critical notice because of their simplicity and ring of cliché',[4] and yet romances are similar to proverbs in the way they function to reinforce social ties, beliefs, attitudes, values, fears and perceptions. Where Bradbury concentrates on their use in the construction of peasant identity, Cichon looks more broadly at the ways in which *Eger and Grime* 'deploys its traditional

---

1   *Mediaeval Studies* 27 (1965), 91–116.
2   'The Pleasure of Popular Romance', below, p. 11.
3   Bradbury, 'Representations of Peasant Speech', below, p. 22.
4   Cichon, 'Proverbial Context', below, p. 43.

paroemiological material to control audience response and to establish itself within a referential context wider than that normally associated – at least by modern readers – with medieval romance'.[5] Even (or perhaps especially) the most banal examples of proverbs and proverbial comparisons resonate with wider literary or cultural traditions, and it is this that allows them to work as a kind of embedded gloss on the narrative – explaining and justifying or, conversely, introducing shades of doubt and ambiguity.

A different technique for amplifying meaning is explored by Nicholas Perkins' study of the rhetorical figure of ekphrasis – the vivid description of things and actions – in the representative Middle English romances of *Emaré* and *Eglamour of Artois*. Ekphrasis, he argues, is the means by which romance interacts with material culture to generate meaning. Middle English romances are known and valued for their 'liveliness and brisk pace and sheer appetite for narrative';[6] rather less so for their rhetorical powers of description. Their characteristic fascination with luxury objects tends to be dismissed as mere surface decoration or a simplistic expression of social aspiration. Perkins offers a useful corrective here in stressing 'how natural was the integration of the visual and verbal/textual to a late-medieval public ... reminding us that certain contexts are neither easy nor necessarily productive to separate'.[7]

Where the first three papers dealt with juxtapositions, that of Marianne Ailes deals with an often confusing proximity: the genres of romance and *chansons de geste* in Anglo-Norman literature. *Otinel* and *La Destruction de Rome* have traditionally been categorised as *chansons de geste* while the *Roman de Horn* is assigned instead to the genre of romance. Ailes demonstrates that, despite their differing modern labels, all three texts inscribe their works carefully and consciously within a *chanson de geste* tradition. This is only to be expected in the case of the first two texts, which are both attached to continental *chanson de geste* cycles, but to move the purely insular narrative of *Horn* into this category is to recognise in Anglo-Norman literary culture a different, more creative kind of participation in the wider context of continental literary traditions.

Phillipa Hardman also explores generic identity, in this case that of the fragmentary Middle English *Song of Roland* (as its editorial title has it) in relation to both the French *Chanson* and the fragment's more immediate context – the local tradition of Middle English romance. Reading the *Song of Roland* within the latter context, rather than simply against the *Chanson de Roland*, Hardman demonstrates that this text is not an inept mishandling of the *Chanson* tradition written for a safely ignorant English readership, but a distinct, innovative treatment of the material which depends for its full effect on the audience's familiarity with the story. One is reminded of Pearsall's renewed appreciation of Middle English romance in his prefatory essay when

5 Cichon, 'Proverbial Context', below, p. 44.
6 Pearsall, 'The Pleasure of Popular Romance', below, p. 11.
7 Perkins, 'Ekphrasis and Narrative', below, p. 47.

she concludes: 'this version of the *Roland* legend can thus offer both the pleasure of recognition in the retelling of a familiar story, and the accompanying pleasure of difference, as the reader or listener becomes aware that new episodes and changed emphases are producing a fresh take on the story'.[8]

Hardman's probing of the validity of the identity given to a Middle English text by its modern editors shares similarities with the essay by John A. Geck. He also looks at insular English literature in relation to continental French traditions, although the focus of his study of the Middle English *Floris and Blancheflor* and its source, the Old French *Floire et Blanceflor*, is more precisely on the relationship of the Old French source to variants that occur across the manuscript tradition of the Middle English romance. He observes that although the Auchinleck manuscript version of the Middle English *Floris* is usually accorded the greatest textual authority by modern editors thanks to its closer agreement with the Old French, variants in the other three Middle English manuscripts work to present a heightened ambiguity in the presentation of Floris's faith throughout which parallels the much more obvious ambiguity in the presentation of his gender. This additional English highlighting of the themes of ambiguity and transgression is largely absent from the Auchinleck manuscript version which modern readers are likely to encounter in critical texts edited on a 'best-text' principle. Geck's analysis reaffirms the value of studying variation in a medieval romance's manuscript tradition, no matter how authoritative one version may seem. It also reconfirms the keen interest of the medieval English audience in questions of faith, an interest that will be brought to the fore in the essay by Calkin.

In the remaining essays by Calkin, Weiss, Rouse, Liu, Field and Wingfield, the volume shifts its focus from principally literary contexts to the interaction of romances with their wider social, intellectual and cultural surroundings. Siobhain Bly Calkin compares baptism scenes in the Middle English romances of *The King of Tars* and *Sir Ferumbras* to writings on baptism by such authorities as Thomas Aquinas or John Myrc, observing that 'although it is not particularly helpful to sift romance depictions of religious ceremonies for evidence about liturgical practices, it is intriguing to reverse the process and consider the ways in which romances engage the cultural ideas of their day'.[9] Her finely detailed study reveals that, where theologians emphasised the efficacy of the words of the baptism ceremony, romances instead 'suggest that physical acts, experiences and sights, not words, change religious identity', a surprising finding which, however, is entirely consistent with romances' 'artistic ability to translate emotional and mental states into physical actions'.[10] Calkin's analysis illustrates the ability of romances to

---

8   Hardman, 'Roland in England: Contextualising the Middle English *Song of Roland*', below, p. 104.
9   Calkin, 'Romance Baptisms and Theological Contexts in *The King of Tars* and *Sir Ferumbras*', below, p. 105.
10 Calkin, 'Romance Baptisms', below, pp. 108 and 119.

capture and transmit an aspect of medieval thinking on baptism not registered in the formal theological writings of the day.

Judith Weiss investigates another area of interaction between wider medieval learning and romance in her study of the controversial swoon of Troilus in Chaucer's *Troilus and Criseyde*. To interpret this action, she looks first to the literary context of swoons in a variety of Anglo-Norman and Middle English romances. She then tests the viability of the meanings imputed by modern readers to these literary swoons against medieval *medical* understandings of swooning: 'the latters' objective accounts and explanations of the phenomenon provide a welcome antidote to some of the twentieth- and twenty-first-century approaches adopted in recent studies of Chaucer's masterpiece'.[11] This study offers a particularly good example of how much would be lost if such robustly historicist approaches (whether New or Old) were to be abandoned in the modern criticism of medieval literature: the meanings attributed to the fainting heroes and heroines of romance by medieval authors and audiences are radically different from those generated by reading from within a modern cultural context, and the individual romances do not offer enough clues on their own as to how we might adjust our view.

With an amused nod to modern cultural contexts, Robert Rouse's essay offers to set medieval romances such as *Guy of Warwick* in the unexpected context of 'the aspirational reading of Lonely Planet guidebooks'.[12] He argues for the ability of romance to articulate geographical knowledge and provide its medieval readers with a context in which to understand the world. It is widely accepted that romances communicate moral values, social attitudes and even lessons in conduct, but Rouse demonstrates that they could both encode and influence more esoteric branches of knowledge too.

This idea of a two-way interface between medieval romance and other branches of knowledge is also at the heart of Yin Liu's essay, for which *Guy of Warwick* is again the catalyst. In this case, it is the interface between romance and genealogy which is put under the microscope as she studies the use made of *Guy of Warwick* by the fifteenth-century Warwickshire chantry priest, John Rous, in the preparation of armorial rolls for his patrons, the earls of Warwick. Rous's work is dismissed by modern historians thanks to his use of the romance *Guy of Warwick* as a source, but Liu carefully demonstrates how much more tightly interwoven were what we now label 'fiction' and 'history' in Rous's day: 'the fictionality of incendiary shields from heaven, tree-wielding giants, pilgrim-knights recognised only on their deathbeds, or – for that matter – Saxon earls bearing Norman coats of arms, would not have been obvious even to a scholar like John Rous, who had, after all, authorities like Geoffrey of Monmouth and artefacts like the Cup of the Swan to back

---

11 Weiss, 'Modern and Medieval Views on Swooning: the Literary and Medical Contexts of Fainting in Romance', below, p. 121.

12 Rouse, 'Walking (between) the Lines: Romance as Itinerary/Map', below, p. 135.

him up'.[13] This reminder of the difficulty of modern-style historical research in the medieval period – without the benefit of carbon-dating, palaeographic study or even, in some cases, records of any kind beyond the twin repositories of memory and imaginative literature – puts Rous's efforts to reconstruct Warwick family history into perspective. It also reframes the medieval relationship between historical writing and romance, granting the latter a far greater role: 'romance in the fifteenth century was not necessarily an escapist genre but directly relevant to immediate social and political concerns'.[14]

The complex web of relationships between medieval authors, patrons and texts remains the subject of the final two essays of this volume by Emily Wingfield and Rosalind Field. Wingfield's essay studies the relationship between the fifteenth-century Scottish *Buik of King Alexander the Conquerour* and the flamboyant late sixteenth-century owner of both its extant manuscripts, a Sir Duncan Campbell of Glenorchy who grandly described himself as 'the blakest laird in all þe land'.[15] His keen interest in all things Alexandrian (he also owned the only known fragment of the Alexander-cycle romance *Florimond of Albany*) suggests that he found pleasingly personal relevance in the romance's combination of advice to rulers with an exciting narrative of empire-building. Through a study of manuscript signatures and inscriptions combined with a survey of Campbell's other known books, Wingfield reconstructs the lively literary community in which the *Buik of King Alexander the Conquerour* was read in the late sixteenth century, over a century after its original composition.

Where the rest of the essays in this volume have tended to focus on one or two representative texts, Field's concluding essay raises questions about some fundamental aspects of Anglo-Norman romance as a whole, questions which are also relevant to romance in Middle English. She suggests that what she terms the 'chivalric glamour' of the noble patrons of medieval romance has distracted us from another agenda, that of the clerical bureaucrats, lawyers and churchmen engaged in an examination of rule and rights: 'any attempt to understand the position of the authors in their local and literary culture has to take into account this network; the picture of the household cleric in an isolated castle clobbering together a pedestrian narrative to entertain the family in the winter evenings is not adequate'.[16] Comparing the interaction between nobles and clerical writers in the creation of Anglo-Norman romance to the collaboration between these same two groups in the drawing up of Magna Carta, Field argues that the romances, too, are more concerned with matters of good government than with individual or dynastic ambition. She finishes by calling for the lessons of her study of Anglo-Norman clerical

13 Liu, 'Romances of Continuity in the English Rous Roll', below, p. 159.
14 Liu, 'Romances of Continuity', below, p. 159.
15 Edinburgh, NAS MS 112/22/2 (containing the fragment of *Florimond of Albany*), p. ii.
16 Field, '"Pur les francs homes amender": Clerical Authors and the Thirteenth-Century Context of Historical Romance', below, p. 180.

authorship to be applied to Middle English romance, where they may be used to break down the often unhelpful binary opposition in modern critical writing between 'courtly' and 'popular'.

All of the medieval contexts explored in this volume contribute something vital to our understanding of medieval romance, and the romances, in turn, inform our understanding of those same contexts. The medieval contexts for romance are of course not the only ones that signify: modern readers cannot pretend that they do not carry their own assumptions and beliefs with them even when they attempt to resituate a medieval text in some of its original medieval contexts. The self-awareness brought about by modern literary and historiographical theories can mediate this, but there are aspects of medieval texts that will remain stubbornly inaccessible in any context other than a medieval one. We hope that readers will find their understanding of the medieval romances discussed in this volume deepened by the various medieval contexts in which our contributors have set them.

1

The Pleasure of Popular Romance:
A Prefatory Essay

DEREK PEARSALL

This piece aims to provide a particular context for the essays that follow by revisiting an essay on Middle English popular romances that I published nearly fifty years ago.[1] It is an essay that has been frequently cited, though in a manner that is instructive of historical change. In early years, it was quoted with sometimes enthusiastic approval, but in recent years it has been increasingly singled out for criticism as an example of an outdated mode of approach. A recent scholar, writing on *Havelok*, is representative: she quotes one of the essay's many caustic criticisms of popular romance and says that it 'typifies an early tradition of reading romance as hack-work written for a peasant or bourgeois audience'.[2]

The ostensible point of the 1965 article was to provide a place for Middle English popular metrical romance in a formalist literary history, and to do so by concentrating on metre. The main body of Middle English metrical romance – the term 'metrical' being conventionally understood to exclude alliterative romance – was to be recognised, it was argued, as belonging to one of two significantly different metrical traditions, the one characterised by its use of the short octosyllabic couplet, the other by its use of tail-rhyme, in its various forms. The latter had been identified as a group and discussed at length by Trounce in a series of essays thirty years before, but his attempt to define a specifically East Anglian cultural milieu for tail-rhyme romance was flawed and his other arguments therefore subsequently neglected.[3] The aesthetic distinction I saw between the two formal traditions, and in particular

---

1   D. Pearsall, 'The Development of Middle English Romance', *Mediaeval Studies* 27 (1965), 91–116. Reprinted in D. Brewer (ed.), *Studies in Middle English Romances: Some New Approaches* (Cambridge, 1988), pp. 11–35.
2   J. Nelson Couch, 'The Vulnerable Hero: *Havelok* and the Revision of Romance', *Chaucer Review* 42 (2008), 330–52 (p. 347).
3   A. McI. Trounce, 'The English Tail-Rhyme Romances', *Medium Ævum* 1 (1932), 87–108, 168–82; 2 (1933), 34–57, 189–98; 3 (1934), 30–50. For an up-to-date account of the provenance of the tail-rhyme romances, see R. Purdie, *Anglicising Romance: Tail-Rhyme and Genre in Medieval English Literature* (Cambridge, 2008), pp. 151–242.

the difference in emotional 'affect', was only briefly developed, the formal classification succumbing from the first to an item-by-item classification of the romances in terms of literary value. I had read all the fourteenth-century Middle English romances for that paper, and I was determined to mention them all. And so I did, usually with some scathing dismissal of them for their triviality, banality, incompetence and general all-round inconsequence:

> 'grotesquely inept' (*Arthur*); 'hack-work' (*Guy*); 'every possible conces-sion to popular taste ... vivid, gross and ridiculous by turns, though never dull' (*Beves*); 'a not at all contemptible example of what the professional romancer could knock together when pressed' (*Degarre*); 'third-rate fumbling in an enfeebled tradition ... a wretched piece of work' (*Roland and Vernagu*); 'a mechanical shuffling-together of stock incidents' (*Eglamour*); and finally, 'There may not be much interest in what is going on, but at least there is always something going on.' (*Tryamour*)[4]

It is easy and tempting to ladle out abuse in this way and there is much fun to be got out of it. Some of the phrases were recycled in my 1977 book on *Old English and Middle English Poetry*, and so acquired a wider and continuing currency.[5]

This sneering and laughing often disguised itself as what was usually called judgement of literary merit, or aesthetic valuation, in those days. It involved belonging to a sect of self-appointed high panjandrums who dispensed killing judgements with easy confidence, comparing all literary works against a few accepted classics, and assigning them to classes and leagues, like univer-sity degrees or football teams. Thus C. S. Lewis, the model for many of us budding 'new critics', speaking of Gower:

> 'That first line is business-like, but it is poetry.' And again, 'The art of Gower is always on the same level of achievement – always somewhere beneath the highest, but very high.'[6]

The judgements that were pronounced in this confident manner were often quite arbitrary and, in the absence of evidence, incapable of being examined.

The fashion for value-judgement of this kind died out in the 1970s with the dissolution of the consensus of white male middle-class would-be Inklings that had sustained it, along with the increasing domination of the field by women and the general professionalisation of the field. What replaced it, as the volume of writing on Middle English popular romance stepped up, was a greater concentration on definitions of the genre of romance, on manu-script study and reception history, on historical, social and cultural contexts, on narratology and the analysis of narratological motifs. There was too an

---

4   Pearsall, 'The Development of Middle English Romance', pp. 95, 99, 100, 104, 110, 112.
5   D. Pearsall, *Old English and Middle English Poetry* (London, 1977), pp. 143–9.
6   C. S. Lewis, *The Allegory of Love: A Study in Medieval Tradition* (Oxford, 1936), pp. 207, 209.

increase in theoretically informed feminist and post-colonial reading and, above all, a renewed emphasis on Anglo-Norman romance and its French and English connections. A glance at the contents of the present volume will show how vigorously these approaches are being pursued, sometimes in relation to the genre as a whole, sometimes in relation to particular romances. Nearly all are represented, some more fully than others. The essay by Nicholas Perkins is exceptional in attempting a formalist analysis, albeit of a new kind and perhaps an indication of developments to come.

Having offered a personal retrospect on the study of romance over the past fifty years, and provided a context for understanding the relation of the essays in the present volume to that history, I now wish to attempt a different kind of formalist analysis of romance, in the hope of arriving at a better kind of understanding of its unique *value*. It is explicitly, though still a form of evaluation, a recantation of the historically determined bad opinion of romance that swayed that earlier essay out of orbit.

The truth is that whenever I find myself reading one of these romances, usually to remind myself what it is about, I always seem to enjoy myself and – the most telling evidence of absorption – stop watching the line-numbers. It is possible to detect this realisation of the pleasure to be taken in romance – its liveliness and brisk pace and sheer appetite for narrative – struggling to break through the diatribe of abuse quoted earlier. The reasons for this enjoyment are the 'wrong' reasons, according to the usual critical canons. Where I should be demanding originality, sharpness of detail and striking language, I am delighting in the repetition of old plots, repetition of conventional descriptions, repetition of conventional phrases and images. The leap of understanding is in realising that in asking for the wrong things, asking for 'literariness', one misses all that is particular to the pleasure of romance, all those elements that have to do originally and essentially with oral presentation. The popular romances are not a special case: they are the hard core of medieval narrative poetry. It is the Knight's Tale and *Sir Gawain and the Green Knight* that are the special case, with their digressions, reflections, elaborate descriptions, stylistic self-awareness, depth and density of reference. Repetition of motifs, a common stock of language and metaphor and incident, fast pace, predictable outcome, are what is to be enjoyed in medieval popular romance – anathema to any form of post-medieval aesthetic. The romances do not require the reader (or listener) to dwell on words or images or narrative singularities, where language crystallises into the thing in itself and achieves that magic of non-transparency that is called 'literariness'. Romance is transparent and has no design on us but that we should be absorbed and take pleasure in the stories. All the formulaic features I have hinted at have been widely recognised by scholars, though not in a spirit of whole-hearted approbation and usually briefly before passing on to some point that is said to be special or unique to a particular romance. All that needs to be done to release the energies of romance is to put these features at the centre rather than at the margins of our attention.

The typical romance is about a thousand lines, more or less (or episodes of a similar length in longer romances), in origin a brisk reading of about an hour or so, entertainment for both men and women, recited in performance or read from a book, after dinner, say, in some rich wool-merchant's house in East Anglia, as has been suggested for *Emaré*.[7] From the list of what I think of as 'typical' romances, I exclude the Matters of France and Antiquity and also anything written (as distinct from surviving from) after 1400. What is left is a compact group, all written within about a hundred years, mostly in tail-rhyme. They might plausibly be called 'The Family Romances'. They are not all the same, of course. They all have their individual quirks and excellences, and some are better than others.

Their dedication is to the story, and the stories run to a pattern – there are many Constance-sagas and Eustace-sagas and exile-and-return sagas, and composites of these story-types, any of which might be called 'Breton lays'.[8] The character and style of narrative in this core group of romances have much in common with other forms of traditional narrative, such as folk-tale and ballad. There is little reflection and no dwelling on events, and in one's memory the stories tend to merge into a common stock. This is the central value of popular romance: the individual romances do not stand alone, but draw for their effectiveness upon the resonance and accumulated associations in the audience's memory of many such stories. Like the best soups, they are made from non-specific well-matured stock.

The story is told briskly, with few pauses or digressions other than those sanctioned by tradition, such as the introductory description of the hero and heroine. As to plot, expeditious dispatch is the rule. Events are abruptly announced without preliminaries or comment, even animal abductions:

> He bare hym over the water wylde;
> A lyon took his othir chylde
>   Ar he to lond come. (*Isumbras* 172–4)[9]

> A grype come in all hir care,
> The yong chyld away he bare
>   To a countré unkende. (*Eglamour* 816–18)

A whole nation is converted to Islam in an instant:

> [He] comaundyd crystenyd to be swythe
>   Tho that hethene ware.
> The hethene were at on asent. (*Isumbras* 692–4)

[7] See A. Laskaya and E. Salisbury (eds), *The Middle English Breton Lays* (Kalamazoo, 1995), p. 145.

[8] The categories are those of the standard bibliographies: *A Manual of the Writings in Middle English*, general editor J. Burke Severs, Fasc. I: The Romances, by M. J. Donovan et al. (New Haven, 1967); *The New Cambridge Bibliography of English Literature*, general editor G. Watson, Vol. I (Cambridge, 1974), cols. 383–454.

[9] A list of editions cited is given in an Appendix. In the quotations, þ and ȝ are regularised.

Jousts are formulaic:

> Than rode they two togedur aright,
> Wyth scharp sperys and swerdys bright,
> Thay smote togedur sore. (*Tryamour* 1210–12)

They end abruptly when their narrative job is done:

> Syr Tryamowre faght on fote,
> What schall we more of hym mote?
> The tothur brothur was slayne. (*Tryamour* 1438–40)

Journeys are over in an instant and the next adventure begins:

> 'Have good dai! I mot go henne'.
> The knight passede as he cam. (*Degarre* 132–3)

Transitions are abrupt:

> In Jerusalem thus gan scho dwelle;
> Of hir other childe now will I telle,
> That the ape away bare. (*Octavian* 529–31)

> Nou wille we of Gij duelle,
> And of his lyoun ichil you telle. (*Guy of Warwick* 4239–40)

Characters whose function in the narrative is over are swiftly disposed of:

> This olde erld, Sir Prynsamoure,
> Fell down bakward of a towre
> And brake hys nekke belyve. (*Eglamour* 1283–5)

Emotion is conveyed in a kind of formulaic shorthand, most characteristically in the tail-line of the tail-rhyme stanza, which may act also as minimal commentary on the action:

> Grete dele hyt ys to telle. (*Octavian* 1674)
> Sore hys herte can blede. (*Octavian* 1689)

'Gamen and gle' is a very useful little all-purpose phrase of this kind, whether it is to celebrate the joyous moment when the wicked mother-in-law cuts her own head off,

> And therat alle the kynges loghe,
> There was joye and gamen ynowghe;
> Alle tuke thaire leve that tyde; (*Octavian* 1831–3)

or the hilarity when Clement and his wife fall over backwards in the effort of pulling the rusty old sword out of its ancient scabbard:

13

> Gret gamen it es to telle
> How thay bothe to the erthe felle,
>   And Clement laye in swoghe; (*Octavian* 956–8)

or simply sexual pleasure:

> The kynge belafte wyth the qwene;
> Moch love was hem betwene,
>   And also game and gle. (*Emaré* 472–4)

As the story races on ('unfolds' would be the wrong word), one never asks what is happening, meanwhile, to other characters: they have no existence if they are not in the foreground of the story. Inexplicable events are simply placed before us: there are no explanations. In *Octavian*, the queen sleeps through the whole episode when the servant crawls in beside her and then is slain by the king, blood all over the place, and only wakes up when the severed head of the servant is dumped upon her (142–83). In the same romance the young son is seized by the lioness and carried off in her mouth, and then the lion is carried off in its claws by a griffin, and then they land, and then the lioness fights with the griffin and kills it, and only then does the child wake up, and equably starts suckling the lioness (340–75). If only, some mothers might say. The truest romances are those that are least articulated, most elliptical, with fewest explanations. The telling of the story can be so compressed, in *Sir Tristrem* for instance, that it would be difficult for the audience to follow if they didn't already know the story. It is almost as if such romances have all been subjected in advance to the encrypting abbreviatory techniques of Ezra Pound with Eliot's *The Waste Land*. They are modern without trying.

The audience is not interested in suspense or the unexpected unexpected, only in the expected unexpected: the satisfaction of familiar appetites in familiar ways is what pleases them. The wicked we are told are wicked as soon as they are introduced. In *Sir Launfal*, Guenevere's promiscuity and general bad reputation are explicitly referred to as early as the fourth stanza. In *King Horn* we are told immediately about Horn's two friends:

> Athulf was the beste
> And Fikenylde the werste. (*King Horn* 29–30)

There is a community of response, and a participation in the story so full and so intense that the only kind of suspense the audience can bear is the pleasant dramatic suspense of expectation delayed and fulfilled, for there would be an agony of unfulfilled expectation, a shock wave through the audience, if a story did not keep to the rules or if some favourite violent or outrageous act were omitted. When Degarre marries his mother the terrible secret is openly confided to the audience before anything is revealed to the participants,

> So dede Sire Degarre the bold –
> Spoused there his moder hold –

> And that hendi levedi also
> Here owene sone was spoused to
> That sche upon here bodi bar. (625–30)

So too when he fights his father:

> Lo, swich aventure hem gan bitide –
> The sone agein the fader gan ride,
> And neither ne knew other no wight! (1028–30)

The fight between father and son is a well-known outrageous turn of events that has the audience delighting in excited anticipation that the familiar thrill of horror will inevitably be resolved into a happy outcome.

In language, metaphor and simile, too, the romances draw their power from a familiar stock, with its accumulated resonances and rich associations. The repetitive style and conventional phraseology began in the economies of orally rendered narrative, but they come to have an important effect in inducing an appropriate response of solidarity in the audience. They reinforce shared cultural meaning, pre-empt differences and doubts, confirm the audience in their views. The repetition of formulaic phrases is a feature of romance that has long been recognised and routinely castigated as the work of lazy hacks. But such repeated phrases, with their familiarity, memorableness, accumulated emotional resonance and their role in creating community and a sense of shared values are vital to the aesthetic economy of romance, and have a distinguished ancestry in the 'epic formulae' of the older heroic poets, writing for a listening audience and, in the earliest days of Homeric epic, composing impromptu according to certain stylised conventions. Layamon and the Middle English alliterative poets and metrical romancers have a large repertory of such phrases, but confusion has often arisen from the failure to distinguish between oral-formulaic composition, oral delivery, and reading aloud. The first was long ago firmly ruled out for Old English and Middle English alliterative poetry and should be ruled out too for the popular metrical romances as they are known from written copies. Reading aloud from a written text, 'romanz-reding on the bok', whether by the author or not, becomes increasingly the norm, alongside performance from memory, and eventually private reading supersedes both.[10] In the fifteenth century there are, significantly, examples of written romances which have been adapted

---

10 For 'romanz-reding on the bok', see *Havelok*, 2332. For the practice of oral delivery, and the close connections between oral tradition and the extant written texts, see N. Mason Bradbury, *Writing Aloud: Storytelling in Late Medieval England* (Urbana and Chicago, 1998). The important essay by A. C. Baugh, 'Improvisation in the Middle English Romance', *Proceedings of the American Philosophical Society* 103 (1959), 418–54, analyses a large sample of formulaic phrases to show how romance-reciters would improvise to cover lapses of memory or to embroider cadenzas into a favourite episode. For the custom of reading aloud, or 'prelection', as she calls it, see J. Coleman, *Public Reading and the Reading Public in Late Medieval England and France* (Cambridge, 1996). For a general discussion of questions of oral delivery, including memorial transmission,

so as to convey the impression of oral delivery by the insertion of familiar phrases suggestive of a listening audience and so as thereby to recapture something of that feeling of a listening community bonded together by shared ideals, aspirations, values and feelings. Simon Horobin and Alison Wiggins show how revisions of the text of the romance of *Merlyn* and of an A-text of *Piers Plowman* in Lincoln's Inn MS 150 'would have enhanced the impact of these texts for a listening audience'.[11] In its less successful form, the hackneyed and unthought repetition of stereotyped phrases, images and vocabulary ceases to be evocative of a rich cultural past and descends into cliché.

Repetition is specially effective in the expression of emotion – a type of stylised verbal equivalence where certain familiar phrases trigger certain emotional responses. The tail-rhyme latter half of the Auchinleck *Guy of Warwick* is especially rich in this stylised language, as it is employed particularly in the last three lines of the twelve-line stanza:

> 'Allas', he seyd, 'that Y was born;
> Bodi and soule icham forlorn.
> Of blis icham all bare.' (*Guy*, stanza 22/1–3)

> 'Therfore ich wot that icham lorn;
> Allas the time that Y was born!
> Of blis icham al bare.' (25/10–12)

> And when thai founde him nought that day
> There was mani a wayleway,
> Wringand her hondes tuo. (38/10–12)

> Mani a moder child that day
> Wepe and gan say 'waileway',
> Wel sore wringand her hond. (43/10–12)

Tail-rhyme in particular can always flower into a lyrically expansive mode, as in *Guy* and also in *Amis and Amiloun*, where the conventional phraseology establishes a poetic context in which a particular situation is invested with great narrative emotional power, perhaps by a single phrase within a context of laconic simplicity:

> And when he hadde hem bothe slain,
> He laid hem in her bed ogain –
> No wonder thei him were wo –
> And hilde hem, that no wight schuld se,
> As noman hadde at hem be –
> Out of chaumber he gan go. (*Amis and Amiloun* 2311–16)

---

  see Putter's part of the Introduction to *The Spirit of Medieval English Popular Romance*, ed. A. Putter and J. Gilbert (London, 2000), pp. 1–15.
[11] S. Horobin and A. Wiggins, 'Reconsidering Lincoln's Inn MS 150', *Medium Ævum* 77 (2008), 30–53.

The development of the twelve-line tail-rhyme is the triumph of form in the popular romance.[12] Unpromising from many points if view – as Chaucer demonstrated – it is the perfect medium for this kind of orally rendered narrative. It was an ephemeral flowering, was born and died in about 100 years.[13]

The stock of adjectives that is used to describe characters, often in similes – 'bryght of blee', 'bryght as blosme on brere', white as foam, white as whale's bone, 'also white so lylie-flour', 'red as rose of here colour' – has a similar function in creating a common audience response, a pleasure in familiarity, and a bond of emotional engagement. Likewise the exact internal formulaic repetition of some key wording – incremental or 'enchained' repetition (concatenation), or the words of a promise or command repeated in its fulfilment, as in *Athelston*,[14] or the words of an errand in its delivery, as in the climax to *Sir Launfal* – has an important effect in creating a heightened emotional awareness. In *Sir Launfal*, Launfal says to Guenevere that his lady's lowliest maiden is more beautiful a queen than she is; she, outraged, repeats the claim word for word to Arthur, he to the court, Launfal agrees that that was what he said, and then when the first ten maidens arrive the lowliest is agreed by all to be more beautiful, and when the Lady Tryamour arrives she too repeats it and confirms it in her person – she performs it, so to speak.[15] The six repetitions burn Guenevere into blindness.

Such repetitions in syntax and diction are reminiscent of the repetitiveness of the traditional ballad (towards which a romance like *King Horn* always seems to want to approximate) and the classic Hollywood western. There too the secret is in the bond with and among the audience created by the repetition of familiar elements. Who was not delighted to watch for the umpteenth time the same unlikely gunfight or daring horseback rescue, the same lone horseman against the landscape of Monument Valley or solitary woman in a long skirt waving goodbye, or bullet being extracted by knife with help of alcohol? But perhaps I am the only one left that relishes such things. These are all simplicities, it will be readily admitted, but simplicities are not alien to popular literature. No doubt individual romances break out occasionally into an unexpected questioning of genre, or reversal of expectation, or subversion of the prevailing ethos, and a general 'multiplicity of inscribed reader-positions and ideological identifications', and if there are such elements present it is certain that modern scholars will find them, or, if not, supply them.[16] Such interpretation is the familiar result of reading popular romances in the light of

---

12 For the stylistic excellences of a particular tail-rhyme romance, see M. Mills, '*Sir Isumbras* and the Styles of Tail-rhyme Romance', in C. M. Meale (ed.), *Readings in Medieval English Romance* (Cambridge, 1994), pp. 1–24.

13 See 'The Era of Tail-Rhyme Romance' in Purdie, *Anglicising Romance*, pp. 149–50.

14 *Athelston*, stanzas 18/10–12 and 19/1–3, 20/4–6 and 21/1–3, 54/4–5 and 56/4–5, 53/1–6 and 73/1–6, and for the repeated command, 66/7–12 and 67/7–12.

15 See *Sir Launfal*, 698, 720, 763, 780, 852, 1005.

16 For the quotation, see the part of the Introduction by J. Gilbert to *The Spirit of Medieval English Popular Romance* (see note 11, above), pp. 15–31 (p. 24).

modern expectations and preoccupations, but it is hard to see how a romance-style so direct and transparent could nourish such indirection and idiosyncrasy among its historical audience. Understanding something *different*, that is, the pleasures taken in romance by that historical audience, which has been the preoccupation of this piece, goes against the modern grain. Yet it is clear that the narrative economy and formulaic style of the popular romances are dominantly those productive of cultural and moral conformity and the reinforcement of communal values. Hidden depths there may be, but they are on the surface. The cumulative effect of the Middle English popular romance is the irresistible bonding of the audience into the story, almost independent of any teller or reciter. The romances do what they do consummately well. The more pertinent question is, can we ever call up again their special 'moment' – when song turned into poetry, texts developed from and into improvisation, and audiences were bound with story-teller in a commonalty of deeply felt experience – except through the power of historical imagination? Can we learn to understand how *Emaré* might be perceived as a better telling of the Constance-story than Chaucer's? Who was ever brought to tears by the Man of Law's Tale?

Appendix: Editions of Romances Cited

Guy of Warwick, ed. J. Zupitza, EETS ES 42, 49, 59 (London, 1883, 1887, 1891).

Havelok, Athelston and *Sir Degarre*, in *Medieval English Romances*, ed. A. V. C. Schmidt and N. Jacobs, 2 vols. (London, 1980): I.37–121, I.123–50 and II.57–88, respectively.

Emaré and *Sir Launfal*, in *The Middle English Breton Lays*, ed. A. Laskaya and E. Salisbury (Kalamazoo, 1995), pp. 145–99 and 201–62, respectively.

Sir Isumbras, Octavian, Sir Eglamour of Artois and *Syr Tryamour*, in *Four Middle English Romances*, ed. H. Hudson (Kalamazoo, 1996), pp. 7–44, 45–114, 115–71 and 173–232, respectively.

Amis and Amiloun, in *Amis and Amiloun, Roberd of Cisyle, and Sir Amadace*, ed. E. E. Foster (Kalamazoo, 1997).

2

Representations of Peasant Speech:
Some Literary and Social Contexts for
*The Taill of Rauf Coilyear**

NANCY MASON BRADBURY

This essay offers some fresh contexts for reading *The Taill of Rauf Coil-year*, one of many late medieval narratives that sit uneasily, and therefore intriguingly, within the generic category 'medieval romance'. Preserved in a printed edition of 1572, the tale is nevertheless 'medieval': its composition is generally dated to the later fifteenth century, and scholars regularly extend the boundary of medieval Scots poetry well into the sixteenth.[1] *Rauf Coilyear*'s claims to the designation 'romance' include the appearance of the cyclical romance hero Charlemagne among its characters, the adaptation of an alliterative stanza form shared by a subset of English romances, and the extreme elasticity of the romance category itself. The existing scholarship examines *The Taill of Rauf Coilyear* within a variety of contexts, including Scottish romances, alliterative romances, Charlemagne romances, romances depicting Saracens, and encounters with unrecognised kings.[2] I hope to

* My thanks to Richard Firth Green, Thomas Hahn, and Rhiannon Purdie, who invited me to give talks (the last a conference paper) in which I tried out versions of the arguments made here.

[1] The 1460s is the decade suggested by H. M. Smyser, '*The Taill of Rauf Coilyear* and Its Sources', *Harvard Studies and Notes in Philology and Literature* 14 (1932), 135–50, at p. 136. That the poem is pre-1500 is indicated by its casual citation in Gavin Douglas's *Palis of Honoure*, completed by 1501: see Gavin Douglas, *The Palis of Honoure*, ed. D. Parkinson (Kalamazoo, 1992), p. 2 and line 1711. On the question of periodisation, see R. Purdie, 'Medieval Romance in Scotland', in *A Companion to Medieval Scottish Poetry*, ed. P. Bawcutt and J. H. Williams (Cambridge, 2006), pp. 165–77, at p. 167, and R. J. Goldstein, 'Writing in Scotland, 1058–1560', in *The Cambridge History of Medieval English Literature*, ed. D. Wallace (Cambridge, 1999), pp. 229–54. On the problem of genre, see M. K. Morris, 'Generic Oxymoron in *The Taill of Rauf Coilȝear*', in *Voices in Translation*, ed. D. Sinnreich-Levi and G. Sigal (New York, 1992).

[2] On Scottish romance: Purdie, 'Medieval Romance in Scotland'; on alliterative romance: J. P. Oakden, *Alliterative Poetry in Middle English* (1930, 1935; rpt in one vol. Hamden, Conn., 1968). On *Rauf Coilyear* in connection with Charlemagne romances and Saracens, see G. Wright, 'Convention and Conversion: the Saracen Ending of *the Taill of Rauf Coilȝear*', *Al-Masaq: Islam and the Medieval Mediterranean* 14 (2002), 101–12. On 'unrecognised king' analogues, see Smyser, '*The Taill of Rauf Coilyear* and its Sources'; E. Walsh, 'The King in Disguise', *Folklore* 86 (1975), 3–24 and '*The Tale of Rauf Coilyear*: Oral Motif in Literary Guise', *Scottish Literary*

expand *Rauf*'s frame of reference in two ways: first, by comparing the main character's peasant identity and his use of language to that of the peasant speaker in the Middle English prose *Dialogue of Solomon and Marcolf* (c.1492) and, second, by attending to two subgenres embedded within *Rauf Coilyear*, the proverb and the popular complaint or 'poem of social protest'. These contexts for *The Taill of Rauf Coilyear* help us to see more clearly what is at stake in its representation of a speaking voice only rarely heard in the realm of romance.

My interest in the representation of peasant language began with the numerous late medieval texts that depict peasants as lacking reason, incapable of coherent speech, comparable mentally to beasts. In England, the Rising of 1381, with its haunting spectre of 'the cherles rebellyng', occasioned fearful and derisive portrayals of peasant speech and behaviour.[3] Contemporary descriptions of the revolt depict the insurgents as rustics or peasants, although historians have shown that a great many of them were not, and, as Steven Justice and others have pointed out, contemporary accounts are particularly condemnatory of peasant language, which they repeatedly compare to the inarticulate noise made by animals.[4] To the ears of John Gower's dreamer in Book I of the *Vox Clamantis*, these supposed peasants seemed to

> bray in the beastly manner of asses, some bellow the lowings of oxen. Some give out horrible swinish grunts ... and fierce barking weighed heavily upon the air of the city as the harsh, angry voice of the dogs flies about. The hungry fox wails and the cunning wolf howls into the air and calls together his runningmates. ... Behold the loud din, the wild clangor, the savage brawling – no sound was ever so terrible before.[5]

The chronicler Thomas Walsingham writes that the shouting of these *rustici*

> became horrendous, not like the shouting that men normally make, but ines-timably louder than any human shouting, and could be likened in particular to the wailing of the inhabitants of Hell.... No words rang out amidst their horrifying clamour, but their throats bellowed forth all kinds of noises, or, to tell the truth, sounds more like the diabolical cries of peacocks.[6]

Journal 6 (1979), 5–19; R. Snell, 'The Undercover King', in *Medieval Insular Romance*, ed. J. Weiss, J. Fellows, and M. Dickson (Cambridge, 2000), pp. 133–54, and G. Wright, 'Churl's Courtesy: *Rauf Coilȝear* and Its English Analogues', *Neophilologus* 85 (2001), 647–62.

3   Quotation from line 2459 of Chaucer's 'Knight's Tale', *The Riverside Chaucer*, ed. L. D. Benson et al. (Boston, 1987). All Chaucer citations are from this edition.

4   *Writing and Rebellion: England in 1381* (Berkeley, 1994), pp. 205–16.

5   Quidam sternutant asinorum more ferino, / Mugitus quidam personuere boum; / Quidam porcorum grunnitus horridiores / Emittunt ... Latratusque ferus vrbis compresserat auras, / Dumque canum discors vox furibunda volat. / Vulpis egens vlulat, lupus et versutus in altum / Conclamat, que suos conuocat ipse pares; ... Ecce rudis clangor, sonus altus, fedaque rixa, / Vox ita terribilis non fuit vlla prius. From *The Complete Works of John Gower*, ed. G. C. Macaulay, Vol. 4: The Latin Works (Oxford, 1902), Liber Primus, lines 799–816. I quote E. W. Stockton's translation, *The Major Latin Works of John Gower* (Seattle, 1962), pp. 67–8.

6   Quo cum peruenisset, factus est clamor horendissimus, non similis clamoribus quos edere solent homines, set qui ultra omnem estimacionem superaret omnes clamores humanos, et maxime

Chaucer too makes use of – or possibly parodies – such images in the 'Nun's Priest's Tale', when the tale's narrator compares the raucous barnyard sounds made by the pursuers of the fox to the cries of fiends in hell and to the 'hideous' noise made by the rebels of 1381.[7]

These representations of peasant speech are of course the most heightened of examples because their writers are reacting to what they understand to be rebelling peasants, but even an admirably balanced study like Paul Freedman's *Images of the Medieval Peasant* shows how commonly the ordinary, non-rebelling, *rusticus* was portrayed by his contemporaries as a creature of beast-like stupidity or rapacity, his words heard only as inarticulate noise.[8] These outright denials of mental life or expressive speech in peasants make all the more interesting late medieval texts such as the Middle English *Dialogue of Solomon and Marcolf* and *The Taill of Rauf Coilyear*, where peasant figures are depicted as engaged in skilled use of language and reasoning. (Chaucer's *Canterbury Tales* is another such text.) The modern English word *peasant* may seem problematic to some, in that late medieval English writers tended to group all 'common men' under the more general word *cherl* (or, in the dialect in which *Rauf Coilyear* is composed, *carll*), which includes agricultural workers but also well-off tradesmen who lived in towns and cities. Most of the points made here apply to literary representations of the speech of *cherls* or 'common men' in general, but, as we will see, both Marcolf and Rauf are vividly depicted as rural cottagers: Marcolf's family keeps a cow and farms a plot of land, and, as a seller of wood charcoal, Rauf is what Jean Birrell calls a 'forest peasant'.[9] Thus both heroes qualify as medieval peasants in the narrower sense as well.

Although precursors of the extant texts may be as old as c.1000, versions of the *Dialogue of Solomon and Marcolf* flourished in the fifteenth century, as attested by some twenty-seven Latin manuscript versions dating from 1410 onwards and forty-nine early printed editions, as well as translations into a wide variety of late medieval vernaculars, including German, Dutch, Swedish, Italian, English, and Welsh.[10] In all its versions, the *Dialogue* features a peasant who holds his own against a king proverbial for his wisdom and justice. Although early allusions to such a dialogue abound, no texts survive before the fifteenth century, and I suggest that their sudden prolifera-

---

posset assimulari ululatibus infernalium incolarum.... Non tamen resonabant uerba inter horrificos strepitus, set replebantur guttura multisonis mugitibus, uel quod est uerius, uocibus pauonum diabolicis. Translation and text from *The St Albans Chronicle: The Chronica maiora of Thomas Walsingham I 1376–1394*, ed. and trans. J. Taylor, W. R. Childs, and L. Watkiss (Oxford, 2003), pp. 426–7.

7   'Nun's Priest's Tale', *CT* VII.3375–97, with the word *hydous* at line 3393.
8   P. Freedman, *Images of the Medieval Peasant* (Stanford, 1999).
9   'Peasant Craftsmen in the Medieval Forest', *Agricultural History Review* 17 (1969), 91–107 and 'The Medieval English Forest', *Journal of Forest History* 24 (1980), 78–85.
10 A Latin text of this multiform dialogue was edited by W. Benary, *Salomon et Marcolfus* (Heidelberg, 1914). Benary's edition is reprinted with a full scholarly study of the Latin work in J. M. Ziolkowski, *Solomon and Marcolf* (Cambridge, Mass., 2008).

tion in that historical period reflects the heightened interest in *cherls*, their tales, and their rival wisdom that characterised European literature in the late fourteenth and fifteenth centuries. *The Taill of Rauf Coilyear*, another depiction of the encounter between *rex* and *rusticus*, the extreme poles of medieval social and political life, is shaped by the same interest. The Middle English *Dialogue* and *Rauf Coilyear* both survive as single copies of a printed edition, the former printed by Gerard Leeu in Antwerp in 1492, the latter by Robert Lekpreuik at St Andrews in 1572. The lone text of the English *Dialogue* is shelved in the Bodleian Library, Oxford, as Tanner 178 (3); the sole copy of *Rauf Coilyear* resides in the National Library of Scotland.[11]

In *The Dialogue of Solomon and Marcolf*, the fictional peasant Marcolf contends with a royal personage even more illustrious than Charlemagne, King Solomon. Marcolf and his wife are depicted as awkward and rustic outsiders at Solomon's court, much as Rauf appears when he visits Charlemagne's court to sell his charcoal. After a long and competitive exchange of proverbial wisdom and other remarks, the scene shifts to reveal Solomon's own class-inflected awkwardness as he sits on his horse, half in and half out of Marcolf's peasant house, an awkwardness Charlemagne too exhibits as his missteps violate Rauf's ideas about the prerogatives of a man in his own home. In the *Dialogue*, Solomon's awkwardness is verbal as well as physical: he is stumped by a series of riddles posed by Marcolf with solutions drawn from the everyday lives of peasants. Unable, for example, to grasp what it is that 'the more that they ascende, the more they downe falle', Solomon must seek from Marcolf the solution: 'They are the benys boylyng in the pott' (Duff p. 14). In a series of hard-fought verbal contests, Marcolf holds his own against the patriarch proverbial for his wisdom. By doing so, he proves himself an eloquent peasant wisdom figure, paradoxical as that title might have sounded to those contemporary writers who questioned whether peasants were capable of thought or articulate speech.[12]

As I began to look closely at what Marcolf and Rauf actually say to their kings, the first surprise, to me at least, was the extent to which their represented speech makes use of recognisable verbal genres, as opposed to ordinary, unstructured 'talk'. Unlike Rauf, Marcolf knows very well with

---

[11] Facsimiles of the Middle English print are available with a diplomatic transcription in E. Gordon Duff, *The Dialogue or Communing between the Wise King Salomon and Marcolphus* (London, 1892); with a modernised text in *The Dialogue of Solomon and Marcolphus*, ed. D. Beecher (Ottawa, 1995), and at Early English Books Online (eebo.chadwyck.com/). With S. Bradbury, I am preparing a TEAMS edition of the Middle English *Dialogue* in parallel to the Latin text from which it is likely to have been translated. All quotations from the *Dialogue* are by page number from Duff's transcription, with some minor changes in capitalisation and punctuation. All quotations from *The Taill of Rauf Coilyear* are from *Longer Scottish Poems*, Vol. 1. 1375–1650, ed. P. Bawcutt and F. Riddy (Edinburgh, 1987), pp. 94–133. I have also consulted the editions by E. Walsh, *The Tale of Ralph the Collier* (New York, 1989) and by A. Lupack in *Three Middle English Charlemagne Romances* (Kalamazoo, 1990), pp. 161–204.

[12] For Marcolf as a peasant wisdom figure, see N. M. Bradbury, 'Rival Wisdom in the Latin *Dialogue of Solomon and Marcolf*', *Speculum* 83 (2008), 331–65.

whom he is speaking: he meets his sovereign at his court, sitting on his throne, and Marcolf's royal interlocutor states that he is 'Salomon the king', descended from generations of patriarchs.[13] King Solomon and the peasant Marcolf contend in a series of verbal contests more formally structured than Rauf's exchanges with his king, though Rauf too has a habit of scorekeeping: 'Now is anis', 'Now is twyse', he counts as Charlemagne fails to respond adequately to the dictates of his peasant host (lines 126, 148). The first verbal genre in which Solomon and Marcolf compete is an exchange of genealogies. Solomon's demand to know 'of what lynage they were comyn' (Duff p. 5) seems designed at least in part to humble Marcolf and his wife, Polycana, by contrast to his own regal descent from twelve generations of Old Testament patriarchs. However, Marcolf's quick and improvisatory wit enables him to parody Solomon's impressive biblical series of 'begats' with twelve generations of peasant ancestors he has presumably made up on the spot: 'Rusticus gat Rustam, Rusta gat Rustum, Rustus gat Rusticellum' (Duff p. 5), and so on. Acknowledging that Marcolf is 'subtyle of wyt' despite being 'mysshapyn and chorlyssh', Solomon proposes that he and Marcolf engage in an 'altercac[i]on' or formal disputation: 'I shal make questyons to the, and thou shalt therto answere' (Duff p. 5).

What ensues, however, is not an academic disputation, but a battle of duelling proverbs. Solomon does not pose 'questyons' per se; rather, he speaks a piece of sententious biblical wisdom to which Marcolf replies in aphoristic form with scathing parody, homely folk wisdom, apt social criticism, or just random crudity. Marcolf often transposes Solomon's lofty idealising to a discourse of barnyard animals and human bodily organs of reproduction and defecation. Their 'proverb contest' takes up nearly half the dialogue; the two then go on to contend in other small but recognisable genres as well: riddles, arguable propositions, and a praise and blame contest, or argument on both sides of an issue.

The proverb contest is the longest of these exchanges, and the most relevant to Rauf Coilyear's use of language. Marcolf responds in varying ways to the long series of *sententiae* with which Solomon challenges him. Many of his responses are verbal parodies of biblical proverbs attributed to Solomon, a relationship that is easier to see in Latin but often survives translation as well:[14]

---

13 The opening verbal confrontations in which Marcolf and his wife appear as rustic outsiders at Solomon's court should perhaps, in linear, chronological terms, come after the next confrontation, in which Solomon comes upon the house where Marcolf is living with his parents and siblings, with no mention of a wife. J. M. Ziolkowski makes the plausible suggestion that the order of these verbal confrontations may at one time have followed the same pattern we see in *Rauf Coilyear* and its analogues: the peasant meets his sovereign first on the peasant's own territory and then at court (*Solomon and Marcolf*, p. 195).

14 I cite the Latin text in these three examples to illustrate the close verbal parody: these proverb exchanges are numbered 17ab, 116ab, and 117ab in Benary's edition.

Solomon: Qui seminat iniquitatem metet mala. (See Proverbs 22.8)
Marcolf: Qui seminat paleas metet miseriam.
Solomon: He that sowyth wyckydnesse, shal repe evyll.
Marcolf: He that sowyth chaf shal porely mowe. (Duff p. 7)

In the exchange above, Marcolf merely responds to an abstract moralising statement with a practical, agricultural one, but others of Marcolf's verbal parodies are more disruptive of Solomon's moral solemnity:

Salomon: Ex habundancia cordis os loquitur.
Marcolfus: Ex saturitate ventris triumphat culus.
Salomon: Of habundaunce of th'erte the mouth spekyst.
Marcolphus: Out of a full wombe th'ars trompyth. (Duff p. 12)

Salomon: Duo boves equaliter trahunt ad unum iugum.
Marcolfus: Due torciones equaliter trahunt ad unum culum.
Salomon: Two oxen in one yocke drawen lyke.
Marcolphus: Two veynes go lyke to oon ars. (Duff p. 12)

In the family of printed texts and vernacular translations to which the Middle English version belongs, many of the most transgressive verbal parodies present in the fullest manuscript versions have been omitted, and the remaining exchanges turn, not on verbal parody of sacred scripture, but on sharp social satire. In the example below, Marcolf takes Solomon's metaphor of coercion as an insurmountable natural force and turns it instead into a harsh image of predation:

Salomon: Agenst a strong and myghty man thou shalt not fyghte, ne stryve agenst the streme.
Marcolphus: The vultier takyth the skyn of stronge fowles and makyth thaym neked of theyr fethres. (Duff pp. 7–8)

Marcolf rebukes Solomon's resolute monologism by taking literally his warning against following any but the single righteous path:

Salomon: Whoo to that man that hath a dowble herte and in bothe weyes wyll wandre.
Marcolphus: He that woll two weyes go muste eythre his ars or his breche tere. (Duff p. 11)

Marcolf's proverbs insist vividly and repeatedly that, in a fallen world, bodily necessity overrides abstract idealism. To Solomon's directive, 'We haue well fyllyd oure beliys, lete us thanke God,' Marcolf replies, 'As the owsell whystelyth so answeryth the thrusshe, the hungery and the fulle synge not oon songe' (Duff p. 10). In a similar exchange, Solomon offers the familiar biblical consolation for the sorrows of mortality, 'Lete us ete and drinke, we shall alle deye,' to which Marcolf responds, 'The hungery dyeth as wele

24

as the full fedd' (Duff p. 10). Throughout his bravura performance, Marcolf insists upon the bodily realities of digestion, defecation, aging, disease, and death, which may afflict the poor more severely, but ultimately cut across the wide social gap that separates the two speakers.

Solomon eventually professes himself too weary to continue and the contest ends with Marcolf the victor; I take this as an indication that the ancient, book-based, and finite fund of sententious remarks upon which Solomon draws is growing weary and is in danger of running out of precepts, whereas Marcolf's discourse is inexhaustible because, where he lacks a precept of his own, he simply improvises a fresh parody of Solomon's latest entry in their verbal contest, thus making an old text new. Marcolf acquits himself ably in all these contests, but eventually wears out the patience of the outwitted king, who condemns him to hang. As a last favour, Solomon grants him the right to choose his own tree. Marcolf searches the known world but cannot find a tree he would like to hang from, and therefore, in the Middle English text, he goes home to his own peasant house, where he lives on 'in pease and joye'. Rauf Coilyear, by contrast, partakes of the fairy-tale transformation of medieval romance: rather than living on as the peasant he was, in the end he is made Marshal of France, moves with his wife to court, and converts the house where he lodged the king to a shelter for travellers.

Both peasant figures, Marcolf and Rauf, show themselves skilled in the traditional art of wielding proverbs. Perhaps the smallest of recognisable genres (or subgenres), the proverb often comes with a strong ideological charge as a result of a vast field of prior textual and extratextual uses.[15] Its authority is therefore much greater than the statements of a single individual, and yet access to proverbial wisdom requires no formal education, nor even literacy. It would of course be a serious mistake to identify the medieval proverb literally or exclusively with lower class or uneducated speakers – nearly all medieval English writers use proverbs, and some of the most well read, such as Chaucer, use them in greatest profusion, and assign them to their highest born and most learned characters. Nevertheless, the idea that the 'common man' was an important source and carrier of proverbial wisdom had considerable currency in medieval Europe, as we can see from the titles of collections that circulated under such names as *Proverbia rusticorum*, *Proverbia Rustici*, and *Proverbes au Vilein*.[16] In his foundational study of the proverb, Archer Taylor cites a fourteenth-century German legal document

---

15 For this property of traditional expressions that circulate orally as well as in writing, see J. M. Foley, *Immanent Art: from Structure to Meaning in Traditional Oral Epic* (Bloomington, 1991) and *The Singer of Tales in Performance* (Bloomington, 1995).

16 See N. Zemon Davis, 'Proverbial Wisdom and Popular Errors', in her *Society and Culture in Early Modern France* (Stanford, 1975), pp. 227–67; R. N. B. Goddard, 'Marcabru, *Li Proverbe au Vilain*, and the Tradition of Rustic Proverbs', *Neuphilologische Mitteilungen* 88 (1987), 55–70; and B. Taylor, 'Medieval Proverb Collections: The West European Tradition', *Journal of the Warburg and Courtauld Institutes* 55 (1992), 19–35.

that advises pleaders before juries, 'Whenever you can attach a proverb, do so, for peasants like to judge according to proverbs.'[17]

An English collection called *The Proverbs of Hendyng* that circulated in the thirteenth and fourteenth centuries attaches the idea of proverbial wisdom to the peasant Marcolf himself. In the version found in MS Harley 2253, Hending is identified as 'Marcolves sone', and at the end of the moral proverbs assigned to Hendyng in Cambridge University Library MS Gg.1.1, the reader finds this pragmatic Marcolfian grumble, deprecating the ultimate utility of sententious wisdom: '"Al to late, al to late / Wan the deth is at the 3ate," Quod Marcol'.[18] Marcolf's special affinity for deploying proverbs also turns up in the 'Marcolf' poem of John Audelay, believed to have been written in the 1420s, which adopts the voice of Marcolf as a vehicle for some sharp criticism of church and state. Richard Firth Green has pointed out that Audelay's 'Marcolf' poem cites the ominous English proverb 'Be war or ye be wo' in contexts that recall its politically charged use in the letters associated with John Ball and his followers in contemporary accounts of the Rising of 1381.[19]

Both Marcolf and Rauf prevail as a result of their verbal agility, using proverbs, and, in Marcolf's case, a mock genealogy and a series of riddles, as ideological weapons deployed against their superiors in learning and in political power. Marcolf's language shares with Rauf's a stubborn insistence on 'reason' and 'law' above royal authority.[20] For example, Solomon promises Marcolf rich rewards if he can hold his own in the proverb contest, but when he does, Solomon's courtiers suggest that it would be more suitable to throw him to the bears or to blind him than to exalt him 'to any dignyte or honour' (Duff p. 13). Solomon settles for giving the unexpected victor a good meal and allowing him to go in peace. Chagrined at the king's broken promise, Marcolf's aphoristic response gives him a certain dignity as he departs: 'I suffre ynough what that ye haue sayde. I shall alweyes saye, "There is no king were no lawe is"' (Duff p. 14).

Like Marcolf, Rauf Coilyear is a verbally assured rustic who holds his own in agonistically toned encounters with his king, though Rauf is at the disadvantage of not knowing who his sovereign is. Charlemagne's jest is at Rauf's expense when he claims to be a particularly favoured attendant of the queen's chamber: 'And thocht myself it say, maist inwart of ane' (line 236). From its opening stanzas, *The Taill of Rauf Coilyear* is hyper-attentive to

---

[17] *The Proverb* (Cambridge, Mass., 1931), p. 87.

[18] C. Lewis, 'XXII. Proverbs, Precepts, and Monitory Pieces', in *A Manual of the Writings in Middle English 1050–1500*, ed. J. Burke Severs (New Haven, 1993): 2957–3048, 3349–408, at 2975 and 3360.

[19] 'Marcolf the Fool and Blind John Audelay', in *Speaking Images: Essays in Honor of V. A. Kolve*, ed. R. F. Yeager and C. C. Morse (Asheville, 2001), pp. 559–76.

[20] Two articles that explore this more serious side of *Rauf Coilyear* with its apt social and political commentary are S. H. A. Shepherd, '"of thy glitterand gyde haue I na gle": *The Taill of Rauf Coilȝear*', *Archiv für das Studium der neueren Sprachen und Literaturen* 228 (1991), 284–98 and G. Wright, 'Churl's Courtesy'.

rank, an attention as socially polarising as the contrastive genealogies at the beginning of *The Dialogue of Solomon and Marcolf.* Charlemagne becomes lost while travelling to Paris with a retinue said to include emperors, earls, prelates, princes, dukes, 'douzepeers', barons, and bachelors. Separated from this socially distinguished company, the king meets his polar opposite, a 'cant carll' (line 42), or 'bold and lively common man'. The tale insists on Rauf's status as *carll*, a Northern form of *cherl*: alliterative phrases throughout the narrative oppose *carll* to both *king* and *knicht*, until the *carll/knicht* polarity resolves itself into identity at the end. When Charlemagne finally commands that Rauf be knighted, 'courtasie' becomes the alliterative shared middle term that mediates the opposition: 'That carll for his courtasie salbe maid knicht' (line 746). Prior to his elevation, Rauf is also called a 'husband man' (lines 520, 597) or peasant farmer, his clothing described by the courtier Roland as 'husband weid' (line 593). He dwells in rural isolation on a barren, windswept moor bounded by high, rugged country subject to violent storms. It has often been noted that this countryside resembles the poet's native Scotland much more than the tale's supposed setting outside Paris. Like the outdoor scenery, Rauf's peasant house is also concretely imagined: its owner describes it as the most substantial house in its remote area, and indeed it turns out to include barn, stable, hall, a large hearth with a roaring fire, and at least one private chamber where the unexpected guest will sleep in a curtained bed. Rauf's material comfort is another link to Marcolf, who sits at his hearth tending his pot of beans in a house that possesses at least one separate chamber where his unwed sister weeps because her flirtation has resulted in a pregnancy (Duff p. 15).

As early readers sometimes paid more attention to Marcolf's crude antics than to the considerable verbal acumen he displays in the proverb contest and in succeeding verbal competitions, so some readers of *Rauf Coilyear* have been more aware of the heavy blows he delivers as rebukes to the manners of his unrecognised king than of his deft use of proverbial wisdom to negotiate a delicate situation of potential class conflict. In *The Taill of Rauf Coilyear*, proverb tradition serves as a universal wisdom source upon which both peasant and high-ranking guest can plausibly draw for guidance in how to negotiate a situation of acute social tension. Despite his comfortable material circumstances, Rauf betrays considerable apprehension about lodging what he believes to be a knight. His wariness about sharing his private space with his socially superior guest is acute: two whole stanzas are devoted to his concern about whether his lodging will suit his guest (lines 66–91). Rauf's apprehension, however, is expressed more by aggression than by submission. He repeatedly warns that he and his guest may quarrel (lines 60, 79, 129–30), and most of their dialogue in this scene establishes the principles by which the high-born guest can spend the night without offending his host.

For Rauf, the situation requires no fewer than five proverbs. The idea that proverb tradition represented an accumulated store of peasant wisdom was a powerful idea upon which medieval and early modern writers could draw. Rauf's first proverb, 'With-thy thow wald be payit of *sic as thow fand* / Forsuith, thow suld be welcum to pas hame with me' (lines 70–1), is a version of the expression 'to take as one finds' indexed by Whiting (T15).[21] Interestingly, Chaucer uses the same expression in a very similar context in the 'Reeve's Tale', in which two Cambridge scholars agree to make do with what they find in the house of the Miller Symkyn, a *cherl* even more aggressively sensitive than Rauf Coilyear about taking lodgers from a different social status. As is frequent in Chaucer, the student John marks his expression quite clearly as a pre-existing proverb, ' "*I have herd seyd*, Man sal *taa* of twa thynges: / *Slyk as he fyndes*, or taa slyk as he brynges" ' (*CT* I.4129–30). The idea that one must accept simple accommodations for what they are is obviously much less tactful coming from the socially superior guest than from the host, and we can measure Rauf's proverb use against the boorishness of Symkyn's two well-educated, but ill-mannered, houseguests.

Charlemagne gives his heartfelt thanks for Rauf Coilyear's offer of shelter, and Rauf replies with two more proverbs, both of which warn against premature praise that may soon give way to criticism: 'Pryse at the parting how that thow dois' (line 86), and 'first to lofe and syne to lak, Peter, it is schame!'.[22] Affronted when his guest does not allow him to dictate who shall take precedence in passing through the door of the house, Rauf admonishes his high-born visitor with two more proverbs: 'kynd aucht to creip / Sen ellis thow art unknawin / To mak me lord of my awin' (lines 126–8). Rauf's 'Kynd aucht to creip' adapts the first half of the well-attested saying 'Nature crawls where it cannot walk' (Whiting K34). The implication here seems to be that if an individual is well born, as is Rauf's unidentified knight, his superior nature should, by one means or another, manage to find expression (Whiting K34 cites eight examples in addition to this one). Finally, the expression, 'to make someone lord of his own' appears to have been proverbial in Scotland, as it appears in a similar context in *Gologras and Gawain* when Gawain courteously defers to his host: 'To mak you lord of your aune, me think it grete skill' (line 147).[23] Proverbs are not at all unusual in medieval narrative, and they occur in the represented speech of all classes, including Charlemagne and Roland in the tale in question, but here it is the density and the skill with which they are wielded that interest me, as well as their assignment to a peasant speaker. Rauf's proverbs, five in a row, all serve to get a knight over a peasant threshold, to mediate relations between men of unequal status forced by unusual circumstances into close proximity. Although he is a rustic, Rauf is mentally acute and adept at manipulating the proverb, a tiny but culturally important verbal form.

---

[21] B. J. Whiting with H. Wescott Whiting, *Proverbs, Sentences, and Proverbial Phrases from English Writings Mainly Before 1500* (Cambridge, Mass., 1968).

[22] See Whiting P39, 'Praise at the parting', and L17, 'Lack ['blame'] not where you have loved ['praised']'.

[23] *The Knightly Tale of Gologras and Gawain*, ed. T. Hahn, in *Sir Gawain: Eleven Romances and Tales* (Kalamazoo, 1995).

Two of the other genres wielded skilfully by the peasant Marcolf – the argu-able proposition and the argument on both sides of an issue – suit the mock-scholastic dialogue in which they appear, with its more formally structured set of verbal contests, but there is no place for them in the traditional folktale of the peasant and his unrecognised king that underlies the first half of *The Taill of Rauf Coilyear*. Instead, the tale's representation of Rauf Coilyear's peasant speech draws upon another recognisable genre, the popular complaint or 'poem of social protest'. J. R. Maddicott has suggested that poems of social protest in English and Anglo-French begin to appear rather suddenly in the early decades of the fourteenth century in part because it was an historical moment in which there was a great deal for the working man to protest about: the weight of taxation in England, for example, may have been the heaviest of the entire Middle Ages, exceeding even the years just prior to the 1381 Rising.[24] Russell Peck offers another possible impetus: the new emphasis on examining individual consciences that followed the Fourth Lateran Council in 1215 gave rise to a developing social conscience, a concern for the poor and dispossessed that rose in intensity late in the fourteenth century, when what contemporaries understood as a 'peasants' revolt' drew attention to the social conditions of the lowest sectors of English society.[25]

Rauf Coilyear's 'complaint' is broken up into parts and embedded in the narrative, not delivered as a single formal unit, but its language and themes resemble those of the free-standing complaint poems circulating in the four-teenth and fifteenth centuries. We learn from Rauf's first-person speeches that he travels long distances in all kinds of weather with his horse and his two heavy charcoal baskets; his clothing is ragged and his feet muddy; if he poaches a fat deer for his dinner, the king's foresters threaten to have him up before the king for punishment. Despite these hardships, Rauf describes himself as a law-abiding man who continues to transport his heavy loads and live 'with mekle lawtie ['uprightness'] and laubour':

> 'Men callis me Rauf Coilyear, as I weill wait.
> I leid my life in this land with mekle unrufe,
> Baith tyde and time, in all my travale.
> Hine ovir sevin mylis I dwell,
> And leidis coilis to sell.
> Sen thow speiris, I the tell
>   All the suith hale.' (lines 46–52)

> … 'I have deir coft all this dayis hyre,
> In wickit wedderis and weit walkand full will.' (lines 105–6)

24 J. R. Maddicott, 'Poems of Social Protest in Early Fourteenth-Century England', in *England in the Fourteenth Century*, ed. W. M. Ormrod (Woodbridge, 1986), pp. 130–44.
25 R. Peck, 'Social Conscience and the Poets', in *Social Unrest in the Late Middle Ages*, ed. F. X. Newman (Binghamton, 1986), pp. 113–48.

... 'the forestaris, forsuith, of this forest,
Thay have me all at invy for dreid of the deir!
Thay threip that I thring doun of the fattest.
Thay say I sall to Paris, thair to compeir
Befoir our cumlie King, in dule to be drest.
Sic manassing thay me mak, forsuith, ilk yeir.' (lines 195–200)

'I have na myster to matche with maisterfull men,
Fairand ovir the feildis fewell to fet,
And oft fylit my feit in mony foull fen,
Gangand with laidis my governing to get.' (lines 442–5)

'I war an fule gif I fled and fand nane affray,
Bot as ane lauchfull man my laidis to leid,
That leifis with mekle lawtie and laubour, in fay.' (lines 507–9)

Particularly characteristic of popular complaint is Rauf's claim at lines 51–2 to be telling the whole truth, his subsequent affirmation of his integrity and law-abiding intentions at lines 507–9, and the hostility he expresses toward local officials – the faces that enforced the lord's or the crown's exactions – in this case the foresters at line 195.

An example of complaint in the voice of a peasant from about 1340 is the 'Song of the Husbandman', found in MS Harley 2253, a poem distant in time from the fifteenth-century tale of *Rauf Coilyear*, yet allied to it by the similarity of its octet/quatrain alliterative stanza (abababababcdcd),[26] a stanza with some resemblance to *Rauf Coilyear*'s more unusual alliterative 13-line form, which rhymes $ababababc_4dddc_2$. Thanks to the enduring quality of alliterative formulas, both Rauf (line 106) and the first-person speaker of 'The Song of the Husbandman' lament 'wickede wederes' among their other hardships:

Thus I kippe and cacche cares ful colde,
Seththe I counte and cot hade to kepe.
To seche selver to the kyng I mi seed solde;
Forthi mi lond leye lith and leorneth to slepe.
Seththe he mi feire feh fatte I my folde,
When I thenk o mi weole wel neh I wepe.
Thus bredeth monie beggares bolde,
And ure ruye ys roted and ruls er we repe.
Ruls ys oure ruye and roted in the stre,
For wickede wederes by broke and by brynke.
Thus wakeneth in the world wondred and wee
Ase god is swynden anon as so forte swynke. (lines 61–72)[27]

---

[26] For a study of the dating and affiliations of these stanza forms, see S. Greer Fein, 'Twelve-Line Stanza Forms in Middle English and the Date of *Pearl*', *Speculum* 72 (1997), 367–98.
[27] *Medieval English Political Writings*, ed. J. M. Dean (Kalamazoo, 1996).

The peasant speaker also protests the obstacles to earning one's livelihood imposed on the working man by haywards, bailiffs, and 'woodwards' or keepers of the lord's timber (lines 15–17), grievances that would resonate with Rauf, who protests in lines 195ff. the vigilance of the 'foresters' who guard against game poaching.

Closer in time to *The Taill of Rauf Coilyear* are the fifteenth-century alliterative complaint poems in the *Piers Plowman* tradition.[28] These often have a religious fervour and a strong bent toward allegory absent from *Rauf Coilyear*, but they share Rauf's conviction that the ruling classes betray their own ideals when they express contempt for those below them: in Rauf's words to Roland, 'Schir knicht, it is na courtasie commounis to scorne' (line 429). The Langlandian passage below from *Mum and the Sothsegger* argues in a similar vein that scorn for the weakest injures those in power as well as the dispossessed themselves:

> This same cursid custume the coroune doeth a-peyre
> And bringeth a bitter byworde a-brode among the peuple,
> And is in euery cuntre but a comune tale
> That yf the pouer playne, though he plede euer
> And hurleth with his higher hit happeth ofte-tyme
> That he wircheth al in waste and wynneth but a lite.
> Thus laboreth the loos among the comune peuple
> That the wacker in the writte wol haue the wors ende;
> Hit wol not gayne a goky a grete man forto plede,
> For lawe lieth muche in lordship sith loyaute was exiled,
> And poure men pleyntes penylees a-bateth. (lines 1574–84)[29]

The 'cursid custume' that injures the crown and embitters the people in this particular passage is maintenance at law, and the 'pleyntes' of poor men are legal rather than literary complaints, but the speaker's conviction that 'lawe lieth muche in lordship' resonates with Rauf's own protests of the forest laws and the intimidation he suffers at the hands of the local officials who preserve timber and game for the king (lines 195–200).

It should be said that Rauf's speeches in context are more comic, less earnest, than those of the speakers in the freestanding complaint poems: in particular, his protest about the foresters who protect the king's deer, unknowingly made to the king himself, raises a laugh at Rauf's own expense. Yet an undercurrent of earnestness, and indeed of historicity, underlies *The Taill of Rauf Coilyear* and links Rauf's complaint to more serious expressions of social protest. Although Rauf nominally resides in France, forest laws such as those that raise his ire governed the forests of the poet's native Scotland from

---

28 In *The Palis of Honoure*, Gavin Douglas mentions 'Peirs Plewman that maid his workmen fow [i.e. 'full']' in the same stanza as 'Raf Coilyear' (ed. Parkinson, lines 1714 and 1711).
29 *The Piers Plowman Tradition*, ed. H. Barr (London, 1993), pp. 137–202, at p. 195.

the twelfth century onward.[30] Jean Birrell has examined the records of the fourteenth-century forest courts for instances of deer-poaching by peasants and found that prominent among the culprits were woodcutters and charcoal-burners, who exploited their legitimate presence in the king's forests in order to put venison on their tables.[31]

Rauf's lament that he practises only a minor craft – 'I have na myster to matche with maisterfull men' – also rings true. It appears that those whom Birrell calls 'forest peasants' often could not live by a forest trade such as woodcutting or charcoal burning alone. Thirteenth- and early fourteenth-century peasants with the surname 'Colier' were more often granted seasonal than full-year licences to burn charcoal, which Birrell takes to 'indicate that charcoal burning was normally a subsidiary, not a main, occupation'.[32] The documentary sources studied by Birrell suggest that, at least at this earlier period, a peasant usually had to farm his smallholdings as well as practising a forest trade such as woodcutting or charcoal burning, 'work which could be done part time, and concentrated at the time of the year when the peasant was not fully occupied on his holding'.[33] The fictional Rauf speaks only of transporting and selling charcoal; whether we are to imagine that his trade also involved burning is not made explicit, though that activity lay within the range of the designation 'Colyear', and Rauf shows himself opinionated about laws governing the management of forests. By all accounts, dealing in charcoal was a difficult, dirty occupation that did indeed call for endurance of 'wickit wedderis and weit walkand', as Rauf's complaint registers.[34]

I have argued, then, that reading the encounter between Rauf Coilyear and Charlemagne in the light of Marcolf's encounter with Solomon is illuminating because each work uses recognisable genres to constitute a discourse for its peasant speaker that is pointed and meaningful as well as comic. As one of relatively few verbal genres valued by clerical and court culture and yet also accessible to ordinary people, the proverb in particular serves as a vital form of argument for fictional outsiders like Marcolf and Rauf, who use this tiny but potent form, which circulates both inside and outside literary texts, to mediate relations with a different sector of a hierarchical society. Just as Marcolf's proverbs insist upon truths absent from high Solomonic sententiousness, so Rauf Coilyear's segmented but recognisable complaint asserts truths and perspectives often lacking in chivalric romance. Although

---

[30] Bawcutt and Riddy, note to lines 195ff, with a reference to J. M. Gilbert, 'Hunting Reserves', in *An Historical Atlas of Scotland c.400–c.1600*, ed. P. McNeill and R. Nicholson (St Andrews, 1975), pp. 33–4.

[31] 'Peasant Deer Poachers in the Medieval Forest', in *Progress and Problems in Medieval England: Essays in Honour of Edward Miller*, ed. R. Britnell and J. Hatcher (Cambridge, 1996), pp. 68–88 (p. 77).

[32] 'Peasant Craftsmen', p. 96.

[33] 'Peasant Craftsmen', p. 96.

[34] For an illustrated account of the craft, see J. Bond, 'Medieval Charcoal-burning in England', in *Arts and Crafts in Medieval Rural Environment (Ruralia VI)*, ed. J. Klapste and P. Sommer (Turnhout, 2007), pp. 277–94.

he is clearly presented as a rustic, Rauf is not barely sentient, but verbally adept. His genres are the proverb and the popular complaint and these generic choices are the more effective and plausible because they correspond to wider cultural ideas about peasant self-expression.

3

'As ye have brewd, so shal ye drink': the Proverbial Context of *Eger and Grime*

MICHAEL CICHON

At first glance, the Older Scots romance *Eger and Grime* seems to be a stereotypical medieval tale about prowess, revenge and love. Perhaps this is why *Eger and Grime* has not been extensively studied. In general, medieval romances entertain, and this is certainly true of *Eger and Grime*. However, romances also convey, strengthen and uphold social bonds, opinions, prejudices, hopes and fears. In this they function very much like proverbs. Proverbial sayings 'propose a world of moral implications to those who pause to consider them'.[1] By pausing thus over the proverbs deployed in romances, one may gain a better understanding of what the authors of these texts were trying to convey. From the thirty categories of paroemial segment (proverbs and proverbial phrases) identified in *Eger and Grime* by Bartlett Whiting in his two-part article 'Proverbs and Proverbial Sayings from Scottish Writings before 1600', supplemented by twelve not noted by Whiting, I have identified groups of proverbs in the romance which exhibit some common characteristics.[2] This chapter will consider three of these groups – proverbial comparisons; proverbs touching on the condition of women; and reciprocity. The proverbial comparisons are fairly conventional phrases one would expect to find in a tale of knights, combat and love, but should not be overlooked for this reason. Traditional phraseology generates meaning by deploying well-established conventions that function similarly each time they are used.[3] Thus, proverbs evoke a web of associations within a specific narrative and appeal to the overarching authority of larger tradition.[4] The two that treat the unfortunate condition of women are interesting because

---

[1] R. Harris, 'The Proverbial Heart of Hrafnkels saga Freysgoða: "Mér þykkir þar heimskum manni at duga, sem þú ert"', *Scandinavian-Canadian Studies* 16 (2005–6), 28–54 (p. 46).

[2] These paroemial segments are listed in an appendix at the end of the chapter. Whiting's identifications are indicated by a bold-type **W** after the proverb.

[3] J. M. Foley, 'The Implications of Oral Tradition', in *Oral Tradition in the Middle Ages*, ed. W. F. H. Nicolaisen (Binghamton, NY, 1995), pp. 31–57 (p. 33).

[4] L. A. Garner, 'The Role of Proverbs in Middle English narrative', in *New Directions in Oral Theory*, ed. M. D. Amodio (Tempe, 2005), pp. 255–77 (p. 267).

they exemplify well-known medieval and proverbial misogynist stereotypes, and proverbs can indicate an appropriate audience response – when characters speak a proverb and thus align themselves with traditional wisdom, they sanction action.[5] What is said about women in *Eger and Grime* also fits with the broader theme of reciprocity. Reciprocity seems of utmost importance to the authors, and this should be no surprise since the romance is about, among other things, brotherhood. Moreover, the concern for revenge that drives the narrative fits with the reciprocity theme as well – revenge is standard reciprocal behaviour in feuding cultures, of which pre-modern Scotland was certainly one, so reciprocity in *Eger and Grime* can be contextualised in terms of a feuding society.[6] Because these proverbs and proverbial phrases line up with the broader themes of the narrative, examining the values represented by traditional wisdom as it is conveyed by the paroemes offers the reader a valuable extra interpretative tool for use with a romance such as *Eger and Grime* which, like so many popular romances, is easy to read but rather resistant to scholarly analysis.[7]

It is slightly misleading to speak of *Eger and Grime* as if it were a single text since it survives in two versions of substantially different length and rather different endings. In both of its manifestations, *Eger and Grime* stands as a 'problematical text, riddled with gaps, errors and clumsy modernizations'.[8] James Caldwell's 1933 edition – still the standard one – presents the shorter 1474-line version found in the Percy Folio manuscript of c.1650, British Library Additional MS 27879 (hereafter cited as P), in parallel with the longer 2860-line version represented by a 1687 black letter print and known as Huntington-Laing after, respectively, the library that now holds it and its most illustrious former owner and editor, the nineteenth-century scholar David Laing (hereafter cited as HL).[9]

The story as we have it is a version of a common medieval tale-type, that of the two brothers, which has roots as early as the thirteenth century BC.[10] In

---

5 Garner, 'Role of Proverbs', p. 262.
6 Feud occurs when central government is weak or absent, and is driven by the participants' belief that their honour has somehow been threatened or compromised. See J. Black-Michaud, *Cohesive Force: Feud in the Mediterranean and the Middle East* (New York, 1975) and C. Boehm, *Blood Revenge: the Anthropology of Feuding in Montenegro* (Lawrence, Kan., 1984).
7 On this feature of 'popular' romance see Pearsall's Prefatory Essay to the present volume.
8 R. Purdie, 'Medieval Romance in Scotland', in *A Companion to Medieval Scottish Poetry*, ed. P. Bawcutt and J. H. Williams (Cambridge, 2006), pp. 165–77 (pp. 168–9).
9 *Eger and Grime: A Parallel-text edition of the Percy and the Huntington-Laing Versions of the Romance, with an Introductory Study*, ed. J. R. Caldwell (Cambridge, 1933). The 'Huntington-Laing' version of 'The history of Sir Eger, Sir Grahame, and Sir Gray-Steel' is in fact represented by three almost identical prints: 1) Glasgow, Robert Sanders?, 1687: now San Marino, Calif., Huntington Library, shelfmark 55193 (Wing H2140 [CD-ROM, 1996]); 2) Glasgow, Robert Sanders, 1669: now British Library, shelfmark C.57.aa.44(6) (Wing H2139 [CD-ROM, 1996]); 3) Edinburgh?, 1711: now Oxford, Bodleian Library, Douce R 267(1).
10 Caldwell and Van Duzee both note correspondences with the Two Brothers motif: Caldwell, *Eger and Grime*, pp. 68, 81–95 and M. Van Duzee, *A Medieval Romance of Friendship: Eger and Grime* (New York, 1963), p. 15. See also A. Dundes, 'Projective inversion in the ancient Egyptian "Tale of Two Brothers"', *Journal of American Folklore* 115 (2002), 378–94.

this late-medieval version, Eger, a landless second son, loves the noblewoman Winliane (or Winglayne in the Percy version), who for her part will only love someone who has never been defeated in combat. Eger is this man until one day he seeks a foe, Sir Graysteel, in the 'land of doubt' (HL 1447, 1864) or the 'forbbidden countrye' (P 410). Graysteel defeats Eger, who confesses his loss to his sworn brother Grime, but Winliane has been eavesdropping and decides that she no longer loves Eger. Grime then proposes a plan whereby he masquerades as Eger and defeats Graysteel so his sworn brother can regain the love of Winliane. P ends shortly after this point with marriages all round, while in HL, Eger confesses the truth after Grime has died. He is rejected by his wife who enters a nunnery; he goes on crusade and later marries Grime's widow after Winliane herself has died.

Apart from being nearly twice the length of the Percy version, the Huntington-Laing version significantly alters the ending of the romance – Eger and Winliane do not live happily ever after, and eventually Eger marries Lillias, the widow of his sworn brother Grime and the lady who healed him after his loss to Graysteel. The origins and textual history of *Eger and Grime* before the appearance of the extant versions remain a mystery: the surviving P and HL versions are almost certainly revisions of an earlier romance, but neither derives from the other and they do not share an immediate common source.[11] The story is, however, mentioned in a number of seventeenth-, sixteenth-, and fifteenth-century sources. Robert Gordon of Straloch's lute book of 1627–29 contains a tune called 'Gray Steel',[12] and *Eger and Grime* is listed in the c.1550 *Complaynt of Scotland*.[13] It is also mentioned in Sir David Lyndsay's mid-sixteenth-century poems *Squyer Meldrum* and *The Cupar Banns*.[14] The earliest reference to the tale comes from the records of the Lord High Treasurer of Scotland, which note that two fiddlers sang 'Graysteil' in 1497 for James IV.[15] There is, unfortunately, no way of knowing if the aforementioned allusions are to texts anything like the surviving seventeenth-century witnesses.

Eger and Grime has not, until recently, enjoyed sustained critical attention. Apart from Caldwell's inter-war edition, there is only one extended study of the romance, Mabel Van Duzee's 1963 monograph *A Medieval Romance of Friendship: Eger and Grime*. Van Duzee's study is typical of the early- to mid-twentieth-century sources and analogue scholarship: based on lengthy

---

11 Caldwell, *Eger and Grime*, pp. 20–42.
12 John Purser argues that the longer HL version would take about two and a half hours to perform when set to this tune: see 'Greysteil' in *Stewart Style 1513–1542: Essays on the Court of James V*, ed. J. Hadley Williams (East Linton, 1996), pp. 142–52 (p. 146).
13 Ed. A. M. Stewart, STS 4th series 11 (Edinburgh, 1979), fol. 51r (p. 50).
14 *Squyer Meldrum*, line 1318; *Cupar Banns*, line 242. For *Squyer Meldrum*, see *Sir David Lyndsay: Selected Poems*, ed. J. Hadley Williams (Glasgow, 2000); for the *Cupar Banns*, see *The Works of Sir David Lindsay of the Mount, 1490–1555*, ed. D. Hamer, 4 vols., STS 3rd series 1, 2, 6, 8 (Edinburgh, 1931–6): II, 10–32.
15 *Compota Thesaurariorum Regum Scotorum*, ed. T. Dickson (Edinburgh, 1877), I, 330 (entry for 19 April 1497).

comparative studies of various romances, it argues that *Eger and Grime* was originally an Arthurian romance which derived from a story of combat at a ford, much like that depicted in the *First Branch* of the *Mabinogi*. Her work is thorough, but her conclusions are highly speculative. Beyond the introduction to Caldwell's edition and Van Duzee's study, the romance has received a few lines, albeit favourable ones, in larger anthologies and literary histories,[16] but has been examined in less than ten scholarly articles, book chapters and published conference proceedings. These treatments have ranged from attempts to prove the Scottishness of the romance based on word choice[17] and geography,[18] to Lacanian[19] and Freudian[20] readings of loss, a comparative study of *Eger and Grime* alongside the middle English *Ywain and Gawain*,[21] a study of the romance as a source for Scott's *Redgauntlet*[22] and an interpretation of the romance as a deliberate questioning of the entire medieval romance tradition.[23] The text continues to attract occasional critical attention: a new scholarly edition is in preparation,[24] and a recent study of medieval masculinity features a highly theorised interpretation of the romance.[25] At this stage in the history of *Eger and Grime*'s critical reception, then, there is both need and room for a micro-structural approach to the romance.

---

[16] Beyond praising the romance for its accurate description of combat, C. S. Lewis notes that the poetry of *Eger and Grime* is '… hard, plain, vivid, and economical in manner, effortlessly and unobtrusively noble in sentiment': *English Literature in the Sixteenth Century excluding Drama* (Oxford, 1954), p. 68. See also *A Manual of the Writings in Middle English 1050–1500*, gen. ed. J. B. Severs, Vol. I (New Haven, 1967), pp. 151–2.

[17] Caldwell contends that the parent source of the romance was a north-eastern or central Scots version, using rhyme-evidence to make his claim. However, H. A. Basilius looks at all the rhymes common to both versions and notes that of 127, only nine are distinctively Scots. He argues that, while it is not improbable that the romance was composed in Scotland, based on linguistic evidence the best one can say is that the source for the romance was northern English or Scottish: 'The Rhymes in *Eger and Grime*', *Modern Philology* 35 (1937), 129–33 (p. 133).

[18] D. Delmar Evans argues that place-names, personal names and topography in the romance place it in the Borders: 'Re-evaluating the Case for a Scottish *Eger and Grime*', in *The European Sun: Proceedings of the Seventh International Conference on Medieval and Renaissance Scottish Language and Literature*, ed. G. D. Caie, R. J. Lyall, S. Mapstone and K. Simpson (East Linton, 2001), pp. 276–87. In this Evans counters Van Duzee, who argues that place- and personal names are probably continental: *Medieval Romance of Friendship*, pp. 122–3.

[19] A. J. Hasler, 'Romance and its discontents in *Eger and Grime*', in *The Spirit of Medieval English Popular Romance*, ed. A. Putter and J. Gilbert (London, 2000), pp. 200–18.

[20] L. C. Ramsey, *Chivalric Romances: Popular Literature in Medieval England* (Bloomington, 1983), pp. 135–50.

[21] D. E. Faris, 'The Art of Adventure in the Middle English Romance: *Ywain and Gawain, Eger and Grime*', *Studia Neophilologica* 53 (1981), 91–100.

[22] D. Delmar Evans, 'Scott's *Redgauntlet* and the late Medieval Romance of Friendship, *Eger and Grime*', *Studies in Scottish Literature* 31 (1999), 31–45.

[23] S. Mainer, '*Eger and Grime* and the Boundaries of Courtly Romance', in *'Joyous Sweit Imaginatioun': Essays on Scottish Literature in Honour of R. D. S. Jack*, ed. S. Carpenter and S. M. Dunnigan (New York, 2007), pp. 77–95.

[24] R. Purdie, *Shorter Scottish Medieval Romances*, STS (Cambridge, forthcoming).

[25] T. Pugh, 'Queer Castration, Patriarchal Privilege, and the Comic Phallus in *Eger and Grime*,' in his *Sexuality and its Queer Discontents in Middle English Literature* (New York, 2008), pp. 123–44.

Just as the history of *Eger and Grime* before 1650 proves elusive, the definition of a 'proverb' is equally hard to pin down. In fact, coming to a definition of a proverb is as fractious an enterprise as defining romance. The proverb has been characterised as a rhetorical strategy that expresses a relative truth[26] as well as the strategic social use of metaphor.[27] A logician's definition might be that a proverb is a traditional communication to persuade, exhort and criticise.[28] A linguist would suggest that proverbs are form-meaning units and analysable complexes of independently occurring units, and that proverbs belong to the study of phraseology both as a linguistic item and an item of folklore.[29] Folklorists consider them a genre or a subgenre of folksay, along with proverbial phrases, comparisons, conventional phrases and ditties.[30] Archer Taylor, the grandfather of modern paroemiology, simply says that proverbs are sayings common among the folk, impossible to define precisely, but that 'an incommunicable quality tells us this sentence is proverbial and that one is not'.[31] My simple, working definition is that a proverb is a pithy statement that expresses traditional wisdom or a general truth, and which stems from a society's need to 'formulate, preserve and transmit its collective wisdom'.[32]

The conventional approach to proverb analysis is that paroemes, however they are defined, emerge from the people. In fact, Taylor contends that proverbs have meant more to the folk than to the learned classes at all times, and that in literature from classes removed from the folk, proverbs rarely occur.[33] Taylor's contention is too limited and limiting, for examples of proverbial use in high literature abound – Kurt Wittig finds in the writings of Barbour 'popular language full of mother wit' including many proverbs;[34] the composer of *Clariodus*, who very deliberately presents his romance as 'innovative, high-brow, and above all Scottish',[35] sprinkles his narrative liberally with proverbs;[36] Geoffrey Chaucer deploys at least one proverb for every

---

26 B. Kirshenblatt-Gimblett, 'Toward a Theory of Proverb Meaning', in *The Wisdom of Many: Essays on the Proverb*, ed. W. Mieder and A. Dundes (Madison, 1994), pp. 111–21.

27 P. Seitel, 'Proverbs: A Social Use of Metaphor', in *The Wisdom of Many*, ed. Mieder and Dundes, pp. 122–39.

28 P. D. Goodwin and J. W. Weinzel, 'Proverbs and Practical Reasoning: A Study in Socio-logic', in *The Wisdom of Many*, ed. Mieder and Dundes, pp. 140–60.

29 N. R. Norrick, *How Proverbs Mean: Semantic Studies in English Proverbs* (Berlin, 1985): see chapter 3, 'Defining the Proverb' (pp. 31–79).

30 D. Buchan, 'Folk Tradition and Literature till 1603', in *Bryght Lanternis: Essays on the Language and Literature of Medieval Scotland*, ed. D. McClure and M. R. G. Spiller (Aberdeen, 1989), pp. 1–13 (p. 8).

31 A. Taylor, *The Proverb* (Cambridge, 1931), p. 1.

32 Harris, 'Proverbial Heart', p. 45.

33 Taylor, *The Proverb*, pp. 171–2.

34 K. Wittig, *The Scottish Tradition in Literature* (Edinburgh, 1958), p. 18.

35 R. Purdie, '*Clariodus* and the Ambitions of Courtly Romance in Later Medieval Scotland', *Forum for Modern Language Studies* 38 (2002), 449–61 (p. 450).

36 B. J. Whiting counts at least 103 proverbs in *Clariodus*. 'Proverbs and Proverbial Sayings From Scottish Writings Before 1600. Part One: A–L', *Mediaeval Studies* 11 (1949), 123–205; 'Proverbs

sixty-four lines of his *Troilus and Criseyde*.[37] Late-medieval romance has roots in both the most popular and most refined segments of society,[38] and material from each tradition crosses into the other: participation in the audience of more refined romances did not preclude participation in the audience of more popular romances.[39] Certainly, 'Chaucer's use of proverbs reminds us that medieval culture cannot be divided into mutually exclusive categories of elite versus popular'.[40] Moreover, because of their constant repetition of phraseology, distinct vocabulary and omission of conjunctions, proverbs are extremely well suited for use in poetry.[41]

Thematic Groups

Proverbial Comparisons

By far the largest group of proverbial phrases in *Eger and Grime* is the comparisons: ladies are as white as foam or as white as swans; a knight's mail is milk-white and shines like the moon; gear is red as blood or hard as flint; warriors are wroth as boars or wild as lions; a wounded knight falls dead as a stone; Grime is to Lillias worth his weight in gold; the healing draught is green as grass, and so on. Certainly here, the composer often chooses a ready-made utterance, a familiar stock phrase with a standard meaning.[42] While some of these phrases are ornamental or used as filler, this is not to say that all proverbial comparisons in the romance are mere embellishment. Two examples stand out; both are colour comparisons. The first instance involves red – Graysteel (despite his name) wears red armour and carries red weapons (HL 136–8; HL 1501; P 117); Lillias wears red and has a red spot between her eyes (HL 251; P 215). Laura Hibbard, Roger Sherman Loomis, Caldwell and Van Duzee all make much of the colour symbolism, asserting that red is a traditional colour marker for denizens of the Otherworld.[43] This assertion seems more credible when one considers that such colour associations are prominent in the ballad tradition, which in Scotland overlaps with the flourishing of metrical romance,[44] and that *Eger and Grime* is replete with other features common to the ballad tradition: a special sword, rivers and wilder-

and Proverbial Sayings From Scottish Writings Before 1600. Part Two: M–Y', *Mediaeval Studies* 13 (1951), 87–164.

[37] Garner, 'Role of Proverbs', p. 267.

[38] C. Lindahl, 'The Oral Undertones of Late Medieval Romance', in *Oral Tradition in the Middle Ages*, ed. Nicolaisen, pp. 59–75 (pp. 59–60).

[39] Buchan, 'Folk Tradition', p. 3.

[40] Garner, 'Role of Proverbs', p. 268.

[41] A. C. Spearing, *Readings in Medieval Poetry* (Cambridge, 1987), p. 138.

[42] Norrick, *How Proverbs Mean*, p. 25.

[43] Caldwell observes that red is a favourite fairy colour: *Eger and Grime*, p. 115. Hasler also observes that Loosepaine ('Lillias' in HL), like Graysteel, is clad in red and gold: 'Romance and its discontents', p. 209. Ramsey categorises the romance as a fairy mistress type and notes red and gold among several conventional markers for the otherworld: *Chivalric Romances*, p. 141.

[44] Purdie, 'Medieval Romance in Scotland', pp. 174–5.

nesses as barriers to the Otherworld, and a heroine who resembles a fairy mistress.[45] What is on the surface a stock colour reference actually evokes all the associations that go with an Otherworldly encounter. Furthermore, the grassy green healing draught offered to Eger is not merely a proverbial commonplace description of a strange brew: in the ballad tradition, green is associated with love and lust, as well as death, ill-luck, and has otherworldly associations.[46] Without doubt, Eger is a victim of all these hardships during and after his unsuccessful combat. So, in the case of these colour comparisons, the composer of the romance has deployed the traditional proverbial material in such a way that what appear to be, on the surface, merely filler or local pithy sayings really do inform the work on a deeper level.

Women

Two proverbs dealing with women merit consideration. The first, 'of women I can never traist,/ I find them fikle, false and right untrew' (HL 715–16), is spoken by Grime after Eger has divulged his secret failure and laments the unlikelihood of a continued relationship with Winliane. The second, 'Thus she was so set all to ill,/ as wanton women that gets her will:/ amongst thousands there is not one/ can govern them but wit of none' (HL 2827–30), occurs toward the end of the romance, when Winliane has discovered Eger's deception and vows to leave him. Both proverbs fit into the broader paroemiological category of the capriciousness of women, and one could easily analyse these proverbs in terms of the well-documented tradition of medieval misogyny.[47] Such proverbs express a perceived truth, and are both the result and cause of cultural practice, passing the practice from generation to generation, entrenching it and upholding what is deemed to be culturally acceptable behaviour.[48] They make a declarative statement about the social universe and strengthen an audience's faith in that statement.[49] Reading the proverbs in this way reinforces the oft-made point that if women in romance are kept in their place, all will be well.[50]

Beyond the obvious anti-feminist focus of these proverbs, the composer achieves added effect when he deploys them both in terms of character and to reinforce the theme of reciprocity. Speakers often resort to proverbs when revealing their own preferences or wishing to avoid hurting someone.[51]

---

45 M. P. McDiarmid, 'The Scots Makars and the Ballad Tradition', in *Bryght Lanternis*, ed. McClure and Spiller, pp. 14–23 (p. 17).

46 McDiarmid, 'The Scots Makars', p. 15.

47 See R. H. Bloch, *Medieval Misogyny and the Invention of Western Romantic Love* (Chicago, 1991); M. Schipper, *Never Marry a Woman with Big Feet* (New Haven, 2003); J. A. Brundage, *Law, Sex, and Christian Society in Medieval Europe* (Chicago, 1987).

48 D. A. Malmgren, 'Gender-related Proverbs: A Cultural and Cognitive Approach', *Proverbium* 24 (2007), 231–3.

49 S. Wittig, *Stylistic and Narrative Structures in the Middle English Romances* (Austin, 1978), p. 45.

50 Hasler, 'Romance and its discontents', p. 205.

51 Norrick, *How Proverbs Mean*, p. 27.

Grime's statement follows almost immediately on his discovery of the eaves-dropping Winliane outside their apartment. Instead of telling Eger the truth, namely that Winliane has heard his entire confession and has resolved to no longer love him, Grime utters the proverb and then concocts a plan to restore Eger to Winliane's good graces.[52] We have here an instance in which a proverb is used to deflect Eger's attention from the immediate reality of his botched engagement. Furthermore, when one deploys a proverb it can signal a wish to teach: 'the speaker shows with a proverbial utterance that he has the right, or at least can afford to act as if he had the right, to council [sic] his hearer, and thereby that the relationship is either one between equals or one in which the speaker is one-up'.[53] Grime has already berated Eger for ignoring his advice and going after Graysteel in the first place, a didactic 'I-told-you-so': the proverb occurs in a context in which Grime instructs Eger to follow his plan and undo the consequences of ignoring Grime's original advice. Inter-estingly, Grime offers himself as a replacement for Eger, but Winliane refuses his advance. Perhaps by claiming Eger's woman after uttering the proverb, Grime is heightening the one-upmanship implicit in his proverbial utterance. Whatever his intentions toward the woman Hasler reads as a dominatrix who subjects her lover to 'senseless, outrageous, impossible, arbitrary, capricious ordeals',[54] Grime has no qualms about lying to protect his sworn brother, using cunning and pretence to restore Eger's honour and relationship.[55] We can also see in the deployment of anti-women proverbs the concept of reci-procity, insofar as the proverbs are a response to Winliane's rejection and the context is part of a series of actions to win her back, albeit punishing her first. Eger, after Grime has slain Graysteel, is pressed to dismiss Winliane, just as she earlier had dismissed him, and she eventually comes to him on her knees begging that he take her back (HL 2374 ff.). What goes around comes around. Not surprisingly, this retroactively justifies and reinforces the attitude in the misogynist proverbs.

Reciprocity

In this tale of two sworn brothers, one of whom helps out his comrade in terms of winning a bride and getting revenge, it is no surprise that several proverbs deal with reciprocity. Here are three which touch that theme: 'Thus ungracious deeds without mending/ can never Scape without an ill endinge' (P 1088–90); 'He that slays, he will be slain' (HL 2004); 'As ye have brewd, so shal ye drink' (HL 2384). Eger utters the third of this trio after he returns, ostensibly to exonerate himself in the eyes of the court and Winliane. He has been instructed by Grime to 'keep no kindness to her now,/ And love

---

[52] A plot Hasler reads as an effort to reassert male symbolic authority, fitting nicely with the theme of misogyny exemplified by these proverbs: 'Romance and its discontents', p. 210.
[53] Norrick, *How Proverbs Mean*, p. 29.
[54] Hasler, 'Romance and its discontents', p. 207.
[55] Mainer, '*Eger and Grime*', pp. 85–6.

her as she loveth you' (HL 2365–6). He tells her that he will not do to her as she has done to him, but announces that he is leaving for another locale, and Grime informs her that Eger has a new paramour. This proverb, then, is connected with the scheme to regain Winliane's affection after making her suffer for spurning Eger earlier in the romance. The first two, each from roughly the same point in the narrative in the Percy and Huntington-Laing versions respectively, occur in the context of blood revenge. Grime has slain Graysteel, and in the Percy version the narrator reports that this is vindication for the upward of one hundred knights Graysteel has unceremoniously and shamefully killed (P 1093–4). Graysteel is now vilified well beyond his role as the architect of Eger's shame. The same holds true in the Huntington-Laing version. Lillias utters the proverb 'he that slayes, he will be slain' (HL 2004) when she reports Graysteel's death to her father (HL 1995–2020). In this version, we have learned that Graysteel is responsible for the death of Lillias's brother as well as her fiancé, and has routinely terrorised her father's land, so it is not surprising that a proverb is deployed to emphasise that ill leads to ill. The theme of reciprocity is certainly common in medieval romance, as is its correlative, revenge, and this is consistent with the societies that produced the literature. Late-medieval Scotland was characterised in some respects by feud, the hallmarks of which are retaliation and reciprocity.[56]

Eger and Grime may very well be stereotypical in terms of its plot, and chock-full of predictable and commonplace themes and formulae. Nevertheless, its romancer has consciously laid out groups of proverbs that help the tale express social beliefs, attitudes, values, fears and perceptions.[57] Within the work, a deployed proverb, by quoting traditional material, signals the audience to look for contextual meaning.[58] The proverbial comparisons are frank and sometimes even inartistically ordinary – 'white as milk', 'green as grass' – and they may appear to be little more than ready-made filler. Indeed, proverbs have tended to escape serious critical notice because of their simplicity and ring of cliché. As has been demonstrated, however, they may also resonate with wider literary or cultural traditions, and it is their very commonality and predictability that allows the audience to tap into those traditions. Proverbs and proverbial comparisons therefore serve to blur the boundaries between so-called high and low literatures, highlighting the interconnectivity among various genres and traditions. The proverbs about women reinforce misogynist stereotypes, and when characters speak such proverbs they use aspects of traditional wisdom to endorse the action of the narrative and the

56 See especially K. M. Brown, *Bloodfeud in Scotland 1573–1625: Violence, Justice and Politics in an Early Modern Society* (Edinburgh, 1986) and J. M. Wormald, 'Bloodfeud, Kindred and Government in Early Modern Scotland', *Past and Present* 87 (1980), 54–97.
57 S. Douglas, 'Scotland on the European Storytelling Map', in *The European Sun*, eds. Caie et al., pp. 24–9 (p. 25).
58 Norrick, *How Proverbs Mean*, p. 27.

so-called wisdom that informs it. These particular proverbs also reinforce the characterisation of Winliane as callous and manipulative, and demonstrate that Grime has the upper hand in his relationship with Eger. Moreover, they illustrate the theme of reciprocity, which is itself communicated by means of proverbs which not only reinforce misogyny but also sanction and celebrate blood revenge. One might analyse other related thematic strands in terms of their proverbs – *Eger and Grime* contains proverbs that deal with good governance and finality, duplicity and failure, all of which contain elements of reciprocity. These might be considered from a strictly literary point of view, or explicated in terms of Scotland's socio-political history at the time of the romance's composition and during its period of popularity. *Eger and Grime* thus deploys its traditional paroemiological material to control audience response and to establish itself within a referential context wider than that normally associated, at least by modern readers, with medieval romance.

Appendix: Proverbial phrases in *Eger and Grime*
(P Percy; HL Huntington-Laing)[59]

1. Her rud was red as rose in raine (P 217; 795) **W (Rose 1)**
2. The drinke shee gave mee was grasse greene (P 291) **W (Grass 1)**
3. That Ladye with her milke white hand (P 311) **W (Milk)**
4. Her own hands white as the milk (HL 323) **W (Milk)**
5. I fell down dead as any stone (HL 429) **W (Stone 7)**
6. Armour they may be fresh and new,/ and yet be false and right untrew (HL 625–6)
7. For weapons may be both fresh and new,/ fikle, false, and full untrue; when a weapon faileth when a man hath need,/ all the worse then may hee speede; (P 545–8)
8. I strake the nail upon the head (HL 663) **W (Nail)**
9. Of women I can never traist,/ I find them fickle and never fast (HL 715–16)
10. The Ladies white as lake (HL 723; 981; 2497; 2511; 2687) **W (Lake 1. 1)**
11. The man that loves, and als is leel./ is worthiest to keep counsel (HL 795–6) **W (Love VB. 1. 3)**
12. Teugh as the wax when it was wrought,/ Hard like the flint, and faileth nought (HL 837–8) **W (Wax 1)**
13. There is no fault in any thing,/ but it was in misgoverning/ for a man of evil guiding,/ may tine a kinrick and a king (HL 845–8) **W (Grace 1)**
14. Als as trew as the steel (HL 1003) **W (Steel 7)**

---

[59] **W** indicates Whiting's original identification. I include in parentheses the heading under which Whiting classifies his proverbs as well as a number when he assigns one.

15. For want of grace and good governing/ may loose a Kingdome and a King (P 595–6) **W (Grace 3)**
16. And was as fresh as any lyon (HL 1035) **W (Lion 9)**
17. But when there is a knight for a knight,/ they must do more to try a right:/ knight for knight, and steed for steed,/ then to do well were all the need (HL 1077–8)
18. He spowted forward as he had beene a deere (P 652) **W (Deer 2)**
19. He rydeth fiercely out of the towne/ as he were a wild Lyon (P 662–3) **W (Lion 3)**
20. Hee may make great boast and shoure/ when there is noe man him before;/ but when there is nam to nam, and steed to steede,/ to prove his manhood, then were it neede! (P 665–8)
21. But all men in loving shall never be wise (P 798) **W (Love VB. 1. 1)**
22. There is no leech in all the land,/ can put a finger to an hand (HL 1273–4)
23. There is noe Leeche in all this land/ can sett a finger to a hand (P 808–9)
24. Scorn and heeding goes together (HL 1284)
25. But game and bourd Let goe together;/ scorning I can well consider (P 811–12)
26. His gear was red as any blood (HL 1501) **W (Blood 1)**
27. Then he waxt brim as any bare (HL 1506) **W (Boar 2)**
28. That both in earnest and in play,/ it were better who might it hint,/ get the first strake nor the last dint (HL 1546–9) **W (Stroke)**
29. Like a lyon in his woodest time (P 990) **W (Lion 3)**
30. Thus ungracious deeds without mending/ can never Scape without an ill endinge (P 1089–90) **W (Deed 3)**
31. It shone as Moone doth in the night (P 970) **W (Moon 4)**
32. He is worth to her his waight in gold (P 1154) and He is worth his waight in gold (P 1228) **W (Weight)**
33. So wight in the world was never none/ But where two meets them alone,/ And departs without company,/ But one must win the victorie (HL 1607–10) **W (Two 2)**
34. But a fair tale it may be shown,/ Another in the heart be known (HL 1901–2) **W (Word 9)**
35. Falset is ay a fained friend/ and it cometh ay at the last end (HL 1903–4) **W (Falset)**
36. And in lawtie there is no lack (HL 1908) **W (Lewty 1)**
37. He that slays, he will be slain (HL 2004) **W (Slay 1)**
38. A man may covet many a year,/ that many right hastilie appear (HL 2009–10) **W (Year 2)**
39. The Lady was as white as Swan (HL 2085) **W (Swan 2)**
40. And Ladies quyet as any fame (HL 2371) **W (Foam)**
41. As ye have brewd, so shal ye drink (HL 2384) **W (Brew 2)**
42. Parting is a privye payne,/ but old friends cannot be called againe! (P 1341–12) **W (Friend 4)**

43. The swiftest hound that ever was made,/ may run so far into a stade,/ will suffer ere he come to lack,/ a simple hound the game to take (HL 2421–4)
44. For both their hearts they were so light,/ as ever Falcon was of flight (HL 2519–20) **W (Falcon 2)**
45. And your two maidens myld as mood (HL 2655) **W (Mud)**
46. Thus she was so set all to ill,/ as wanton women that gets her will:/ amongtst thousands there is not one/ can govern them but wit of none (HL 2827–30)

4

Ekphrasis and Narrative in *Emaré*
and *Sir Eglamour of Artois*

NICHOLAS PERKINS

The worlds created by Middle English romances are frequented by important objects (often gifts), by exchanges of tokens and promises, and by
protagonists who are regularly both party to and subjects of exchange. One
way of reading these objects and exchanges is to categorize them as narrative
clutter: a naïve or aspirational fascination with luxury materials, or clumsy
plot devices that rely on formulaic social actions. Another is to assign symbolic
or associative meaning to them: in these readings, objects and exchanges
provide structural or psychological motifs denoting a larger arena of meaning.[1] While not discounting such approaches, this essay shifts the focus to the
relationships between description and narration in two romances. In them, I
argue, the techniques of describing objects and the people who own, carry
or wear them bear on aspects of romance narrative itself, and in particular
on how romances engage or provoke their reading or listening audience. The
contexts in which I shall read them are initially those of rhetoric and material
culture. In particular, the rhetorical figure of ekphrasis – a trope character-
ized by vivid description of things and actions – helps to draw together the
arenas of poetic style, materiality and audience engagement, reminding us
that certain contexts are neither easy nor necessarily productive to separate.

Sir Eglamour of Artois and *Emaré* survive in London, British Library, MS
Cotton Caligula A.II (first part), a rather plain, paper manuscript dating from
the mid-fifteenth century containing eight romances amongst practical and

---

[1] In *Sir Eglamour of Artois*, ed. F. E. Richardson, EETS OS 256 (London, 1965), Richardson
comments on its 'rather thin' use of 'descriptive ornament' and absorption of romance motifs,
like *Sir Thopas* but 'in solemn and naïve earnestness' (pp. xli, xxxix). W. R. J. Barron notes
English romances' 'fabulous trappings, and properties which function as images as much as
objects' (*English Medieval Romance* [London, 1987], p. 5). John Stevens, citing Northrop Frye,
writes of the 'stage-properties' that enable romance's 'claim of the ideal' to be achieved (*Medieval
Romance* [London, 1973], p. 169). Derek Brewer's *Symbolic Stories: Traditional Narratives of the
Family Drama in English Literature* (Cambridge, 1980; repr. London, 1988) influentially reads
symbolic story patterns across a wide range of texts.

religious texts in English.[2] *Eglamour*, a poem of about 1400 lines in tail-rhyme stanzas, is the second item in the manuscript. While little discussed now, it survives in whole or part in four pre-1500 and two sixteenth-century manu-scripts, six early printed editions and the seventeenth-century Percy Folio (London, British Library, MS Additional 27879).[3] Helen Cooper, recording what she calls *Eglamour*'s 'inexplicable popularity', notes that Shakespeare styles the first of Julia's suitors in *Two Gentlemen of Verona* 'the fair Sir Eglamour', and that a lost play of 'Eglemour and Degrebelle' was acted at St Albans in 1444.[4] I shall trace *Eglamour*'s narrative now, focusing on its use of objects not only as important markers for status and relationships, but also as cues for certain emotional responses to the romance. Eglamour is a knight 'of lytyll lond' (64) who loves the Earl's daughter Cristabell. The jealous Earl sets him three onerous tasks, but to help him Cristabell gives Eglamour two greyhounds and a sword. These gifts match the first task: to bring back a hart from the forest guarded by the giant Arrok. The baying hounds awake Arrok, and in a transposition of Eglamour's generational struggle against the Earl for his dear daughter, he accuses Eglamour: 'Thefe! traytour! what doos þou here / In my forest to stele my dere?' (313–14).[5] Eglamour blinds and then decapitates Arrok with Cristabell's sword. He returns with the head, which not only forms a wondrous spectacle in itself, synecdochal of the slain giant, but also suggests the transfer of power from Earl to aspiring knight.

> Before þe erle he hit bare:
> 'Lo, lorde, I haue ben þare!'
>   That bere þey wyttenes ylkane.
> Make we mery, so haue we blysse!
> For þys ys þe fyrst fytte, iwys,
>   Of Sir Eglamour þat he has tane. (340–5)

---

2   For a description, see G. Guddat-Figge, *Catalogue of Manuscripts containing Middle English Romances* (Munich, 1976), pp. 169–72, and for discussion of quiring and compilation see J. J. Thompson, 'Looking behind the Book: MS Cotton Caligula A.II, part 1, and the Experience of its Texts', in *Romance Reading on the Book: Essays on Medieval Narrative presented to Maldwyn Mills*, ed. J. Fellows et al. (Cardiff, 1996), pp. 171–87. The other romances are the Southern *Octavian*; *Launfal*; *Lybeaus Desconus*; *The Siege of Jerusalem*; *Chevelere Assigne*; and *Isumbras*. I quote *Eglamour* and *Emaré* from *Eglamour*, ed. Richardson (using the Cotton text), and *Six Middle English Romances*, ed. M. Mills (London, 1973, repr. 1988) respectively.

3   For a recent summary including copies discovered since Richardson's edition, see R. Purdie, *Anglicising Romance: Tail-Rhyme and Genre in Medieval English Literature* (Cambridge, 2008), pp. 178–9.

4   H. Cooper, *The English Romance in Time: Transforming Motifs from Geoffrey of Monmouth to the Death of Shakespeare* (Oxford, 2004), pp. 261–2, 416–17; see pp. 39–40 for Samuel Rowlands' parody of *Eglamour* in his *Melancholie Knight* (1615). On printed texts, see further J. Fellows, 'Printed Romance in the Sixteenth Century', in *A Companion to Medieval Popular Romance*, ed. R. L. Radulescu and C. J. Rushton (Cambridge, 2009), pp. 67–78 (pp. 68–70).

5   On problematic fathers, see J. Charbonneau, 'Transgressive Fathers in *Sir Eglamour of Artois* and *Torrent of Portyngale*', in *Discourses on Love, Marriage, and Transgression in Medieval and Early Modern Literature*, ed. A. Classen (Tempe, 2004), pp. 243–65, which, however, does not develop the father–giant connection.

Briefly commenting on this scene, Jeffrey Jerome Cohen nicely draws out the dynamics of spectacle here, noting that this stanza 'maps lines of sight that pass from the gathered spectators to the severed head to the hero, and finally to the earl [...] The narrative gaze finally centers on and is transfixed by the young Eglamour.'[6] The stanza's end merges the imagined speech of the intradiegetic spectators with its narrating voice's exhortations. Cohen suggests that 'the physical inscription of the romance and the production of Eglamour's heroic body [become] one and the same activity' here.[7] We might add that the passage's energy moves in the other direction too, co-opting the romance's audience as exactly those witnessing spectators who can reinforce or relive Eglamour's claim 'Lo, lorde, I haue ben þare'.

Eglamour's next task is to kill a rampaging boar. The poem again attends to objects as a way to interpret narrative – 'Sleyn men' and 'Bryȝt helmes' (368, 376) providing 'Tokenyng' (367) of the animal. A squire witnesses Eglamour's fight with the boar, and reports to his king:

> ȝys, syr, a knyȝt on hym I se–
>   Be God, he has ben hys bane!
> He beris of gold a well fayr syȝt:
> A stede of asar, and a knyȝt
>   All armed for to gon.
> The crest on his hed hit ys
> A lady of golde in hyr ryches;
>   Hys sperys of sabull ylkon. (422–9)

The king declares 'Tho gentyll armes wyll I se!' (431), assimilating Eglamour with his betokening arms and chivalric accoutrements. When Eglamour displays the boar's head as a symbol of defiance against Arrok's brother Marras (who kept the boar as a pet), the giant's lament comically mimics the emotional reaction to signs and symbols elsewhere in the romance:

> The gyaunt loked vpon þe hed:
> 'Allas, my bore, art þou ded?
>   My trust was mykyll in þe!
> Be þe lawe þat I lefe inne,
> My lytyll spotted hogelynne,
>   Dere bowȝt þy lyfe schall be!' (544–9)

Having killed Marras, Eglamour is given a horse and ring with magical properties by the grateful king and his daughter Organata, in lieu of marrying her. After bringing his prospective father-in-law the heads of giant and boar,

---

6   J. J. Cohen, *Of Giants: Sex, Monsters, and the Middle Ages* (Minneapolis, 1999), p. 72.

7   Cohen, Ibid. Cohen's bibliography lists an 1844 edition based on Lincoln, Cathedral Library, MS 91 (the Lincoln Thornton manuscript), but the line that he quotes here, 'that we have undertane', seems to have been supplied from Cambridge, University Library, MS Ff.2.38.

Eglamour goes to bed with Cristabell. The poem merges his recounting his deeds to Cristabell with staying the night: 'So gracyus he con here tell / A poynt of armes þat hym befell / And þere he dwelled all ny3t' (682–4).[8] He gives her a ring on departing for the third task: to defeat a dragon at Rome. The Roman emperor stands in a tower to view the fight and reports Eglamour's victory (751–6); the people then rush out to see the aftermath.[9]

While Eglamour is away, Cristabell gives birth to their son, and her angry father casts them away in a boat. The child is snatched by a griffin and taken to Israel where he is discovered by a king, wrapped in a 'skarlet mantell' (857) with a 'full ryche pane' (858) and 'a gyrdyll of golde' (860). These precious materials, including his eyes, 'clere as cristall stane' (861), help to convince his discoverers that he is of noble birth. Returning to his queen, the king describes the child as a gift from God:

> 'Dame,' he seyde vnto þe qwene,
> 'Mykyll of solas haue I sene—
> Thys chyld God has me sent.' (871–3)

Cristabell, meanwhile, is washed up in Egypt and discovered by another king (her father's brother). Described as 'whyte as floure' (893), she cannot speak for exhaustion, but 'made sygnes with here hond' (900). Mother and child both, then, appear as if from nowhere, bearing with them ambiguous markers of value. The boy, named Degrebell by his surrogate family, grows up using as his heraldic sign a golden griffin with a child wrapped in a mantle and gold girdle – his own biography turned into visual symbol.[10] The description here is reinforced with a call to attention 'Lestenes, lordynges... And 3e wyll vndyrstond' (1030, 1032). Degrebell travels to Egypt with his adopted father, having heard of a beautiful woman for whose hand a tournament has been announced (she is, unbeknownst to Degrebell, his own mother). They ask the king of Egypt if they can view her:

> 'I pray 3ou swythe, yf þat 3e my3te,
> Of 3our dow3tyr to haue a sy3te,
> Als whyte as bon of whall.'
>
> Tyll a chambur þey haue here brow3t,
> With mannes hond as sche were wro3t
> Or coruen on a tre.

---

8   A variant in CUL MS Ff.2.38 allows for more obvious *double entendre* here, with 'Of poyntys of armes he schewed hur hys fylle' at line 683 (*Eglamour*, ed. Richardson, p. 49).

9   The Lincoln Thornton manuscript focuses even more on Eglamour's own damaged body as a readable sign in lines not present in Cotton: 'Bot alle þat euir saw his hede, / Þay sayd þat he was bot dede, / This knyght Sir Eglamour' (772–4; *Eglamour*, ed. Richardson, p. 54).

10 Medieval coats of arms regularly embedded family narratives through their emblems, or such narratives developed as a back-formation to explain a heraldic motif. Degrebell's biographical sign has analogues in, for example, *Octavian* and *Torrent of Portyngale* (whose narrative closely parallels that of *Eglamour*).

> Hys sone stode styll and hyre behelde:
> 'Well were hym þat þe myȝt welde!'
> To hymself sayde he. (1084–92)

She is like whalebone, as if made by craftsmen, or carved in wood, provoking silent appreciation from the men gazing on her, as she mingles with the other precious fabrics and exchangeable objects that form the romance's currency. The denouement of the narrative once again involves affective responses to visual signs. Having married Degrebell, Cristabell is provoked by his coat of arms to remember her child, and they discover one another's identity:

> Hys armes þey bare hym beforen;
> Sche þynkes how hyre chyld away was born—
> Therefore sorow sche hade:
>
> …
>
> 'Lorde, in þyn armes a fowle I se
> That sumtyme raft a chyld fro me—
> A knyȝt dere hym bowȝte.' (1144–6; 1153–5)

A tournament is announced to choose a more suitable husband for Cristabell, and Eglamour (unaware of her identity) arrives to challenge for her. He now wears changed arms, described in detail:

> For Crystabell was don in þe see
> No armes bare he—
> Lystyn and I wyll ȝou say sykurly:
> He bare a schyp in armes of gold,
> And a lady drownyng as sche schold;
> A chyld lyand hyr by.
> The chyld was butt a nyȝt old;
> Hys mast was of syluyre and gold
> In euery poynte to þe ye;
> Of reed gold was hys fane,
> Hys fales and hys ropes ylkane
> Was purtred varely. (1198–1209)[11]

Eglamour defeats Degrebell in the tournament, claims Cristabell and is recognized by her through the story contained in his heraldic device. They finally marry, and Degrebell weds Organata, the princess whom Eglamour helped earlier and who has been warming up on the touchline, as it were, for the last fifteen years.

Eglamour punctuates its narrative with gifts given, trophies brought back, promises exchanged, rich symbols viewed and recognized. We could stop there and say that material culture provides a rich, enabling context for

---

[11] The Lincoln Thornton manuscript reads 'Newe armes' at 1199 (*Eglamour*, ed. Richardson, p. 86).

this romance narrative. Their connection is more active than this, however. Protagonists merge with the objects that they carry with them, or that mark turning points in their lives. Objects and protagonists are involved in networks of exchange between individuals, families and nations, and are gazed on as works of craftsmanship, while Eglamour and Degrebell become moving canvases for the display of their own biographies. The power of people and objects to move, excite and narrate is something that *Eglamour* both builds into its plot, and overtly celebrates. Through such verbal spectacle, the audience too are drawn into participation with the emotional narrative of test, tension and resolution. This is where the trope of ekphrasis (literally 'speaking out') might help our analysis, since it designedly makes a connection between speaker and audience through its lively description of objects and actions. Before discussing its implications more fully, however, I shall turn to *Emaré*, a tail-rhyme romance of 1035 lines uniquely preserved in MS Cotton Caligula A.II, in order to track the relations it develops between protagonist, object and narrative.

Emaré's eponymous heroine is frequently an object acted against: her journeys away from her father's and then husband's homes result from expulsion or false accusation and, like Cristabell in *Eglamour*, she drifts at sea.[12] But the romance also allows for movements back and forth between subject and object position, and moments when that traditional ingredient of romance – formation of or discovery about identity – interacts with relationships of reciprocity and objectification. After a visit by the King of Sicily, the emperor Sir Artyus recalls his daughter Emaré from the woman who has reared her and decides to marry her. Emaré resists her father's desires and is cast out to sea, sustained by the intervention of God's will directing her *aventure*. She does, however, undergo a symbolic death or transformation, casting off temporarily the clinging identifiers of her lineage and apparently becoming a contextless unit of narrative:

> Wyth carefull herte and sykyng sore,
> Such sorow was here yarked yore,
>   And ever lay she styll.
> She was dryven ynto a lond,
> Thorow the grace of Goddes sond,
>   That all thyng may fulfylle. (328–33)

Arriving on the coast of 'Galys', the protagonist (now calling herself Egaré),[13] activates the generosity of Sir Kador, a steward who discovers her, and this

---

12 For *Emaré*'s relations with other legends of accused women, and the motif of sea exile, see M. Schlauch, *Chaucer's Constance and Accused Queens* (New York, 1927), and Cooper, *English Romance in Time*, pp. 106–36.

13 Cf. OF *esgaree*: 'outcast'. Emaré perhaps signifies OF *esmeree*: 'refined, excellent', but also possibly *esmarie*: 'afflicted'.

moment also injects the narrative with that sense of wonder and possibility that romance habitually demands of its beginnings:

> A boot he fond by the brym
> And a glysteryng thyng theryn:
>> Therof they hadde ferly.
> They went forth on the sond
> To the boot, Y unthurstond,
>> And fond theryn that lady. (349–54)

In this stanza, a nameless, nearly dead woman is described through the eyes of the discovers as 'a glysteryng thyng' which produces 'ferly' – astonishment, or wonder – followed by 'pyté' (361).

Despite Emaré/Egaré's rebirth, she is still beautiful and skilful, especially in 'sylky[n] werke' (377), both attributes marking for this genre her aristocratic origins. As Ad Putter has argued, Emaré repeats elements of the story pattern that initially complicate or break down the texture of her social world, but whose repetition has the power to heal those rifts.[14] Aristocratic culture of itself, however, does not provide narrative resolution: of the two wicked acts that propel Emaré from her homes, one is her emperor father's incestuous desire, while the other is the spite of her royal mother-in-law. In the repeating/remaking economy of *Emaré*'s narrative, these parental crimes are compensated for by acts of kindness, one by the steward Sir Kador, and one by Jordan the Roman merchant, who, like Kador, discovers Emaré washed ashore. Jordan thinks that she is 'non erdyly wyght' (701), but nevertheless takes in Emaré and her son Segramour. These surrogates, while they yield up Emaré to her royal husband and father at the end of the narrative, also broaden the social base of virtue in the romance. They play an economic role by supplying the generosity and stability that Emaré lost in her two courtly households, but they also themselves represent alternative models of economic prudence and social virtue that English romances react to with some complexity in the fourteenth and fifteenth centuries.[15]

Furthermore, Emaré's role as a gift object in the narrative, whose circulation accrues debts, obligations and also inspires desire and wonder, is important not only to the narrative cohesion of the plot, but also to the claim that romance itself makes on its audience – that same ability to provoke emotion, bind an audience together and nourish social relations. So far, I have been describing *Emaré* along the same lines as *Sir Eglamour of Artois*: the romance hero acts in networks of financial, social and narrative exchange, and can also be compared to a gift object in the way that his or her power in the narra-

---

14 A. Putter, 'The Narrative Logic of *Emaré*', in *The Spirit of Medieval English Popular Romance*, ed. A. Putter and J. Gilbert (London, 2000), pp. 157–80.
15 See A. Putter, 'Gifts and Commodities in *Sir Amadace*', *Review of English Studies* 51 (2000), 371–94; D. V. Smith, *Arts of Possession: The Middle English Household Imaginary* (Minneapolis, 2003).

tive sometimes derives from unexpected or apparently unmotivated arrival followed by the uncovering of reciprocal bonds.[16] Middle English romances use gifts to highlight those relations or mark transitions, introducing objects that are nurtured and maintained between lovers, friends, or within a family.[17] Moments describing such objects can become important opportunities for reflection, for the mingling of person and object, for narrative patterning and for instances of wonder or otherworldliness that heighten or override standard narrative structures.

A particular object in *Emaré* focuses the power of these moments of exchange, description and scrutiny: the cloth that is given to Emaré's father by the King of Cesyle, is shaped into a robe for Emaré, and which subsequently accompanies her. The emperor is initially blinded by the sparkling stones on the cloth, which provokes wonder and mystery throughout. As a verbal equivalent to the object's visual richness and power, the poem gives a substantial ekphrasis of the cloth, beginning like this:

> The cloth was dysplayed sone;
> The emperour lokede therupone,
>   And myght hyt not se;
> For glysteryng of the ryche ston
> Redy syght had he non,
>   And sayde, 'How may thys be?'
> The emperour sayde on hygh,
> 'Sertes thys ys a fayry,
>   Or ellys a vanyté!'
> The kyng of Cysyle answered than,
> 'So ryche a jwell ys ther non
>   In all Crystyanté.'
>
> The amerayle dowghter of hethennes
> Made thys cloth wythouten lees,
>   And wrowghte hyt all wyth pryde,
> And purtreyed hyt with gret honour
> Wyth ryche golde and asowr
>   And stones on ylke a syde.
> And as the story telles in honde
> The stones that yn thys cloth stonde
>   Sowghte they wer full wyde.
> Seven wynter hyt was yn makynge
> Or hyt was browght to endynge,
>   In herte ys not to hyde. (97–120)

---

16 I am exploring this dynamic in a study in preparation, provisionally entitled *Gifts and Books in Medieval England*.

17 In *Inalienable Possessions: The Paradox of Giving-While-Keeping* (Berkeley, CA, 1992), Annette Weiner responds to the longstanding anthropological debate around the gift by stressing the importance of objects that are restricted from or held out of exchange networks. This focus brings the influence of women to the fore, particularly in their roles as producers and distributors of cloth. Numerous medieval textiles with romance motifs do indeed survive.

The four corners of the cloth are then described. The first three portray pairs of lovers (or perhaps the narrative of their love): 'Ydoyne and Amadas, / Wyth love that was so trewe' (122–3); 'Trystram and Isowde so bryght' (134); 'Florys and Dam Blawncheflour, / As love was hem betwene' (146–7). Sparkling gems are set into the cloth, either accompanying stitched designs or actually forming the pictures. The fourth corner likewise portrays the maker of the cloth and the man she loved:

> In the fowrthe korner was oon,
> Of Babylone the sowdan sonne,
> The amerayles dowghtyr hym by.
> For hys sake the cloth was wrowght;
> She loved hym in hert and thowght,
> As testymo[n]yeth thys storye.
> The fayr mayden her byforn
> Was portrayed an unykorn,
> Wyth hys horn so hye.
> Flowres and bryddes on ylke a syde,
> Wyth stones that wer sowght wyde:
> Stuffed wyth ymagerye.
>
> When the cloth to ende was wrowght,
> To the sowdan sone hyt was browght,
> That semely was of syghte.
> 'My fadyr was a nobyll man;
> Of the sowdan he hyt wan,
> Wyth maystre and wyth myghth.
> For gret love he yaf hyt me;
> I brynge hyt the in specyalté:
> Thys cloth ys rychely dyght.'
> He yaf hyt the emperour;
> He receyved hyt wyth gret honour,
> And thonkede hym fayr and ryght. (157–80)

This is one of the most detailed descriptions in Middle English romance.[18] The gift of the cloth, though not immediately linked to Emaré's exile, seems

---

[18] The cloth/robe has been discussed by, for example, R. G. Arthur, 'Emaré's cloak and Audience Response', in *Sign, Sentence, Discourse: Language in Medieval Thought and Literature*, ed. J. N. Wasserman and L. Roney (Syracuse, 1989), pp. 80–92; M. Robson, '"Cloaking Desire": Re-reading *Emaré*', in *Romance Reading on the Book*, ed. Fellows, pp. 64–76; A. Hopkins, 'Veiling the Text: The True Role of the Cloth in *Emaré*', in *Medieval Insular Romance: Tradition and Innovation*, ed. J. Weiss et al. (Cambridge, 2000), pp. 71–82; see also notes to *Emaré* in *The Middle English Breton Lays*, ed. A. Laskaya and E. Salisbury (Kalamazoo, 1995). Hopkins corrects inaccuracies in previous critics' assimilation of Emaré and the cloth, though I do not find her focus on its 'exteriority … its separateness' (p. 81) from Emaré convincing. Recently, Elizabeth Scala has written on the cloth as a figure for specifically textual production, comparing the cloth's woven narratives with romance manuscript textuality ('The Texture of *Emaré*', *Philological Quarterly* 85 [2006], 223–46). I am sympathetic to her claim that '[t]he cloth *is the*

to provoke and underlie the story of escape and recovery to come, and its description is a rhetorical *nota bene* to the audience, engaging their attention and threading this narrative onto that open weave of texts that forms the romance tradition. In that sense, the description of the cloth provides a way of placing *Emaré* in the contexts of generic intertextuality and symbolic story.

In addition, however, the passage poses questions about narrative and description themselves, some of which are discussed in a valuable essay by the classicist D. P. Fowler.[19] Fowler summarizes three major ways to resolve the perceived problem of the 'gap' between narrative (active, people-centred, open) and description (static, object-centred, didactic); we might note that medieval romances, including *Eglamour* and *Emaré*, are frequently accused of not minding this gap. 'Historically', Fowler says, 'description has tended to make people nervous.'[20] His first possible solution is to stress the role that description plays in bringing the scene before our eyes. This is indeed the purpose of the figures grouped under the heading enargia (Greek *enarges*: 'visible, palpable, manifest') of which ekphrasis forms a part. Much work focuses on description of visual art as the defining activity of ekphrasis, but this can be overly restrictive. As Ruth Webb observes:

> [Ekphrasis] is a form of vivid evocation that may have as its subject-matter anything – an action, a person, a place, a battle, even a crocodile. What distinguishes ekphrasis is its quality of vividness, enargeia, its impact on the mind's eye of the listener who must, in Theon's words, be almost made to see the subject.[21]

This mode shares much with Barthes' 'effet de réel', and helps to expand our range of interpretative possibilities beyond the sense that described objects are formulaic white noise or laden with specific symbolism.[22] More recent approaches via cultural materialism and 'thing theory' have also prompted investigation into objects themselves as subjects of critical scrutiny, whose own contexts or properties help to delineate the position of the literary text in its cultural milieu. Elaine Freedgood, for example, has delved into the historical and political trajectories of Victorian fiction's many objects, before returning to the text in the light of a resultant 'radiance or resonance' that

---

poem' (224), but more sceptical of other links that she makes between the cloth, the poem and specifically manuscript production, especially in relation to MS Cotton Caligula A.II itself.

[19] D. P. Fowler, 'Narrate and Describe: The Problem of Ekphrasis', *Journal of Roman Studies* 81 (1991), 25–35.

[20] Fowler, 'Narrate and Describe', p. 26.

[21] R. Webb, 'Ekphrasis Ancient and Modern: The Invention of a Genre', *Word & Image* 15 (1999), 7–18, (p. 13). Webb's reference is to Aelius Theon (first century AD), author of a *Progymnasmata*. See also C. Preston, 'Ekphrasis: Painting in Words', in *Renaissance Figures of Sepech*, ed. S. Adamson et al. (Cambridge, 2007), pp. 115–29.

[22] R. Barthes, 'L'effet de réel', *Communications* 11 (1968), 84–9; trans. R. Carter as 'The Reality Effect', in *French Literary Theory Today*, ed. T. Todorov (Cambridge, 1982), pp. 11–17. Barthes cites ekphrasis as important to the tradition he describes, though his examples, from realist prose fiction, employ this rhetoric and 'notation insignifiante' (p. 85) to a different end.

might, in terminology borrowed from Pierre Macherey, provide a moment of 'splitting', revealing previously obscured contexts.[23] One example is the mahogany furniture in that dark romance *Jane Eyre*, furniture whose trade from the West Indies opens the narrative, in Freedgood's reading, to the tidal currents of racial histories and people-trafficking embodied in Rochester's secret wife Bertha Mason. In *Emaré*, the richly ornate and exotic cloth, woven by an emir's daughter, engages the analogous dynamics of what Jane Burns has termed 'saracen silk'. The medieval luxury trade in silks and jewellery provides a material context for *Emaré*'s cloth, but also allows for ambivalent associations with the fictional traditions of mysterious, eastern, female-worked fabrics, which themselves help to constitute western Euro- pean definitions of refinement, sexuality and courtliness: 'In economic terms, it is the European west that has been fashioned by material goods crossing its borders. Indeed, in terms of luxury fabric, the east has already begun to define the west from within.'[24] I do not have space to explore this avenue further here, but returning to *Emaré* in the light of such associations, we can specu- late that the rhetorical act of bringing the cloth before the audience's eyes might evoke their own knowledge of luxury fabrics 'stuffed wyth ymagerye' (that is, a contemporary material context for the poem), but also arouse their imaginative notions of exoticism, the marvellous, and the complex origins of romance narrative itself.

The emir's daughter brings us to the second method of analysis discussed by Fowler: the integration of description and narrative by claiming that the description of an object is really 'an account of its making'. This is the approach adopted by G. E. Lessing in the eighteenth century to western literature's founding ekphrasis – the description of Achilles' shield in the *Iliad*. Fowler dismisses this method as something of a 'trick', though he does note here the importance of the observer in the dynamics of ekphrasis.[25] In both *Eglamour* and *Emaré*, ekphrastic description precisely engages this sense of objects (including human bodies) as provoking recollection of their origin or history, whether that is the changed heraldic designs of Eglamour and Degrebell, *Emaré*'s robe, or her son Segramour's noble bearing and cour- tesy, which prompts his father and grandfather to recognition and resolution.

23 E. Freedgood, *The Ideas in Things: Fugitive Meaning in the Victorian Novel* (Chicago, 2006), quoting pp. 6 and 3. See also *The Social Life of Things: Commodities in Cultural Perspective*, ed. A. Appadurai (Cambridge, 1986); and *Things*, ed. B. Brown (Chicago, 2004).

24 E. J. Burns, *Courtly Love Undressed: Reading through Clothes in Medieval French Culture* (Phil- adelphia, 2002), p. 197. For the association of cloth working with female aristocratic virtue, see R. M. Karras, ' "This Skill in a Woman is By No Means to Be Despised": Weaving and the Gender Divison of Labor in the Middle Ages', in *Medieval Fabrications: Dress, Textiles, Clothwork, and Other Cultural Imaginings*, ed. E. J. Burns (New York, 2004), pp. 89–104. The notes in *Middle English Breton Lays*, ed. Laskaya and Salisbury, provide details of the gems and helpful refer- ences. A wider perspective is given by S. Crane, *The Performance of Self: Ritual, Clothing, and Identity during the Hundred Years War* (Philadelphia, 2002).

25 Fowler, 'Narrate and Describe', p. 27.

Fowler's third method of bridging the narrate–describe gap is integrative: for example, making the ekphrasis a symbol of some later plot element, or as a psychological insight into a protagonist. Some of *Eglamour*'s objects, such as Cristabell's gift of the phallic sword with which to decapitate the giant/father, have a clear potential for psychoanalytic or symbolic reading. However, evaluating each object through this lens can also unhelpfully restrict a story's suggestive power. Fowler observes that 'precisely because ekphrasis represents a pause at the level of narration and cannot be read functionally, the reader is possessed by a strong desire to interpret'.[26] He promotes a reading of ekphrasis that is 'neither *narrative* (where description is subordinated to narrative) nor *descriptive* (where it is set free) but *rhetorical*, conferring on the ekphrasis the status of a figure [... and viewing] the relationship with the main narrative as a figured one, in which elements shift and are transformed as we move from detail to whole'.[27] In *Eglamour* and *Emaré*, the reader or listener is certainly 'possessed of a strong desire to interpret'; one way in which *Emaré*'s cloth stimulates this desire is through the slippery relationship between the cloth's awed spectators, the romance's audience, and the acts of making and narration that the cloth inscribes. The description is begun by the King of Cesyle (lines 106–8, quoted above). In Maldwyn Mills's valuable edition, his speech ends here, with the rest of the description assigned to the romance's narrating voice. Edith Rickert, Thomas C. Rumble, and Anne Laskaya and Eve Salisbury do likewise.[28] French and Hale's edition has the king's speech extending up to 'stones on ylke a syde' (114).[29] They also then close the speech, perhaps thinking that the following line's 'as the story telles in honde' seems to relate to a written account, and is thus a narratorial intervention. I would question the absolute boundary that modern punctuation introduces here, and the point of view that it creates. The present tense 'stonde' in line 116 ('The stones that stand (or 'are placed') in this cloth were sought from far and near'), along with the deictic 'thys', implies a continuous description of the object, present before the speaker.[30] Phrases like 'wythouten lees' (110); 'In herte ys not to hyde' (120); and 'Forsoothe as Y say the' (144) also fit as well with the speaking voice of the

---

[26] Fowler, 'Narrate and Describe'. Fowler's 'desire to interpret' is comparable to the movements of 'ekphrastic indifference', 'ekphrastic hope' and 'ekphrastic fear' in W. J. T. Mitchell, 'Ekphrasis and the Other', *South Atlantic Quarterly* 91 (1992), 695–719.

[27] Fowler, 'Narrate and Describe', p. 34, summarizing A. Perutelli, 'L'inversione speculare: Per una retorica dell'ecphrasis', *Materiali e discussioni per l'analisi dei testi classici* 1 (1978), 87–98.

[28] *The Romance of Emaré*, ed. E. Rickert, EETS ES 91 (London, 1908 (for 1906)); *The Breton Lays in Middle English*, ed. T. C. Rumble (Detroit, 1965); *Middle English Breton Lays*, ed. Laskaya and Salisbury.

[29] *Middle English Metrical Romances*, ed. W. H. French and C. B. Hale, 2 vols. (New York, 1930; repr. 1964).

[30] *Emaré*'s phrase 'in honde' is cited by the *Middle English Dictionary*, ed. H. Kurath (Ann Arbor, 1952–) under meaning 1d (b) for *hond(e*: a usage in adverbial phrases of time, meaning 'in due course, soon'. Another possible meaning is 1c. (a), '?assuredly; in an oath'. Scala ('Texture', p. 229) reads the phrase as the story (cloth and/or book) literally being held in the hand, though her related comment on the handy size of MS Cotton Caligula A.II is very speculative.

king as with the narrative voice. Mills's and the other four editions I have mentioned all begin the king's speech again at line 172 in a slightly awkward shift, implying that he must in any case have been saying exactly what we have just heard.[31]

Fluid movement from narrating voice to protagonists' speech is, of course, characteristic of Middle English romance. Nevertheless, the ambiguity of the speaking/narrating voice here – the curious melting effect whereby the King of Sicily's speech merges with at once a narratorial account of this artful object and the story of its making – engages exactly the powerful energies that ekphrasis holds. This moment collapses the distance between speaker, audience and object, which itself contains (though 'contains' is the wrong word) not only further stories, but the story of how those stories were stitched into the cloth's corners. It is both a *mise en abyme* for the powerful genera-tion of romance itself, and an intertextual, 'specular' moment, provoking thoughtful reappraisal of the narrative(s) into which it is woven.[32]

I see this description, then, as responding to a number of material and literary contexts, opening out a variety of interpretative responses to the text/ cloth, and answering to each of the categories of ekphrastic reading that D. P. Fowler describes: vividness of description; ekphrasis as narration of the object's making; and ekphrasis as neither solely descriptive nor narrative, but as *rhetorical* – part of its rhetorical force being to kindle that 'desire to interpret'. The cloth, excessively meaningful, charged with potential desire, arrives into a previously stable situation and makes something happen. Forces of generosity, revenge and redemption help to shape the story of the object/ heroine. Finally, a more thoroughly stabilized, sociable and mutually generous environment has been established in which the protagonist/object repays or renews the ties that had originally been stretched or fractured. The cloth here provides, early in this romance, a series of possibilities for the kind of story, the kind of exchanges, that will take place, and also the demand for a feeling response that the audience should make. Wearing the robe literally involves Emaré with the various possibilities of the romance tradition, and with that previous woman, the heathen emir's daughter, whose stitching of other love stories guaranteed the passing on of her own story. Just as in the legend of Philomela, where the act of stitching a cloth provides a female author who, though tongueless, 'speaks out', so cloth-making in *Emaré* gives a glimpse of female-focalized and female-authored, if rarely female-controlled, narrative.

---

31 In MS Cotton Caligula A.II there are no speech cues here (fols. 71v–72r). There is a cross in the left-hand margin beside line 177, but this looks like a correction mark.

32 For 'specular' encounters in French texts, see D. Maddox, *Fictions of Identity in Medieval France* (Cambridge, 2000), p. 3 *et passim*. The mirroring relations between part and whole, text and image, that ekphrasis provokes are explored in H. Wandhoff, *Ekphrasis: Kunstbeschreibungen und virtuelle Räume in der Literatur des Mittelalters* (Berlin, 2003): 'Die Erzählung in der Erzählung wird als ein Fragment entdeckt, das paradoxerweise das Ganze des Werkes enthalten kann, von dem es doch zugleich eingeschlossen und begrenzt wird' (p. 10: 'The narrative within the narra-tive is rediscovered as a fragment that can paradoxically encompass as a whole the same work that encloses and restricts it').

Charged with the power of returning to its origins; provoking wonder; gener-
ating narrative; working in an open weave of other stories and situations. This
applies to the cloth, to *Emaré* as protagonist and to (the) romance as a whole.

In both *Eglamour* and *Emaré*, then, the descriptions of objects, people
and artworks function integrally to heighten a romance's claim on the audience's attention and memory.[33] Such descriptions signal important contexts
for narrative romance, and reinvent those contexts as part of the romance's
own imaginative landscape. There is a difference in scale and self-conscious-
ness between *Emaré*'s cloth and the heraldic motifs worn by Eglamour and
Degrebell. Nevertheless, each of these acts of narrating and describing works
rhetorically to bring the narrative before the mind's eye of the audience, and
suggests how natural was the integration of the visual and verbal/textual
to a late-medieval public, who encountered narratives in painting, carving,
stained glass and embroidery, clothing, dramatic performance and manuscript imagetexts.[34] It would be possible to argue for MS Cotton Caligula
A.II as a particularly apt environment for this aspect of *Eglamour* and *Emaré*,
given their proximity to other texts concerned with the spiritual dangers or
imperatives of looking, including *A Pistel of Susan* (before *Eglamour*), and
The Charter of Christ (after *Emaré*). Whether or not that specific reading
context is plausible, it should take its place amidst a larger, messier involve-
ment in what we might term medieval imaginative materiality, whose objects,
like *Emaré*'s cloth and the romances themselves, are products of physical
labour and of fantasy, and whose inseparable affiliations with the tangible
and the fictive challenge our notions of context, however indiscretely we try
to use that term.

---

[33] As Mary Carruthers has shown, the integration of pictorial and mental images with textual ones
is central to medieval practices of memory; see her *The Book of Memory*, 2nd edn (Cambridge,
2008), e.g. pp. 291–3.

[34] J. Brantley, *Reading in the Wilderness: Private Devotion and Public Performance in Late Medieval England* (Chicago, 2007) studies this integration in London, British Library, MS Additional
37049. The term imagetext, also used by Brantley, is derived from and discussed in W. J. T.
Mitchell, *Picture Theory: Essays on Verbal and Visual Representation* (Chicago, 1994), pp.
83–107. See also M. Camille, *The Medieval Art of Love* (London, 1998).

5

What's in a Name?
Anglo-Norman Romances or *Chansons de geste*?

MARIANNE AILES

Whilst many Middle English romances were derived from Anglo-Norman texts in the form of *chanson de geste*, there is a long established view that there was no such thing as an Anglo-Norman *chanson de geste*.[1] The Anglo-Norman versions of *Horn* and *Boeve de Haumtone*, both described by Dominica Legge as 'romances in *chanson de geste* form',[2] are usually discussed with the other so-called 'ancestral' romances such as *Gui de Warewic, Waldef, Havelok* and *Fouke Fitz Warin*.[3] Anglo-Norman redactions of continental *chansons de geste* have been labelled '*chansons de geste*' but these are generally seen as 'mere adaptations' and given little attention as independent texts even when (as in the case of the Anglo-Norman *Fierenbras*) the reworking has been considerable.[4]

This discrepancy raises questions regarding the definition of medieval genres. Are our genre labels simply modern critical constructs imposed on medieval texts? Critics have been asking this for nearly half a century.[5] Does it matter if we ascribe different generic labels to these texts? The basic

1 M. D. Legge, *Anglo-Norman Literature and its Background* (Oxford, 1963), p. 3. This view has not gone unchallenged; see M. Ailes, 'The Anglo-Norman *Boeve de Haumtone* as a *chanson de geste*', in *Sir Bevis of Hampton in Literary Tradition*, ed. J. Fellows and I. Djordjević (Cambridge, 2008) pp. 9–24, and M. Ailes, 'Anglo-Norman Developments of the *Chanson de geste*', *Olifant* 25: *Acts of the 17th International Congress of the Société Rencesvals, Storrs, Connecticut, July 22–28 2006* (2009), pp. 97–109 (p. 100).
2 Legge, *Anglo-Norman Literature*, p. 156.
3 For a critique of the term 'ancestral romance' see S. Crane, *Insular Romance: Politics, Faith and Culture in Anglo-Norman and Middle English Literature* (Berkeley, 1986), pp. 13–18; S. Dannenbaum, 'Anglo-Norman Romances of English Heroes: "ancestral romance"', *Romance Philology* 35 (1981/82), 601–8.
4 Ailes, 'Anglo-Norman Developments'. K. V. Sinclair appeals for the Anglo-Norman version of the legend (*Fierenbras*) to be treated as a text in its own right: '*Fierabras* in Anglo-Norman, some cultural perspectives', in *Anglo-Norman Anniversary Essays*, ed. I. Short (London, 1993), pp. 366–77 (pp. 376–77).
5 P. Zumthor, *Essai de poétique médiévale* (Paris, 1972); H. R. Jauss, 'Littérature médiévale et théorie de genres', *Poétique* 1 (1970), 79–98, also published as 'Theory of Genres and Medieval Literature', in *Modern Genre Theory*, ed. D. Duff (Harlow, 2000), pp. 127–47.

premise behind genre classification is the same as that behind other inter-
textual analysis: a clarification of what Northrop Frye called 'traditions and
affinities'.[6] The perceived traditions and affinities will determine the horizon
of expectations of the audience and an analysis of how the poets manipulate
these expectations will bring us to a different appreciation of the texts.

Here the validity of the genre labels ascribed to three texts will be examined; they have in the past been considered to belong to different genres.[7]
These texts are:

Otinel, an Anglo-Norman redaction of a continental *chanson de geste*, and
as such labelled '*chanson de geste*'. The Anglo-Norman version has been
largely ignored because of the lack of an edition.[8] *Otinel* is a thirteenth-
century text, probably written shortly after the continental *Fierabras*; the
Anglo-Norman manuscript dates from the late thirteenth or early fourteenth
century.[9]

La Destruction de Rome, the Anglo-Norman 'prequel' to the *chanson de
geste Fierabras*. It survives in two distinct versions, one in an Anglo-Norman
manuscript containing a version of the Vulgate *Fierabras* dating from the
end of the thirteenth century; the other, shorter version, precedes the Anglo-
Norman *Fierenbras* and dates from the fourteenth century.[10]

The twelfth-century *Roman de Horn*, a text usually referred to as 'romance',
as is suggested in the title. Laura Hibbard, writing before Legge, described
it as having 'in general the spirit of a *chanson de geste* and the romantic
character of the Round Table'.[11] More recently Judith Weiss also refused it
the label of *chanson de geste*, describing it as marking 'a transitional stage
of writing containing elements of the romance genre that developed from
the mid-twelfth century'.[12] This echoes the views of M. K. Pope, the editor
of the text.[13] Pope and Weiss imply a Darwinian evolution by which a genre

[6] N. Frye, *The Anatomy of Criticism* (Princeton, 1957), p. 247.
[7] This builds on work I have published on *Horn, Fierenbras* and *Boeve de Haumtone*: Ailes,
'Anglo-Norman Developments' and 'The Anglo-Norman *Boeve de Haumtone*'.
[8] I am very grateful to Dr Diane Speed of the University of Sydney for allowing me access to her
unpublished transcription of the Anglo-Norman manuscript Bibliotheque Bodmeriana MS 168.
The published edition of the *chanson de geste* is based largely on the continental MS, Vatican
Regina 1616, with lacunae filled from the Anglo-Norman manuscript; see *Otinel*, ed. F. Guessard
and H. Michelant (Paris, 1859, reprint Nendeln, 1966).
[9] A description of the manuscript can be found in F. Vielliard, *Manuscrits français du moyen âge*
(Cologny-Geneva, 1975) pp. 93–99.
[10] The longer version has been edited several times. The edition cited here is that by L. Formisano (ed.), *La Destructioun de Rome: version de Hanovre* (Florence, 1981) [hereafter Formisano (1981)]; a more conservative edition was published by Formisano as *La Destructioun de
Rome*, ANTS Plain Texts Series 8 (London, 1990) [hereafter Formisano (1990)]. The shorter text
contained in BL Egerton MS 3028 was edited by L. Brandin in *Romania* 64 (1938), 18–100. The
translations of both versions are my own.
[11] L. A. Hibbard, *Medieval Romance in England* (New York, 1960), p. 84.
[12] J. Weiss, *The Birth of Romance: An Anthology. Four Twelfth-century Anglo-Norman Romances*
(London, 1992), p. 157. The English translations given here are from Weiss's text.
[13] M. K. Pope (ed.), *The Romance of Horn*, 2 vols., ANTS 9–10, 12–13 (Oxford, 1955, 1964), II, 6.

transmutes from one thing, labelled 'epic', to another, labelled 'romance'. Given that the two genres co-existed for about two hundred years this is not really a tenable position, though the related view that later *chansons de geste* were influenced by romance is more defensible. More difficult to assess is exactly what that impact was.[14]

Each of the three selected texts will be examined in turn with consideration given to their place within the literary tradition and whether the generic labels previously applied to them have any validity.

Otinel

The basic narrative of *Otinel* concerns the conversion of a Saracen messenger, Otinel. He is sent by the Saracen emir Garsi to Charlemagne, where he makes a challenge and engages in single combat with Roland. During the combat a dove descends from heaven to alight on Otinel who consequently submits and converts. Thereafter he proves himself one of Christendom's most worthy defenders in the battles against his former lord. Charlemagne promises his daughter, Belissant, to the newly converted Otinel, who refuses to marry her until the war is won. There are some narrative changes in the Anglo-Norman redaction, mostly concerning combats, which streamline the narrative a little. There is also some development of the expression of piety, in particular more emphasis on Mary. The Anglo-Norman redaction is slightly, but not significantly, shorter than the continental one, at 1908 lines compared to 2133 lines.

Of more interest is the treatment of certain elements of *chanson de geste* discourse and the use of the *laisse*, the basic building block of the *chanson de geste*. Most of the time the Anglo-Norman redactor follows the *laisse* pattern of the continental text but there are several places in *Otinel* where the Anglo-Norman text has a *laisse* division that is not present in the continental one.[15] This, combined with its slightly shorter narrative, has a significant effect on average *laisse* length, the average *laisse* length in the continental text being 35.55 lines (60 *laisses*) and in the Anglo-Norman text, 30.77 lines. This is entirely in keeping with the pattern of insular *chansons de geste* which tend to have shorter *laisses* at a time when the average *laisse* length in continental texts was increasing.[16] It is quite noticeable when the *laisse* divisions are

---

[14] S. Kay, *The Chansons de geste in the Age of Romance* (Oxford, 1995) discusses at some length the issue of romance influence and concludes that in some aspects it is not so much the texts as the critics who are influenced by romance. Jauss, 'Littérature médiévale', rejected the Darwinian model in his consideration of the evolution of medieval genres, along with a concept of 'closed genres'. He suggested that it is by enrichment from other genres that a genre develops (pp. 95–97).

[15] This contrasts with *Fierenbras* where an abbreviating technique is the running together of two *laisses* from the continental version.

[16] Ailes, 'Anglo-Norman Developments', p. 100.

examined, however, that the Anglo-Norman redactor systematically removes a certain type of *vers d'intonation*, or opening line, namely the formulaic battle description, for example:

> Mult fu l'estour orgeillous et felon
>
> ['The fighting was very proud and fierce', line 510]
>
> Molt par fu grant et ruiste la mellée
>
> ['The fight was fierce and violent', line 545][17]

Nor does the text include such formulae in those sections where it departs from the continental text. Some elements of *reprise* are also lost. While these are relatively minor changes they show development in the same direction as other insular *chansons de geste*.

Otinel is formulaic in both versions and there are a few additional formulaic phrases which seem to echo other *chansons de geste*, in particular the *Chanson de Roland* and *Fierabras*.[18] In both continental and Anglo-Norman redactions the emir Garsi is described in the same terms as Marsile in the *Roland*, 'un fel paien que deu naime nient' (line 1772); in the continental text he is in fact called 'Garsile' and the editors refer to him as 'Garsile or Marsile', though he cannot be Marsile as he is taken prisoner by Charlemagne before the end of the text.[19] A pagan called 'Balan' appears in the Anglo-Norman *Otinel*, recalling the Fierabras tradition, while a Christian not named in the continental text becomes 'Baldwin d'Aigremunt' (line 174) – the patronym of a major *chanson de geste* family. In such small ways the Anglo-Norman *Otinel* continues to be consciously linked to the wider *chanson de geste* tradition.

By the thirteenth century the presence of a love interest in a *chanson de geste* is not unusual. Though this has in the past been interpreted as 'romance influence' the attitude to women in the different genres is very different.[20] In both versions of *Otinel* Belissant, Charlemagne's daughter, can be read as a reply to the feisty and forward *belle sarrasine* of many a *chanson de geste*,[21] a type which seems to challenge the use of the female as part of a dynastic arrangement or a gift exchange between men, an aspect of medieval society

---

[17] See also lines 564, 556.

[18] Thus Otinel is found 'desuz un arbre ariner' (line 1527) in an echo of the finding of Fierabras 'soz l'arbre ramé' (line 377; line 1885), *Fierabras*, ed. M. Le Person (Paris, 2003). Such formulaic echoes on their own would mean little, though they are instances of epic formulaic discourse.

[19] Eds. Guessard and Michelant, p. v.

[20] Kay, *Chansons de geste*; see above n. 13.

[21] J. Weiss, 'The Wooing Woman in Anglo-Norman Romance', in *Romance in Medieval England*, ed. M. Mills, J. Fellows and C. Meale (Cambridge, 1991), pp. 149–61; J. Weiss, 'The Power and Weakness of Women in Anglo-Norman Romance', *Women and Literature in Britain 1150–1500*, ed. C. Meale, 2nd edn (Cambridge, 1996), pp. 7–23. There are many parallels between the continental *Fierabras* and *Otinel* to the extent that *Otinel* could be seen as a response to *Fierabras*; this will be the subject of a forthcoming study.

that is challenged in the world of the *chanson de geste*.[22] It is the *belle sarra-sine* who does not conform to Levi-Strauss's statement that:

> The total relationship of exchange which constitutes marriage is not estab-lished between a man and a woman but between two groups of men, and the woman figures only as one of the objects in the exchange.... This remains true even when the girl's feelings are taken into consideration.[23]

Belissant, on the other hand, content to be given to Otinel but not engineering this, does not conform to the 'type' of female of the *chanson de geste*.

Both redactions, however, evoke the romance concept of *druerie*, or love-service. The Anglo-Norman *Otinel* describes Belissant as being given to Otinel as 'amie' – a romance epithet not used in the continental text. Some more romance influence *is* perceptible generally in the relationships between men and women in both versions of *Otinel*. Throughout the text women are seen as an inspiration to the warrior knights on both sides: thus, for example, the Alfage of Nubie is introduced in a way that connects his ability to fight with the promise of *druerie* he made to his cousin:

> Par le champ broche l'alfage de nubie,
> Un Sarrazin que Dampnedeu maldie,
> Cusins fu [il] à la bele Alfamie.
> Huï matin il promist druerie,
> E il promist colp de chevalerie
>
> ['The lord of Nubia, a Saracen cursed by God, spurs through the camp; he was cousin to the beautiful Alfamie. That very morning he had promised her his love and he promised chival-rous blows', lines 962–66]

This contrasts with the kind of *chanson de geste* attitude which we find in *Horn*, where vengeance and fighting for God are the main motivational factors. Yet it is *Horn* which is more often seen as a romance.

The Anglo-Norman *Otinel* is a *chanson de geste* despite these minor romance elements, also found in the continental text.

La Destruction de Rome

We now turn to the 'prequel' of *Fierabras*, *La Destruction de Rome*. The two surviving versions of the *Destruction de Rome* vary slightly in the order of events and in some details but the essentials are the same. Both lead up to and explain the situation that pertains at the beginning of *Fierabras*:

---

[22] Kay, *Chansons de geste*, pp. 25–48 questions the simplistic view of women as objects of exchange.
[23] C. Levi-Strauss, *Elementary Structures of Kinship*, 2nd edn (London, 1969) pp. 52–68, 115.

Fierabras' father, Balan/Laban, attacks Rome in revenge for an attack made on some of his ships. With him are his son and daughter, Floripas, and a pagan warrior, Lucafer, who has asked to be betrothed to Floripas. Count Savari of Rome sets out to fight the pagans. Lucafer enters the outer bailey disguised in Savari's arms and Savari is killed. Messengers are sent to Charlemagne who sends Gui de Bourgogne to help. Meanwhile a traitor opens the gates of Rome which is then sacked and the Passion relics taken by Fierabras. The pagans return to Spain. Gui arrives in Rome followed by Charlemagne. They then follow Balan to Spain. Fierabras offers battle; Oliver is injured. This leads into the beginning of *Fierabras*.

As a prequel to an established *chanson de geste* it is clearly inscribed into the *chanson de geste* tradition. As a freestanding text it is unsatisfactory in that the ending does not bring any element of closure, but this is true of other *chansons de geste* in cyclical manuscripts. Both manuscripts (the Hanover manuscript and the Egerton manuscript) very clearly mark it as a separate text from the one that follows. It is therefore legitimate to consider the *Destruction* to be a *chanson de geste* – albeit a very short one; the longer of the two redactions is only 1507 lines.

Much debate has centred on whether or not the *Destruction de Rome* is an insular text. The first editor of the longer Hanover text, G. Groeber, mutilated the text to restore it to what he believed to be its original Picard dialect. His conviction was based at least as much on his belief that the *Destruction de Rome* and *Fierabras* were by the same author as on his linguistic analysis of the poem, which is good, though his conclusions are unsatisfactory.[24] He lists the 'nombreux anglicismes' and a number of Picard forms, such as the use of *le* instead of *la* for the feminine article, but both Picard and Norman were important factors in the far from homogenous dialect we generally call Anglo-Norman.[25] Gaston Paris and Paul Meyer argued the case for an Anglo-Norman origin to the text.[26] The idea that the text should be considered in two parts was put forward by Stimming and followed by Formisano, whose detailed analysis of the language of the poem is the most thorough and whose conclusions are the most objective.[27] He argues for 'une anglo-normandisation progressive' dividing the text at line 698. However, while he finds fewer Anglo-Norman traits before line 699, he has difficulty finding traits that point to another dialect, concluding that 'la langue de la première partie

---

[24] G. Groeber, *Romania* 2 (1873), 1–48 (1–5).

[25] M. K. Pope, *From Latin to Modern French*, 2nd edn (Manchester, 1952), ¶1252 (iii), p. 465; I. Short, *Manual of Anglo-Norman*, ANTS Occasional Publications Series 7 (London, 2007), ¶1.8, p. 45. Groeber has been much criticised, most scathingly by Gaston Paris and most recently by Luciano Formisano. See Paris, review of Groeber's edition, *Revue critique d'histoire et de littérature* 4 (1869), pp. 121–26; Formisano (1981), p. 5.

[26] Paris, review, pp. 121–26; P. Meyer, review of Groeber's edition, *Transactions of the Philological Society* 20 (1873–74), 432.

[27] A. Stimming, 'Die Entwicklungsgeschichte der *Destruction de Rome*', *Zeitschrift für Romanische Philologie* 40 (1919–20), 550–88; Formisano (1981), pp. 48–61.

se borne à indiquer la presence d'un "Mischsprache" base septentrionale assez générique'.[28] Ultimately he suggests that either this is a copy of a text composed on the continent with more careful copying in the first section, or it was written by an Anglo-Norman poet 'soucieux de se conformer au bon usage'.[29] It may well have been an Anglo-Norman composition, perhaps originally written by a poet trained in the continental tradition but partially reworked by someone less careful. Formisano himself edited the Hanover version for the Anglo-Norman Text Society.[30]

The other redaction of the text, contained in the Egerton manuscript, has always been considered an Anglo-Norman reworking of an earlier version, whether that version was considered continental or insular.

Given all this evidence it seems appropriate to treat the *Destruction de Rome* in both its extant versions as an insular, Anglo-Norman text. The question less frequently asked is how this text uses the generic conventions of the *chanson de geste*.

Like *Otinel*, the *Destruction de Rome* is highly formulaic but it does not really exploit the possibilities of the *laisse*. Neither redaction uses *laisses similaires* or *laisses parallèles*. Both versions make use of the formulaic *vers d'intonation* and the Hanover version uses similar apostrophes to open the first three *laisses*:

I

Seignurs, ore fetes pes, franke gent honoree,
Gardés k'il n'i ait nois[e] ne corous ne mellee!
S'orrés bone chanchon de bien enluminee;
N'i avra fable dite ne mensonge provee,
Les altres jugelours kels le vous unt countee,
Ne sevent de l'estoire vailant un[e] darree
Le chanchon ert perdu[e] et le rime fausee ...

['My lords, quiet now, frank and honoured people, Let there be no disturbance, no anger and no quarrelling! Listen to a good song, inspired by good. There will be in it no fable nor proven lies; the other minstrels who have told you the story know nothing of it of any value for the song was lost and its rhyme destroyed ...', lines 1–7]

II

Seignors, or m'escotez, si lessés le nois[i]er!
Chanceon de droit' estoire vous voil jeo comenc[i]er:

---

[28] Formisano (1981), p. 55. Throughout the text we find such traits as the reduction of *–iee* to *–ie* (e.g. *herechie* line 319; *drecie* lines 329, 543), a feature of Anglo-Norman and Northern French; a distinction made between *–ant* and *–ent* (*laisse* 7), characteristic of Picard, Walloon and Anglo-Norman; and the use of the feminine personal pronoun *el*, common in western texts but also found alongside *ele* in Anglo-Norman: see Pope, *From Latin to Modern French*, ¶1090 (ii), p. 428, ¶1251, p. 464; Short, *Manual*, ¶8.4, p. 63, ¶1.4, pp. 42–43, ¶32.1, p. 126.

[29] Formisano (1981), p. 55.

[30] Formisano (1990).

L'estoire en est escrit[e] en seint Denis moust[i]er:
Les altres jugelours s'en soilent preis[i]er ...
Par moi orrez le veir, dunt ele muyt prim[i]er,
Jeo ne vous dorray mye fable de loseng[i]er ...

['My lords, listen, leave any disturbance! I wish to begin to
give you a song of true history; the story of it was written at
the abbey of Saint Denis: The other minstrels took pride ...
From me you will hear the truth, as it was in the beginning, I
will tell you no fable or made up story ...', lines 40–44, 47–48]

III

Baron, ore fetes pes, lessés le noise esteer!
Chanceon de vrai estoire plest vous a escouter?

['Nobles, quiet now, stop making any disturbance! Would you
like to hear a song of a true tale?', lines 68–69]

Apostrophising the audience is a standard part of the opening of a *chanson
de geste*, but this is not normally repeated three times. There is over these
three *laisses* a great deal of repetition, mostly in a pattern that is recognis-
ably *chanson de geste* in style. Striking here is the way the epic formulae
are turned round in a semi-chiastic structure so that 'lessés le noiser' (line
40) becomes 'lessés le noise esteer!'. This is not, however, true *rhétorique
scolaire* as such alterations to alter formulae to fit the new rhyme or asso-
nance of a different *laisse* are very common in the *chanson de geste*. The
pattern of *ore fetes pes/ ore m'escotez/ ore fetes pes* and the echo of line 41
in line 69 are also standard *chanson de geste* discourse. The redactor, or poet,
names himself and his collaborator as 'Gautier of Douai' and 'King Louis',
assumed to be a 'king' of minstrels; it is rare but not unknown in *chansons de
geste* for a poet to be named.[31] Our poet's favoured way of linking a series of
laisses is antistrophe, beginning succeeding *laisses* with the same hemistich
or phrase, to the exclusion of other forms of *reprise*:

V

Mult furent grantz les os de la gent l'adversier
['The armies of the devil's people were great', line 221]

VI

Mult fu grant l[i] estorm de la gent payenye
['There was a great uproar from the pagan people', line 314]

VII

Mult fu grant l[i] estorm de la payene gent
['There was a great uproar from the pagan people', line 384][32]

---

31 Pope points out that the poet of *Horn* names himself as Thomas and sees this as an aspect of the
'incoming fashion in romance', something which is not typical of *chansons de geste* ((ed.), *Horn*,
II, 11). There are however several *chansons de geste* in which the poet identifies himself.
32 See also lines 1237 and 1315.

We find in this short text features typical of *chansons de geste* discourse though they are not developed in a sophisticated way or to the extent that they are in the related *Fierenbras*.[33]

If the discourse of the text is standard for the genre, what of the treatment of the subject? It is frequently in the treatment of the woman, or the male–female relationship, that any romance influence is most easily discerned. The character of Floripas in the continental *Fierabras* has attracted comment as a fine example of a *belle sarrasine*, very much a *chanson de geste* 'type'.[34] In the *Destruction* Floripas is presented as a desirable prize for her father's favourite warrior – and she accepts this as her role. There is no real preparation here for what will be her role in *Fierabras*, the *belle sarrasine*, who is already in love with Gui because of his reputation. Here we do not have even the trappings of romance.[35] Floripas is a gift exchanged between men.[36]

Roman de Horn

While *Otinel* is accepted as a *chanson de geste* and the *Destruction de Rome* has only been denied the status to the extent that it is not treated as a text in its own right, the *Roman de Horn* has, as we have noted above, been more consciously denied the label despite the way its prologue invites us to read the text as a *chanson de geste*; its use and exploitation of the *laisse*, the principal generic marker of the *chanson de geste*; and the mix of *rhétorique scolaire* and the more popular rhetoric that is part of the discourse of the *chanson de geste*.[37] Less attention has been given to the narrative of the text. It is a text of disinheritance and repossession, or 'dispossession and reinstatement' identified by Susan Crane as the narrative pattern of the so-called 'ancestral romances'.[38] It has a clear single hero whose adventures are followed but is also the story of a group – or perhaps of several groups. The 'adventures' Horn and his companions undertake are not the single combats of Arthurian romances, but wars, and, moreover, wars against the Saracens.

Horn, the orphaned son of King Aalof, is set adrift in a boat along with his companions by the pagans who have overrun his country, killing his father.

---

33 Ailes, 'Anglo-Norman Developments', pp. 102–04.
34 H-E. Keller, 'La belle sarrasine dans *Fierabras* et ses dérivés', *Charlemagne in the North*, ed. P. E. Bennett, A. Cobby and G. Runnalls (Edinburgh, 1993) pp. 299–307; J-C. Vallecalle, 'Rupture et intégration: l'héroïne révoltée dans les *chansons de geste*', in the same volume, pp. 449–61 (p. 450). On the motif of the *belle sarrasine* see J. de Weever, *Sheba's Daughters: Whitening and Demonizing the Saracen Woman in Medieval French Epic* (New York, 1998); Kay, *Chansons de geste*, pp. 30–48.
35 On romance elements in *Fierabras* see M. Ailes, 'Romance and Epic Elements in the Different Versions of *Fierabras*', *Olifant* 10 (1982–83), 41–49, where I conclude that the influence of romance in the *Fierabras* tradition is largely superficial.
36 Kay, *Chansons de geste*, p. 37; see also above, n. 22.
37 See Ailes, 'Anglo-Norman Developments', pp. 102–6.
38 Crane, *Insular Romance*, p. 87.

They arrive safely in a Christian land. Predictably, Rigmel the daughter of King Hunlaf, the king of that country, falls in love with Horn. The narrative then returns to the Christian–pagan conflict as the brothers of the pagan king responsible for Aalof's death now invade the land. Horn and his companions are armed and help to defeat the invaders. A traitor tells King Hunlaf that Horn is sleeping with Rigmel and Horn is forced to go into exile in Westir (Ireland) where he takes service with the younger son of the king of Westir and the king's daughter falls in love with him. Westir is then attacked by the pagans, this time including the very man who killed Aalof. Horn defeats him in single combat and leads an attack against the pagans, who are defeated, though the king's sons are killed. The king offers his daughter to Horn who refuses her. At this crucial point in the tale a palmer arrives with the message that Rigmel is about to be forced into marriage and the traitor has taken an influential place at court. Horn returns, defeats the traitor and goes back to his father's land where he forcibly ejects the pagans. He finally marries Rigmel.

Striking here is the importance of God and the Christian–Saracen conflict. When Horn and his companions are left to drift out to sea there is an insistence on the protection of God. The Saracens worship Mahomet and Tervagant – as in the continental *chansons de geste*. It is clear that the battles – and most particularly the single combats – are fought over both land and religion. When the Saracen Rollac delivers his message to the king of Westir, he demands that 'henceforth you shall believe in Mahomet and Tervagant'. The two princes respond to the challenge 'to maintain by force of arms that they should not abandon the creed they held, nor should they render tribute' (trans. Weiss, *laisse* 144).[39]

Vengeance for his father's death – another acceptable epic theme – is also a motivational factor for Horn. He is thus fighting to regain his land, as Raoul de Cambrai does; fighting against the Saracens, as countless epic heroes do; and fighting for revenge, again recalling Raoul de Cambrai and the 'feudal cycle' of epics.

Other epic motifs occur with regularity. In the *chanson de geste* the 'prière du plus grand peril' is normally uttered by one of the protagonists either when he is in danger or when another character is in danger. The structure is exemplified in this prayer from *Fierabras*:

> Damledex, Sire Pere, qui en croiz fu[s] penés,
> En la seinte puchele concheus et formés;
> Em Belleem, biau Sire, illuecques fus(t) nés ...
>
> ['My Lord God, Father, who was hung on the cross, conceived and formed in the Holy Virgin; fine Lord, in Bethlehem were you were born ...', lines 1221–23]

---

[39] See also Pope (ed.), *Horn*, II, 21.

Vos feistes Adam, biau Pere esperités,
Puis feistes Evaim …

['You created Adam, fine spiritual Father, then you created Eve
…', line 1231–32]

Dex, tu garris Marcus, qui tout iert enlieprés …

['God, you healed Marcus who was a leper', line 1238]

Si garris Olivier qu'il ne soit afolés

['And you healed Oliver, so that he was not killed', line 1286]

God is addressed; there is a list of miracles attesting to God's power, followed
by an appeal for help.[40] Thomas, the *Horn*-poet, takes this convention and
adapts it, giving it to the narrator. Thus when the pagan king Rodmund takes
the boys and sets them adrift at sea, the narrator comments:

Or les guarisset cil ki salvat Moisan,
Quand fud jecté petit al flum del desruban,
Et ki format Evain de la coste dan Adan
E fist l'asne parler pur le prophete Balaan!

['Now may He protect them, who saved Moses when they
threw the child into the river from the cliff, who formed Eve
out of lord Adam's rib and made Balaam's ass speak!', lines
75–78, trans. Weiss, *laisse* 4)

Here he not only appropriates the prayer for the narrative voice, he also
adapts it by beginning with the most appropriate biblical parallel, another
child who was at the mercy of the waters and was saved by God. Later the
prayer is turned into a benediction uttered by Horn:

'Cil vous rende voz biens ki fist salcatiun
Al vaillant Daniel enz el lai al leun.
Et delivra Jonas el ventre al ceton.'

['May God, who saved the brave Daniel in the lion's den and
delivered Jonah from the belly of the whale, repay your kindness', lines 1403–5, trans. Weiss, *laisse* 70]

Again, the poet takes two of the miracles most frequently alluded to in the

---

40 On the *prière du plus grand peril* see E. R. Labande, 'A Propos des prières dans les *chansons
de geste*', *Recueil de travaux offert à M. Clovis Brunel*, 2 vols. (Paris, 1955), II, pp. 62–80; J. de
Caluwé, 'La Prière épique dans les plus anciennes *chansons de geste*', *Olifant* 4 (1976), 4–20;
J. de Caluwé, 'L'Originialité de quelques prières épiques', *Marche Romane* 20 (1970), 59–74. The
term was first used by Jean Frappier in *Les chansons de geste du cycle de Guillaume d'Orange*,
II, 2nd edn (Paris, 1967), pp. 132–40. On the adaptation of the *prière du plus grand peril* in the
Anglo-Norman *Boeve de Haumtone* see Ailes, 'The Anglo-Norman *Boeve de Haumtone*', pp.
20–21.

'prière du plus grand peril' and incorporates them into Horn's speech, thus exploiting the traditional motif of the *chansons de geste*.

The role of the traitor within the narrative is a common epic topos. In *Horn* this role is taken by 'Wikele', 'grandson of Denerez, who had accused Aalof to the noble Silauf, and this one was to denounce Horn, his lord. He was an evil traitor, in this way faithful to his lineage, because he was cowardly and treacherous' (trans. Weiss, *laisse* 89). In keeping with *chanson de geste* tradition the traitor is a member of a treacherous family. Potentially problematic is the fact that he is also a 'cousin' of Horn (*laisse* 89). Like Hardré in *Ami et Amile* the traitor poisons the king's mind, persuading him to arrange for Rigmel to marry another (*laisse* 177). Surprising in an epic is that after Horn has been restored he forgives the traitor. Any reader of epic would recognise that this is mistaken generosity, for he will betray again – and he does, attacking King Hunlaf and persuading him to hand over Rigmel to him. Wikele then goes on to marry her himself, though Horn comes to the rescue before the marriage can be consummated. This time Horn does not give mercy but kills him, and 'Then he had him dragged out like a stinking cur and hung at the cross-roads as a spectacle' (line 5253, trans. Weiss, *laisse* 243). The treachery is associated with a heterosexual relationship. For Pope it is in this, the treatment of the love-theme, that 'the contrast between epic and romance is most marked', yet she concedes that it is largely in 'superficial details that the influence of the incoming treatment of love in romance is evident'.[41] The love interest in *chanson de geste* is, indeed, very different from that in romance: in epic texts it is about marriage and lineage – it is not normally extra-marital.[42] Rigmel is no submissive and obedient maiden like Belissant in *Otinel*, but, as we have noted, in the *chanson de geste* it is actually the quiet and obedient Belissant who is the exception.[43] Rigmel, having dined apart from the men, ensures that the renowned Horn is brought to meet her. Yet in many ways she is a pawn in her father's politics: twice she is almost married to the 'wrong man' – but she has no agency in this. For all her manipulation to meet Horn, ultimately her role is to reinforce male relationships – and to be part of a dynasty. This is made clear by Horn deferring response to her love on the grounds of his own unworthiness and 'si ne fust par le roi' ('unless it is from the hand of the king', line 1189)[44] and by his concern to know that she is still a virgin when he rescues her from marriage to the traitor. Describing Rigmel as an 'ostur' (goshawk) that he has won, he says:

---

[41] Pope (ed.), *Horn*, II, 8.

[42] F. Sinclair, *Milk and Blood: Gender and Genealogy in the Chanson de geste* (Berne, 2003), see especially chapter 2, pp. 54–105; Ailes, 'Romance and Epic Elements'; see also above nn. 21, 22 and 34.

[43] Vallecalle, 'Rupture et Integration'. Weiss comments on the presentation of both Christian and Saracen women as 'passionate, energetic and resourceful': 'The Wooing Woman', p. 151.

[44] Cf. Gui in *Fierabras* where he says he will only accept Floripas if Charlemagne gives her to him. *Fierabras*, lines 2915–17.

E s'il est si entier cum il fud a ces dis
Quant joe turnai de ci, dunc I ert mien, ço plevis;
Od mei l'enporterai de ci qu'a mes amis.
E cil est depecié u en coë malmis,
Ke penne ait bruséé, dunt rien li seïl de pis,
Ja mes pus nen iert miens si m'aït sant Denis.

['And if it's unblemished, as it was in the days when I left, then
I promise it will be mine; I'll carry it away with me from here
to my friends. And if it's damaged, or its tail feathers injured,
or its wing is broken, and it's the worse in any way, then by
St Denis, it will never be mine', lines 4263–68, trans. Weiss,
laisse 202]

Fortunately, Rigmel is able to reassure him. Weiss succinctly summarises the situation: 'only if she is undamaged may she be carried off'.[45] Pope points out that 'the contrast with the fashionable cult of *amour courtois* could hardly be more complete'.[46] The closing *laisse* of the poem tells us that Horn 'fathered on Rigmel the valiant Hadermod, who conquered, and then ruled, Africa, and took revenge on the heathen for all his kin'. It is marriage and lineage that are valued, rather than love for its own sake.

Elements of the expression of this relationship are taken from the romance tradition and these have been pointed out by Pope in the introduction to her edition: for example, the whole description of Rigmel's state of mind is compared to that of the heroines of the *romans d'antiquité*.[47] The poet may well be drawing upon both traditions but the romance elements are completely appropriated by the *chansons de geste*. While Rigmel's feelings are described like those of a courtly mistress, she behaves as an epic heroine. Similarly when Horn is wearing Rigmel's ring it inspires him to great deeds, a romance motif (*laisse* 152) – but this is within the context of an epic single combat. As Helen Cooper has pointed out, the ring is a symbol of their love and not a magic ring. A second ring given by Rigmel does have magic properties but it is still a desire for vengeance more than the love of Rigmel or the

---

45 Weiss, 'The Power and Weakness of Women', p. 12.
46 Pope (ed.), *Horn*, II, 10.
47 One of Rigmel's ladies describes Horn as having 'the cure for the pain you have had' (*laisse* 49), a topos of *amour courtois*. Rigmel falls in love with Horn on the basis of his reputation, without having seen him (as Floripas falls in love with Gui without meeting him). Pope considered Rigmel's freely expressed desire regarding Horn as too decorous for the *chanson de geste* – but it is very like Floripas's frank admiration of Gui in Fierabras and the language she uses in banter with the peers. In an exchange with the peers in *Fierabras* Floripas banters: '... I cannot see you properly. But I think that you know how to play with the girls and to kiss and cuddle under the covers in the bedchamber' (lines 2125–27: '... ne vous pluis viser; / mais je cuit c'as puciles sivés moult bien juer, / En cambre sous cortine baisier et acoler'). Rigmel's comment to her lady about Horn is that 'Happy she who could have him under her blanket of marten-skins' (*Horn*, lines 726–27, *laisse* 34). See also the contrast in the treatment of swooning between *Horn* and other Anglo-Norman *chansons de geste* as discussed in Weiss's essay in the present volume, 'Modern and Medieval Views on Swooning', pp. 123–4, 133.

possession of the land that spurs him to victory.[48] These 'romance' elements could be described as mere window-dressing, the borrowing of language or motifs from another genre to enrich the expression within a framework that is primarily epic.

It is also worth noting that the narrative is set in a cyclical context. The poem begins 'You will have heard, my lords, from the verses in parchment, how the noble Aalof came to his end'. The last *laisse* refers to a poem yet to be written about Horn's son. Pope even describes it as the 'central poem of a trilogy'[49] – just as the *Destruction* is part of a mini-cycle about Fierabras.

Thomas, in his composition of *Horn*, has taken the characteristic *chanson de geste* form and used characteristic *chanson de geste* discourse and established narrative elements and topoi to tell the story of an insular hero. By calling upon the traditions and affinities of the matter of France, that is, in writing a *chanson de geste*, Thomas gives his insular hero the same status as the heroes of continental *chansons de geste* and begins a process of insular appropriation of the genre.

Conclusion

What, then, is in a name? If the texts under consideration here all share more characteristics than their differing traditional generic labels would suggest, should we reject all attempts at genre classification? But the authors of *Horn*, *Otinel* and the *Destruction de Rome* consciously evoke the *chanson de geste* through their careful exploitation of that genre's forms, traditions and affinities. Romance 'influence', or rather enrichment of the genre by adapting romance conventions, may not be absent, particularly in *Horn*, but the closest link remains with the *chanson de geste* tradition. Thomas, the *Horn* poet, is perhaps the most deliberate in the way he does this. Not writing about traditional *chanson de geste* heroes, he nevertheless ensures that his audience will recognise his poem as a *chanson de geste*. Although the texts are part of insular literary culture they are also part of a Francophone literary culture. There is no impermeable barrier between Anglo-Norman and continental texts. Narratives move in both directions; not only do continental texts move into the insular tradition, Anglo-Norman texts such as *Boeve de Haumtone* and *Gui de Warewic* also move into continental literary tradition. Insular poets, such as the poets and *remanieurs* of *Otinel*, *La Destruction de Rome* and *Horn*, were not ignorant of the *chanson de geste* tradition into which they inscribed their texts and their audiences too would have recognised the

---

[48] H. Cooper, *The English Romance in Time: Transforming Motifs from Geoffrey of Monmouth to the Death of Shakespeare* (Oxford, 2004), p. 154.

[49] Pope (ed.), *Horn*, II, 3. As Weiss points out, 'neither [a poem about Aalof] nor anything about Hadermod, to be composed by Thomas' son "Wilmot" (Gilemot) survive': *The Birth of Romance*, p. xi. This may be no more than a device to link the poem into the cyclical tradition of the *chanson de geste*.

generic markers.[50] Denying *Horn* in particular the label 'chanson de geste' removes the text from that wider context.

When these texts are translated into English we have a different situation as there was no equivalent genre in the Middle English literary tradition; then they become 'romances' by virtue of having been translated from French. It may be this which has led to use of the same label in discussions of the Anglo-Norman texts. Context is crucial here: while 'romance' may suffice as a label in a Middle English literary context that offers no viable alternative generic category, the Anglo-Norman texts belong to a francophone literary culture whose authors and audiences know 'romance' and *chanson de geste* as distinct categories. These Anglo-Norman texts provide a link between continental French literary tradition and a developing insular literary tradition, and are part of both.

---

[50] On the reception of the *chanson de geste* in England see I. Short, 'Patrons and Polyglots: French Literature in Twelfth-century England', *Anglo-Norman Studies* 14 (1991), 229–49; on the potential of tail-rhyme as a Middle English equivalent to the *laisses* of the *chanson de geste* see R. Purdie, *Anglicising Romance: Tail-Rhyme and Genre in Medieval English Literature* (Cambridge, 2008), pp. 104–5.

6

'For Goddes loue, sir, mercy!': Recontextualising the Modern Critical Text of *Floris and Blancheflor*

JOHN A. GECK

The extant manuscripts of the Middle English *Floris and Blancheflor* present certain challenges both to modern editors and to the scholars who rely on their critical editions. Presented in most modern editions – and, thus, behind most modern studies – is the relatively straightforward tale of two young lovers, separated by both class and faith: Floris is a prince and Blancheflor is a slave's daughter; Floris is a heathen and Blancheflor a Christian. The two are forced apart by Floris's father but eventually reunited, at which point Floris converts to Christianity and the two are wed. This simple tale is somewhat more complex in the context of variations across the four manuscript versions: National Library of Scotland, MS Advocates' 19.2.1 (commonly known as 'Auchinleck'); Cambridge University Library, MS Gg.4.27.2; British Library, MS Egerton 2862; and British Library, MS Cotton Vitellius D.III. Scholars draw the identification of Floris as heathen and Blancheflor as Christian from the French tradition; there is no explicit classification as such in the Middle English manuscripts. Each version features at least one instance of Floris or his father beseeching the aid of not just God, but also Jesus, and only in Auchinleck does Floris convert to Christianity at the end. We cannot, however, assume a faith shared by Floris and his love based on the missing introduction, for there are also descriptions within each text that prevent an assumption that Floris is Christian.

This paper aims to explore the differences and similarities between the various Middle English manuscript versions of *Floris*. In doing so, we can see that a major theme of these versions is that Floris occupies a position as both heathen *and* Christian, and that this paradox of character traits is matched in his presentation both as male and female, and in his use of disguise and deceit to reclaim Blancheflor. This paper will attempt to recontextualise our modern readings of *Floris* in light of Auchinleck's deviations from the other manuscript versions. If we assume from this regular and deliberate play that ambiguity is an important theme, then we find that Auchinleck differs from the others in mitigating the most critical ambiguity – religious ambiguity – within the text. Although modern editions treat variants in both the French original and the Auchinleck version as authoritative, we might ask if the Auchinleck version presents *Floris* in the context of later Middle English romance as a whole.

Known across Europe from the twelfth to the sixteenth centuries, the *Floris*-tale was translated and adapted into Old French, Spanish, Italian, Middle High German, Greek, Middle English, Middle Dutch, Danish, Swedish, Old Norse, and Icelandic.[1] The earliest extant manuscript of any significant size is the Old French *version aristocratique*,[2] commonly titled *Floire et Blanche-flor*, dating from c.1200–25. The Middle English romance springs from this version, though in a condensed format. The surviving manuscripts of the French version number between 3000 and 3500 lines, while the longest version of the English romance, Egerton (hereafter E), is 1083 lines, and it is highly unlikely that, even complete, the English version would have been more than 1200 lines.[3] Of these four versions, one is almost unusable for any comparative manuscript study: Cotton Vitellius MS D.III (hereafter V), which dates from the second half of the thirteenth century, was burned in the fire of 1731 and is nearly unreadable. For the purposes of this study, the 180 legible lines and remaining identifiable words will be referenced, but few conclusions can be drawn from so little evidence. The other three texts have suffered considerably less damage. From roughly the same period as V, we have a version of *Floris and Blancheflor* in Cambridge MS Gg.4.27.2 (here-after C). Although 824 lines remain in C, the first quire, containing perhaps 350 lines, has been lost. MS Advocates' 19.2.1, the 'Auchinleck Manuscript' (A), dates from 1330–40, and contains 861 lines. Like C, A has lost a gath-ering at the beginning of *Floris*, and thus lacks perhaps 350 lines. E is the youngest of the Middle English manuscripts, dating from the beginning of the fifteenth century. It is also the largest, most complete, and most error-ridden form of *Floris and Blancheflor*, with 1083 lines remaining, though a lost folio at the beginning of the romance has resulted in a missing eighty lines.[4]

Thus through a twist of fate, modern scholars lack even one extant Middle English version of the beginning of the text. As a result of this, every edition of the romance has turned to the French aristocratic version to supply the expository material. While perhaps inevitable, this approach is not particu-larly helpful for comparative studies: McKnight's introduction to the EETS edition of the romance notes that E's opening line corresponds to line 193 of

[1] For a full catalogue of extant texts across Europe, see V. Schäfer's *Flore und Blancheflur: Epos und Volksbuch: Textversionen und die verschiedenen Illustrationen bis ins 19. Jahrhundert. Ein Beitrage zur Geschichte der Illustration* (Munich, 1984), pp. 176–227.

[2] Found in Paris, Bibliothèque Nationale fonds français MSS 375, 1447, 12562, and Rome, Biblio-teca Apostolica Vaticana, Palatinus Latinus 1971.

[3] Both the Old French and Middle English versions are composed in octosyllabic lines. Though economy of language may allow for some compression in the Middle English versions, the three-fold-length of the Old French versions is primarily the result of extra details.

[4] See F. C. De Vries' analysis of the Egerton manuscript and its consistent errors in versification and rhyme: *Floris and Blancheflur: A Middle English romance edited with introduction, notes and glossary* (Groningen, 1966), pp. 4–5, 11–12.

the French text, while it is known that only eighty lines can be missing.[5] The opening line of A corresponds to line 1001 of the French text, but to line 367 of E. Clearly a direct borrowing from the French text did not occur. What is lost, however? In the preserved openings from other languages, we find a relatively consistent story:

A pagan king of Spain raids Galacia and slaughters pilgrims to Santiago de Compostela, one of whom is a French knight with his daughter. His daughter, a young widow, is taken into slavery by the king and given as a servant to his wife the queen. Both the queen and the widow give birth on the same day to two children: Floris (by the queen) and Blancheflor (by her servant). E begins at this point.

The two children are very close, and show great affection for one another. When the children reach the age of twelve, Floris's father begins to worry that Floris will refuse to marry anyone but Blancheflor, and considers killing her. Floris's mother suggests a gentler scheme: Floris will be sent to his uncle's castle. Floris pines for Blancheflor and refuses food and drink. Floris's father returns to the idea of killing Blancheflor, and is again stopped by the queen, who convinces him that she should be sold to Babylonian merchants and taken across the seas, and that they need then only claim she has died. The king agrees; Blancheflor is sold to the merchants, and then sold to the Emir of Babylon, who puts her in his harem and considers her a potential wife. At this point, V begins.

Back in Spain, the king and queen contrive to deceive Floris into thinking that Blancheflor has died. They build a church and put a tomb for Blancheflor within it. When Floris returns home, he is shown the grave and prepares to kill himself out of grief. Blancheflor's mother begs the king to permit the two children to wed. He consents, and Floris is told the truth. Floris's father gives his son fine clothes, horses, and gold to take to Babylon in the guise of a merchant. A and C begin here, and at this point all four manuscript versions follow the same plot.

Floris's mother gives him a magic ring that she claims will render him invulnerable. On his way to Babylon, Floris stays at two inns where Blancheflor also stayed, and his sorrow is evident to all around him. Both innkeepers offer Floris aid and advice on his journey; the second, named Darius, tells Floris that he should bribe the porter of the Emir's tower to gain entrance in order to rescue Blancheflor. Floris follows Darius's advice and is smuggled into the tower in a basket of flowers picked by maidens of the harem. When the two young lovers are reunited, they 'clippe and kisse' and make 'joie and mochele blisse' (A 542–3). They fall asleep in each other's arms and are found that way in the morning by the Emir, who is prepared to kill them both immediately, but who defers to the judgement of his barons. The barons

5   *King Horn, Floriz and Blauncheflur, The Assumption of Our Lady*, ed. J. Rawson Lumby, EETS OS 14 (London, 1866). Second edn rev. G. H. McKnight, 1901; rpt. 1962, p. xlii.

condemn them to death, at which point Floris urges Blancheflor to take the ring he was given by his mother. She refuses, and insists that he should keep it. The piteous scene sways the Emir to mercy, and Floris and Blancheflor are immediately wed. When the Emir hears that Floris is a prince of Spain, he dubs him a knight and offers him a kingdom if he will remain. Floris, however, hearing that his father has died, refuses the offer and returns to Spain with Blancheflor to take the throne there.

Many scholars have commented on the peculiarity of *Floris and Blancheflor* in comparison to other romances, particularly those of the Matter of Araby, which deal with East–West interaction. Metlitzki notes, among other eccentricities, how 'the emir of Babylon's fairness and moderation contrast with the habitual rashness and temperamental excesses which characterise the stereotyped sultans of the romances composed in the West'.[6] Barnes proposes a generic distinction that separates *Floris and Blancheflor* from the traditional French *roman idyllique* based on 'some characteristics associated with two very different literary traditions in which Love also conquers all, the saint's life and Greek New Comedy', namely 'Christian–heathen conflict [and] "miraculous" same-day conception' for the former, and 'the Youth *versus* Age situation of Greek New Comedy'.[7] Calkin observes that unlike the darker stories of Saracen–Christian intermingling found in the Auchinleck manuscript, '*Floris and Blauncheflur*, too, depicts an inter-faith relationship', and that it 'suggests the possibility of a harmonious integration of Saracen and Christian, and even if it, too, in the end, insists on conversion to deal with the union, this tale of the East represents that conversion as a much less violent process'.[8]

Despite the peculiarities noted above, however, the romance was popular in fourteenth- and fifteenth-century England; its appearance in four manuscripts, two of which (A and E) are noted collections of romances and popular tales, attests to this. Closer study of the most conspicuous peculiarity – the sympathetic treatment of the Saracens – reveals that this treatment is not the result of simple tolerance, but is in fact a sign of a deeper underlying aesthetic, one of ambiguity wherein the main Saracen character, Floris, is not only pagan, but also Christian, and not only masculine, but also feminine. In tandem with this we see ambiguity in acts of disguise and deceit. Among these ambiguities, it is ambiguities of faith that are most pronounced and have received the most scholarly attention. The presence of these ambiguities in all Middle English versions of the romance, albeit mitigated in the

[6] D. Metlitzki, *The Matter of Araby in Medieval England* (New Haven, 1977), p. 191.
[7] G. Barnes, 'Cunning and Ingenuity in the Middle English Floris and Blauncheflur', *Medium Aevum* 53 (1984), 10–25 (p. 12).
[8] S. Bly Calkin, *Saracens and the Making of English Identity: the Auchinleck Manuscript* (New York, 2005), p. 128.

Auchinleck version, attests to the popularity of the theme in the context of later medieval English romance.

Lacking the first 200 lines of the poem, we have no explicit identification of Floris as Saracen and Blancheflor as Christian. This identification is never made in any Middle English version as baldly as it is in the Old French versions,[9] with the possible exception of the Auchinleck manuscript version, which concludes with an apparent, though brief, conversion scene:

> Thai bitaught the Amerail oure Dright,
> And thai com hom whan thai might,
> And let croune him to king,
> And hire to quene, that swete thing,
> And underfeng Cristendom of prestes honde,
> And thonkede God of alle His sonde. (A 848–53)[10]

The other Middle English manuscripts offer even less than Auchinleck. The ending of V is lost and cannot be taken into account here, but E ends succinctly, saying only of Floris: 'Hom he went with royal array / And was crownyd within a short day' (E 1082–3). C gives a hint of a Christianised Floris, ending with a coronation scene, and adding that Floris 'bitaʒte hem alle God Almiʒte, / And com hom whane he miʒte' (C 815–16).

Floris's final commendation of the Saracens to 'God Almighty' does not seem to indicate a sudden and definitive conversion when one considers the semi-Christian qualities that his family display throughout the tale. Earlier in the text, when the king resolves to murder Blancheflor, the queen argues against it vehemently with a nonspecific plea to God: 'For Goddes loue, sir, mercy!' (E 144).[11] All three complete Middle English versions say explicitly that Floris and Blancheflor are wed in a church, with the permission of the

---

9   Cf. 'Flores fu tos nés de paiiens, / Et Blanceflor de crestiiens' (lines 17–18); 'S'ele puet, oblier li fera / La crestiiene Blanceflor' (lines 326–7), from the version aristocratique, in *Li romanz de Floire et Blancheflor in beiden Fassungen nach allen Handschriften mit Einleitung, Namenverzeichnis und Glossar neu herausgegeben*, ed. F. Krueger (Berlin, 1938).

10 Both Calkin and De Vries have commented on the brief and oddly worded nature of this possible conversion. See Calkin, *Saracens*, p. 130, and De Vries, who connects these lines to the French text, 'Floires se fet crestïenner' (line 3006), in his textual notes.

11 These vague references to a monotheistic deity appear in the French version as well: in the above scene, '"Sire," fait el [the queen], "por Diu merchi!"' (414). Such comments have encouraged scholars of the Old French tale to note that 'Nowhere is the romance seriously interested in pagan culture or the problems of inter-cultural romance.' See P. McCaffery, 'Sexual Identity in Floire et Blancheflor and Ami et Amile', in *Gender Transgressions: Crossing the Normative Barrier in Old French Literature*, ed. K. J. Taylor (New York, 1998), pp. 129–51, here p. 135. See also: 'Yet, after the initial episode in which the pagan king Felis captures Blancheflor's mother, the narrative all but abandons the issues of religion, violence, and intercultural relations that separate pagans and Christians in other literary traditions': L. Shutters, 'Christian Love or Pagan Transgression? Marriage and Conversion in Floire et Blancheflor', in *Discourses on Love, Marriage, and Transgression in Medieval and Early Modern Literature*, ed. A. Classen (Tempe, 2004), pp. 85–108, here pp. 93–4.

Emir.[12] Mention of churches begins even earlier on in the romance, and the
buildings seem to be respected, if not always frequented, by Floris's mother
and father as well. Early in the text, when the king sets out to simulate
Blancheflor's death, he and the queen 'lete make in a chirche / A swathe feire
grave wyrche' (E 209–10). The false tomb and the wedding might be read as
an implicit respect for Blancheflor's faith, but one surprising oath to Jesus
appearing in E, made by Floris's father, presents a compelling argument that
the whole royal family may be Christian. When Floris's father prepares his
son to find Blancheflor, he says: 'Al that thee nedeth we shul thee fynde. /
Jhesu thee of care unbynde' (E 338). Since E is unfortunately the only manuscript which preserves this early part of the tale, it cannot be known how
the other three versions would have treated this line. Lest it be considered
'a small slip of the E scribe',[13] however, we can see that such an oath by a
purportedly Saracen character is made again, this time by Floris when he is
reunited with his love:

Floris þen to speke began,
And seid: 'Lord þat madest man,
I it þonke Goddes sone,
Þat al my care I haue ouercome'
        (E 827–30)

Florice ferst speke bigan,
7 saide: 'Louerd þat madest man,
Þe I þanke, Godes sone,
Nou al mi care ich haue ouercome'
        (A 532–5)

Þo Floriz furst speke bigan,
'Ure Louerd', he sede, 'þat makedest man,
Þe ihc þonki, Godes sune,
Þat ihc am to mi leof icum'
        (C 540–3)

...................formest speke bigon
....................d þat makedest man
...........................nou Godes sone
.....[c]are is ouer[c]ome
        (V 301–4)

A modern reader familiar with romances dealing with the conversion of
a Saracen to Christianity might well expect several common tropes. The
Saracen should be verbally definite in his heathenness, by making reference
to the panoply of gods ascribed to Saracens and explicitly denying Christianity. This model holds true for many of the Matter of Araby texts, particularly those relating to Charlemagne: *The Sowdone of Babylone*, existing in
a single manuscript from the mid-fifteenth century,[14] serves well to contex-
tualise the *Floris and Blancheflor* tradition. Within just one hundred lines
of the opening to *The Sowdone of Babylone*, the sultan makes 'a vowe / to

---

[12] 'To a chirche he let hem brynge, / And dede let wed hem with a ryng' (E 1064–5); 'To one chirche
he let hem bringge / 7 wedde here wiȝ here owene ringge' (A 822–3); 'He let hem to one chirche
bringe, / And spusen hem wiþ one gold ringe' (C 787–8).

[13] E. Kooper, note to line 338 of *Floris and Blancheflour* in *Sentimental and Humorous Romances*
(Kalamazoo, 2006).

[14] Princeton University, Robert Garrett Collection of Medieval and Renaissance Manuscripts, MS
No. 140.

Mahounde and to Appolyne'.[15] Utterances by Saracens continue in this vein for the remainder of the text, with references to 'Mahoundis benysone',[16] 'Mahoundes loue',[17] and further pairings of Mohammad with other gods, including Apollo.[18] Indeed, Ferumbras, the sultan's son, whose conversion is one of the major themes of the text, acts in manifestly non-Christian fashion before he consents to be converted. When Ferumbras takes Rome, one of his first acts is to sack St Peter's and seize the holy relics contained within. Ferumbras goes on to give thanks to 'his goddes' for the victory,[19] and explicitly swears to Mohammad no fewer than four times when he faces Oliver in the single combat that leads to his defeat and conversion.[20]

However, even in the specific category of the converted Saracen, should we place Floris there alongside Ferumbras, Floris differs from others in the language applied to and employed by him. Part of this may be due to the fact that while *Floris and Blancheflor* has been considered to be a *roman idyllique*, *The Sowdone of Babylone* falls much more squarely in the genre of *chanson de geste*. As Metlitzki points out, the *chanson* tradition in French literature is a tradition of historicity: '[Saracens] are a crucial public theme – political, militarily, and religious – and what is made fanciful in them is made deliberately so for purposes of patriotism, propaganda, and entertainment'.[21] It is perhaps unsurprising, therefore, that the *chanson* tradition would rely on repeated references to Saracen polytheism in a response to both the desire for historical accuracy and the wish to present the Saracens as a serious external threat. That the Old French *Floire* is almost as devoid of Saracen oaths as its Middle English counterpart speaks to this fact. Despite this, the Old French versions, as noted briefly above, nevertheless retain a large number of markers distinguishing the pagan royal family from Christian Blancheflor. In addition to the explicit division between the two noted in the beginning of the tale, the ending conversion sequence is far clearer: Floire 'se fait crestïener' ('had himself christened', line 3006) before his coronation and 'mena puis crestiiene vie' ('lived thereafter a Christian life', line 3009) for the sake of Blancheflor. Bishops conduct the coronation. After, he persuades his barons to convert and they spend 'plus d'une semaine' ('over a week', line 3027) converting the general populace. As for those who refused, 'Floires les faisoit escorcier, / Ardoir en fu u detrencier' ('Floire had them flayed, burnt or dismembered', lines 3030–1). Floire's forced conversion of his own people and the violence he wreaks on those who refuse are quite at odds with the more gentle interreligious tenor of the rest of this *roman idyllique*.

[15] Quoted here from *The Sowdone of Babylone*, ed. E. Hausknecht, EETS ES 38 (London, 1881), lines 85–6.
[16] *Sowdone*, line 288.
[17] *Sowdone*, lines 413, 425.
[18] *Sowdone*, lines 1020, 2105, 2177, 2431, 2761–2.
[19] *Sowdone*, line 678.
[20] *Sowdone*, lines 1137, 1199, 1221, 1262.
[21] Metlitzki, *Matter of Araby*, p. 119.

Leaving aside genre, however, one can compare Floris to Saracens in Middle English romances not drawn from the Old French *chanson* tradition:[22] here, too, the Saracen characters frequently employ verbal markers of otherness. *Bevis of Hampton* is but one example, and a romance that is found in two of the same manuscripts as *Floris* (A and E). In *Bevis*, the eponymous hero's interactions with Saracens are decisively indicated as a meeting of two incompatible and strictly divided faiths – even if not wholly unfriendly. When Bevis is presented to the 'Ermyn King', the king swears to Mohammad twice:

> 'Mahoun!' a seide, 'þe miȝt be proute,
> And þis child wolde to þe aloute;
> ȝif a wolde a Sarasin be,
> ȝit ich wolde hope, a scholde þe!
> Be Mahoun, þat sit an hiȝ,
> A fairer child never I ne siȝ' (lines 531–6)[23]

Bevis's response is no less clear in maintaining this division of faiths. When the king offers him Josian's hand in marriage if he will convert to the king's faith, he says 'I nolde for-sake in none manere / Iesu, þat bouȝte me so dere. / Al mote þai be doum and deue, / Þat on þe false godes be-leue!'(lines 565–8).

Suffice it to say, the *Floris* model of converted Saracen is considerably more complex than is found in many other romances. Whereas Matter of Araby romances feature a regular and explicit display of Saracen behaviour on the part of their protagonists before they convert, Floris makes no such references before his (apparent) conversion. Indeed, Floris is never referred to as a pagan, heathen, or Saracen, unlike in the *Sowdone of Babylone*, where such references are so common and regular that an accounting of them here would take pages.[24] As Calkin notes:

> Two of the manuscripts do include references to Blauncheflur's mother as 'þe Cristen woman' (E ll. 3, 247, and V l. 46), but all other opening references to the religious differences of Floris and Blauncheflur are lost ... the words 'hethen' and 'paien' do not appear in any manuscript of the tale, the adjective 'Cristen' appears only in the three instances noted above, and the term 'sarazin' appears only once, in Auchinleck. In Auchinleck, however, 'sarazin' describes two of the Amerail of Babiloine's men (647), not Floris.

---

22 Although see Ailes, 'What's in a Name? Anglo-Norman Romances or *Chansons de geste?*' in the present volume on the difficulties of drawing absolute distinctions between these genres in Anglo-Norman literature.

23 This quotation and the next are from the A version of Bevis as edited by E. Kölbing, *The Romance of Sir Beues of Hamtoun*, EETS ES 46, 48, 65 (London, 1885–94).

24 In just the first 250 lines of *The Sowdone of Babylone*, 'heathen' is used six times (lines 22, 147, 151, 158, 164, 237), 'Christiante' (lines 31, 235) and 'Cristen' (lines 128, 145) each twice, and 'Sarysyns' (line 216) and 'Mahound and Appolyne' both once (line 86). In the Auchinleck *Bevis*, the name 'Mahoun' alone is mentioned no fewer than twenty-three times, and is frequently paired with references to Apollo and Termagant (lines 531, 535, 606, 659, 891, 896, 928, 934, 996, 1118, 1124, 1352, 1379, 1625, 1846, 3604, 3695, 3880, 3992, 4036, 4067, 4146, 4221).

Indeed, in the 861 lines of the Auchinleck text that we have, neither lover's religious identification is ever specified.[25]

Can Floris even be considered a heathen in the Middle English versions? There is no reason to assume that he is, beyond the conversion scene at the end of A and reliance on the French source's opening. We might consider the French source, with an opening and a closing that are decidedly clear on the religious division between the two lovers, to fall at one end of a spectrum indicating ambiguity within the *Floris*-story. The Egerton version, with the complicating references to a Christian faith and no conversion sequence, falls at the other end. The other three Middle English versions fall between these two extremes, with Auchinleck falling closest to the Old French version, and C and V falling closer to E. To read the Middle English text in this larger context requires some defence of the more ambiguous versions, so that E's treatment of religious ambiguity is not ascribed to error or textual degeneration. This defence lies in seeing ambiguities beyond religious identity as an important theme in all versions: thus, while the first half of this paper has dealt with the differences between the versions, the second half will look for similarities. And indeed, ambiguities common to the Middle English tradition as a whole are readily apparent, beginning with the striking similarity between Floris and Blancheflor, and the ambiguity of gender this might entail.

In the A, C, and E versions (the comparable section of V does not remain), the nearly identical appearance of Floris and Blancheflor is commented on by the innkeeper's wife, who, when telling Floris where Blancheflor has gone, remarks that 'þou art ilich here of alle þing, /Of semblant 7 of mourning, / But þou art a man 7 3he is a maide' (A 53–5).[26] This similarity between Floris and Blancheflor is tied to Floris's ambiguity of gender, seen in his pronounced effeminate characterisation as a pre-adolescent male. Indeed, the youth of Floris and Blancheflor is the most explicitly presented challenge to the two lovers: even for scholars inured to the idea of children being pledged to marriage at young ages, the protagonists' youth and their passionate attachment are somewhat uncommon for either romances or late medieval French or English custom. For John Stevens, it is precisely this trait that marks the English text's departure from the French version, since 'the English author has managed to retain the innocent charm of their [Floris and Blancheflor's] attachment whilst divesting it of the precocious sexuality which makes it distasteful'.[27] Leaving aside questions of distastefulness, the sexualities of the protagonists are explored in the text in two ways. Firstly, the youth of the protagonists does not only stand in the way of their union, but also challenges Floris's identity as a male lover. Secondly, and resulting from Floris's youth,

---

[25] Calkin, *Saracens*, p. 129.

[26] Compare 'Boþ of semblant 7 of mornyng' (E 412); 'þu art hire ilich of alle þing, /Boþe of semblaunt 7 of murninge, / Of fairnesse 7 of muchelhede, / Bute þu ert a man 7 heo a maide' (C 49–52).

[27] J. Stevens, *Medieval Romance: Themes and Approaches* (London, 1973), p. 45.

is the regular and frequent linking of Floris and Blancheflor in appearance, which further contributes to Floris's ambiguity of gender. While both the French and English texts explore sexual ambiguities through these characterisations, the English text is slightly more complex in its presentation of Floris, revealing an immature and feminised hero, but holding back from the regular reminders of these characterisations that are present in the French.

Floris's characterisation in the French text as a young boy – distinctive in many ways from an adult male, and oftentimes more similar to a woman – has already been well discussed by Gilbert, who points out that not only does the French author repeatedly refer to Floris as 'enfes' ('child'), but that he also meticulously provides the ages of both children.[28] This is a trope carried over to the introduction in the Egerton text, in which the reader is informed 'þat þey were of elde of seuen yere' (E 6) when they are first brought to school, and that they are twelve when the king and queen decide to send Floris away (E 31: 'When þey had v yere to scoole goon'). Unlike in the French versions, further mentions of age are absent from the English texts. Nevertheless, such a characterisation drives much of the story in both the French and English versions: it is only when Floris and Blancheflor approach a marriageable age that their excessive affection becomes problematic, and the young lovers' powerlessness is made clear as adults dictate their separation (as the king and queen do), threaten them with death (as both the king and emir do), or provide them with necessary aid (as the innkeeper, Darius, and the porter do).

However, the English texts depart from the French when it comes to a reading of Floris's gender. Not only does *Floire et Blancheflor* stress Floire's age more consistently than the English version (adding that Floire and Blancheflor are fourteen when they are reunited at the Emir's palace), but the French text is also much more explicit in equating Floire's immature masculinity to femininity: that is to say that as a young boy, Floire has more in common with a woman than an adult man with regard to agency, individual power, and – especially – appearance. Two scenes in particular stress this feminisation of Floire, the first being Licoris's comment that Floris is as beautiful as (the female) Blancheflor:

> 'Sire,' fait Licoris, 'par foi,
> Çou m'est avis, quant jou le voi,
> Que çou soit Blanceflor la bele.
> Jou cuit qu'ele est sa suer jumele'

> ['Sire,' says Licoris, 'in faith, it's my view that when I see him it is as if it were Blancheflor. I think she's his twin sister': lines 1725–8]

---

[28] J. Gilbert, 'Boys Will Be ... What? Gender, Sexuality, and Childhood in *Floire et Blancheflor* and *Floris et Lyriope*', *Exemplaria* 9 (1997), 39–61 (p. 49).

In the second, the Emir, upon catching Floire and Blancheflor together in bed, is confused by what he sees:

> Floires a s'amie gisoit;
> Qu'il fust hom, nul senblant n'avoit,
> Car en face ne en menton
> N'avoit ne barbe ne grenon....
> …
> Au chambrelant dist: 'Les poitrines
> Me descouvrez des deus meschines.
> Leur mameles primes verrons
> Et après les esveillerons.'
> Cil les desceuvre, s'aperçit
> Que li uns des deus hons estoit

> [Floire lay with his sweetheart; he gave no sign that he was a man, for he had neither beard nor moustache on his face or chin … [The Emir] said to the chamberlain: 'Show me the chests of these two young people. We will see their breasts first, and then we'll wake them up.' He uncovered them, saw that one of them was a man: lines 2430–3, 2440–5]

The English versions pare down this emphasis. The comments by the innkeeper's wife are reduced to a remark on their similar appearance, and the Emir's discovery of the two lovers is altered:

> Þe chaumberleyn haþ vndernome;
> Into hir bour he his icome,
> And stant bifore hire bed,
> And find þar twai, neb to neb,
> Neb to neb, an mouþ to mouþ.
> Wel sone was þat sorewe couþ.
> Into þe tour vp he steiȝ,
> & saide his louerd al þat he seiȝ.
> Þe Ameral het his swerd him bring;
> Iwiten he wolde of þat þinge.
> Forht he nimȝ wiȝ alle mayn,
> Himself and his chaumberlayn,
> Til þaie come þar þai two laie;
> Ȝit was þe slep fast in hire eȝe.
> Þe Ameral het hire cloþes keste
> A litel bineþen here breste.
> Þan seȝ he wel sone anon
> Þat on was a man, þat oþer a womman. (A 612–29)

Descriptions of Floris seem to do more than simply feminise him; they also serve to pair Floris with Blancheflor specifically. The close similarity between Floris and Blancheflor is established not only through direct comparisons by the narrator (such as in the inn scene mentioned above), but also through symbolism and word play introduced in Floris's efforts to enter the Emir's castle, a feat accomplished by his hiding in a basket of flowers. This act presents him as an ambiguously gendered figure through two separate interpretations, one literal and the other symbolic. Firstly, the passive entry into the tower on a literal level sets Floris as significantly weaker than the Emir, whose role as a sexually acquisitive mature male is plain. The second, symbolic interpretation follows a somewhat more circuitous path.

Floris's hiding in the flowers makes explicit a connection established earlier in the text through a number of different references. Firstly, it spells out a pun on the protagonists' names: Blancheflor's friend Claris, who carries the basket of flowers to Blancheflor's bower, mentions it explicitly:

> To Blauncheflours bour Clarice wente anon,
> & saide leyende to Blauncheflour:
> 'Wiltou sen a ful fair flour,
> Swiche a flour þat þe schal like
> Haue þou sen hit a lite?' (A 476–80)

This equation of Floris to Blancheflor through floral imagery serves as more than a humorous device, however. Floris's physical concealment in flowers is also matched by Blancheflor in Darius's description of the Emir's garden and the Tree of Love:

> At þe welle-heued þer stant a tre,
> Þe fairest þat mai in erthe be.
> Hit is icleped þe tre of loue,
> For floures and blosmes beþ euer aboue;
> And þilke þat clene maidenes be,
> Men schal hem bringe vnder þat tre,
> And wich-so falleȝ on þat [ferste] flour,
> Hi schal ben chosen quen wiȝ honour;
> & ȝif þer ani maiden is
> Þat þamerail halt of mest pris,
> Þe flour schal on here be went
> Þourh art and þourgh enchantement.
> Þous he cheseþ þourȝ þe flour
> & euere we herkneȝ when hit be Blauncheflour.' (A 311–24)

These pairings of Floris and Blancheflor, the regular references to Floris's youth, his inability to meet the Emir in open challenge to win back his love, and the confusion of gender when the Emir discovers the two, all add to Floris's complex characterisation: just as he is presented as both Christian and Saracen, so too does he appear as both male and female.

Religious and sexual ambiguities are not the only uncertain characteristics of Floris as a protagonist. At his father's advice, Floris travels to Babylon in the guise of a merchant. When first encountering the porter, Floris initially presents himself 'Als [he] were a masoun' (A 337). Floris's attempts at disguise – as a merchant, as a mason, and in a basket of flowers – foreground the theme of ambiguity on two levels. Literally, Floris thrice pretends to be something he is not: while the reader is aware that Floris is Floris, the other characters believe otherwise. Floris's identity is thus fluid, depending on one's perspective. Thematically, the disguises speak to a larger idea within the texts: deceit. The topic of deceit has been discussed by Geraldine Barnes, who argues that '[t]here is no suggestion of moral or religious compunction on the part of the lovers when they deceive Blancheflor's sinister wooer, the Emir of "Babylon"'.[29] Floris's use of cunning and disguise reveals a lack of interest in prowess in open combat, and works in tandem with Floris's hypo-masculinised behaviour and appearance.

With these further ambiguities in mind, we can turn again to the variations between manuscript versions of the tale. All four English versions, where they remain, retain these key elements of the story, an indication that these elements should be seen as integral to a reading of the romance. Thus behind the *Floris and Blancheflor* of any of the manuscripts lies the idea of this romance, and central to this idea is an appreciation of ambiguous characterisation and a deliberate blurring of traditional boundaries. In this way, the Middle English versions realise more completely what the Old French version seems to promise, 'a love story that should be transgressive on every count'.[30]

Despite the blurring of boundaries and heightening of ambiguities present throughout all Middle English versions of *Floris and Blancheflor*, a creative force in the Auchinleck version seems to work to reduce this ambiguity to some degree. One cannot conclude whether this is the result of the wishes of a patron, a scribe, a translator, the cultural milieu of 1330s London, or as mediated through the text from which the Auchinleck version was copied. Regardless of the situation, care should be taken in analyses of *Floris and Blancheflor*, taking into account the context of the other versions. One common approach in reading the romance has been to trust implicitly the French source. This should be done with extreme caution, if at all. Second, and perhaps more important, is the fact that of all four manuscripts, only the Auchinleck text reconciles Floris's paradox of religion through the conversion sequence. Based on this fact, we can characterise Auchinleck as more imitative of the French source than the other English versions, or as less appreciative of this aesthetic of ambiguity, or, indeed, as both. Thus, while the Auchinleck manuscript is frequently cited as an authoritative manuscript in many ways, particularly by virtue of its containing many of the earliest Middle English versions of romances, we should apply any conclusions made from reading Auchinleck very carefully.

---

29 Barnes, 'Cunning and Ingenuity', p. 11.
30 Shutters, 'Christian Love', p. 85. Shutters goes on to argue that 'the poem brings together medieval discourses of love, marriage, religion, and gender to explore and complicate notions of cultural difference' (p. 86).

7

Roland in England:
Contextualising the Middle English *Song of Roland*

PHILLIPA HARDMAN

British Library MS Lansdowne 388 is a composite volume formed by the convenient binding together of a number of quite unrelated smaller manuscripts of different dates. One of these (now folios 381–95) contains the unique Middle English text known as *The Song of Roland*. The incomplete manuscript copy has no title or running head – *The Song of Roland* is the title given to this fragmentary medieval poem by its first modern editor.[1] The Catalogue of the Lansdowne Collection describes it as follows: 'Item 21. A fragment of an old romance, in alliterative metre, on the gests of Charlemagne and Roland. It chiefly relates to the consequences of Ganelon's treachery.' This is a fair account of the text, and it is notable that the cataloguer makes no reference to the *Chanson de Roland* as a source of the English poem.[2] By contrast, the first printed edition of the fragment, which is again placed within a composite volume, now brought together with two romances from the London Thornton manuscript, presents it entirely through the lens of its status as 'the only known English version of the celebrated *Chanson de Roland*' (p. xviii). The title page of Herrtage's edition gives authenticity to the invented name by printing it in the same black-letter type and enclosed in the same quotation marks as the titles transcribed from the Thornton manuscript for the other two texts in the volume. My purpose in this essay is to explore the identity of the text as a fragmentary 'Song of Roland', both in relation to the French *Chanson* and in terms of its new context within the tradition of Middle English romance.

---

1   *The Sege off Melayne, The Romance of Duke Rowland and Sir Otuell of Spayne* and *The Song of Roland*, The English Charlemagne Romances, Part II, ed. Sidney J. Herrtage, EETS ES 35 (1880). Quotations are taken from this edition, with some emendations of punctuation.

2   The Lansdowne catalogue (1812–19) predated the first edition of the French poem (from Oxford, Bodleian Library, MS Digby 23), with the famous title bestowed on it by Francisque Michel (1837). However, the poem was known before that date, being cited in Tyrwhitt's *Canterbury Tales* (1775–78) under the name *Le Roman de Roncevaux* (see Herrtage, p. xviii).

The title *The Song of Roland* implies that what it names is a translation of the Old French epic *La Chanson de Roland*,[3] and Herrtage does nothing to dispel the idea when he provides 'a succinct sketch of the whole story, as told in the French original' (p. xix) to act as a summary of the English poem. This easy identification has proved a barrier to any serious evaluation of the Middle English text on its own terms, even though critics have long recognised that in fact it is not a translation of the illustrious *Chanson* – it combines details from different versions of the tradition and borrows material from the *Pseudo-Turpin Chronicle*.[4] As some have argued, there is no reason to assume with Smyser and Barron that what survives is a poor derivative of a lost French conflated text: it may just as likely represent an adaptation by the English poet of the original materials.[5] Now, with Joseph Duggan's recent edition of all French texts of the *Chanson de Roland*, it is possible to appreciate the complex relation of the Middle English *Roland* to the Anglo-Norman and French texts;[6] to show that the variations in the English *Roland* fragment evident on comparing it with the French source texts constitute a sustained and purposeful programme of rearrangements in the narrative, with a considerable amount of new material not evident elsewhere in the tradition; and to consider the overall effect of these alterations.[7] By reading this new text in the context of the practice of Middle English romance tradition, we can explore how far such changes are likely to represent specific adaptation for a new English readership, versed in the same tradition.

The story of Roland at Roncevaux was of course widely known independently of the *Chanson de Roland* as an episode in the history of Charlemagne's

---

[3] There is also, of course, the prior question of the politically motivated nineteenth-century invention of the title *La Chanson de Roland*, discussed in A. Taylor, 'Was There a Song of Roland?', *Speculum* 76 (2001), 28–65. For discussion of the English poem in relation to the French epic genre, see my 'Speaking of Roland: The Middle English *Song of Roland* in BL MS Lansdowne 388', in *Medieval Historical Discourses: Essays in Honour of Professor Peter S. Noble*, ed. M. Ailes, F. Le Saux and A. Lawrence, *Reading Medieval Studies* 34 (2008), 99–121. I am grateful to the editors for permission to reuse material from this essay.

[4] In their surveys of the Matter of France in English, H. M. Smyser and W. R. J. Barron both take a poor view of the Middle English fragment, judging it almost entirely in terms of its success or failure in rendering the spirit and ethos of the original French *chanson de geste*, and criticising the poet for apparently misunderstanding narrative incidents that are included in the English poem but with altered detail or emphasis: H. M. Smyser, 'Charlemagne Legends', in *A Manual of the Writings in Middle English 1050–1500*, ed. J. Burke Severs, I: Romances (New Haven CT, 1967), pp. 80–100 (p. 96); W. R. J. Barron, *English Medieval Romance* (London, 1987), pp. 90–1.

[5] S. H. A. Shepherd, '"I have gone for þi sak wonderfull wais": The Middle English Fragment of *The Song of Roland*', *Olifant* 11 (1986), 219–36, characterising the text as 'a kind of "researched" compilation'; S. E. Farrier, '*Das Rolandslied* and the *Song of Roulound* as Moralizing Adaptations of the *Chanson de Roland*', *Olifant* 16 (1991), 61–76. Farrier bases her argument in respect of the Middle English poem on J. R. Russ, 'The Middle English *Song of Roland*, a critical edition' (unpublished PhD dissertation, University of Wisconsin, 1968). Both Shepherd's and Farrier's analyses contain some misrepresentations of the ME text.

[6] *La Chanson de Roland – The Song of Roland: The French Corpus*, ed. J. J. Duggan and others, 7 parts in 3 vols. (Turnhout, 2005), I, pp. 39–124. All quotations and MS sigla are taken from this edition.

[7] For a summary of parallels and variations between the English poem and the French corpus of the *Chanson de Roland*, see Hardman, 'Speaking of Roland', Appendix.

conquest of Spain, as related in the *Pseudo-Turpin Chronicle* and its derivatives. The *Chanson de Roland* itself (and it is interesting to note that Michel's original full title was *La Chanson de Roland, ou de Roncevaux*)[8] memorably begins not with Roland, but by asserting the greatness of Charlemagne and his victories and the corresponding hostility of the Saracen king Marsile, and ends with Charles's victorious entry into Saragossa[9] and – the final act – his just trial and punishment of Ganelon for treason, before the concluding reference to a future expedition of Charlemagne's to defend Christendom. The unique copy of the Middle English *Song of Roland* lacks both the beginning and ending of the text, but a similar framing identification with Charlemagne can be observed in the case of the other Middle English romances based on the Matter of France: no matter what the medieval or modern titles attached to them, the manuscripts show evidence of concern that the texts be positively identified as Charlemagne-related – headings, prologues and colophons are provided to make it clear.[10] The Fillingham *Otuel and Roland* and the Auchinleck *Roland and Vernagu* both have or had an extensive prologue summarising the whole Charlemagne cycle, while the Auchinleck *Otuel a Knight* has a unique narrative introduction focusing on Charlemagne. The Fillingham *Firumbras* ends 'Explicit Kynge Charlys'. The Thornton *Roland and Otuell* begins and ends with elaborate title and explicit naming the two heroes, but adds to each on a separate line: 'Off Cherlls of Fraunce' and 'Charlles'. The *Sege of Melayne* in the same manuscript proclaims in its prologue that it will tell of 'Charlles of Fraunce, þe heghe kinge of alle'. After the explicit to the *Sowdone of Babylone*, we find this slightly misleading addition: 'and Kynge Charles off Fraunce with xij Dosyperes toke the Sowdon in the feelde and smote of his heede'. In all these manuscript copies there is a determined reference to the person of Charlemagne, even where the title indicates a narrative focus on the deeds of Fierabras, Otuel or Roland. Similarly, the recently edited Middle English translation of the *Pseudo-Turpin Chronicle* (c.1460) uniquely gives the work an alternative title: *The Storye of the Bataille of Rouncivale of Grete Charles the Emperoure*, and Caxton's translation (1485) of Jean Bagnyon's prose *Fierabras* (1478) is retitled *The Lyf of the Noble and Crysten Prynce Charles the Grete*. Roland is, of course, the heroic Peer at the centre of the *Chanson*, counterpart of the treacherous Ganelon, but also, famously, the companion of Oliver (as Taylor points out, the critical tradition initiated by Bédier reads the text as focused upon 'the central

8   The titles given in the explicit rubrics in four of the later versions (MSS V4, C, P, L) all identify the text as the story of Roncevaux.

9   The episode of Charlemagne's victory over Baligant is thought by many critics to be an interpolation added to an earlier version of the *Chanson*; however, as Marianne Ailes states, 'the Baligant episode is integral to the text as we have it' (*The Song of Roland: On Absolutes and Relative Values* [Lewiston NY, 2002], p. 75).

10 See 'The English Charlemagne Romances' in EETS ES 34–45 (1879–85), 50 (1887), and EETS OS 198 (1935), 322 (2004).

theme of the conflict between Roland and Oliver'),[11] and this central pairing is securely registered in late medieval English culture. In Chaucer's *Book of the Duchess*, for example, the Man in Black distances himself from the perfidy of such notorious traitors as 'the false Genelloun, / He that purchased the tresoun / Of Rowland and of Olyver' (lines 1121–3); the theme of Roland and Oliver's friendship and prowess is also expressed in proverbial English sayings that can be traced in written form back to the fifteenth century, and must have been familiar long before.[12] Perhaps in response to this popular tradition, suggests Shepherd, the Middle English *Pseudo-Turpin* uniquely inserts the names of the heroic pair four times in its account of the battle.[13] In the light of these strong contemporary emphases on the primary importance of Charlemagne and on the mutual bond of companionship between Roland and Oliver, it is a matter of some significance that the Middle English *Roland* fragment shows evidence of contrary concerns in its adaptation of the source material: concerns that relate to its new status in the context of Middle English romance tradition.

Middle English verse romances are often characterised by a preference for logical, sequential action, focused upon the adventures of a single hero,[14] and an analysis of the Gates of Spain section in the Middle English *Roland* (lines 121–380) will demonstrate that the narrative material has been reworked in accordance with just such preferences. In response to Charlemagne's request for nominations to lead both the vanguard and the rearguard through the dangerous pass,[15] Ganelon in this version proposes himself for the former duty, with Roland leading a force of 30,000 at the rear. Against this plausible scheme, Charlemagne reveals his deep knowledge of the treason behind Ganelon's naming Roland: 'For thou louys to slee þat I loue best, / And hym thou hatist, and me next' (lines 155–6), and seeks to persuade Roland not to take the commission: '"Sostir son, … forsak thou þis sondis"' (line 180). Roland, in a further simplification of the scene, addresses himself only to Charlemagne to accept the nomination 'with myld steuyn' (line 158), and the twelve Peers and other knights proclaim their readiness to accompany him with speeches praising his good lordship:

[11] 'Was There a Song of Roland?', p. 37; see the discussion in Ailes, *Song of Roland*, pp. 23–49, significantly, under the heading 'The Heroes'.

[12] See B. J. Whiting, *Proverbs, Sentences and Proverbial Phrases from English Writings Mainly Before 1500* (Cambridge MA, 1968), p. 491: R.170.

[13] *Turpine's Story: A Middle English Translation of the Pseudo-Turpin Chronicle*, ed. S. H. A. Shepherd, EETS 322 (Oxford, 2004), p. xli and n. 95.

[14] Dieter Mehl argues that many Middle English romances demonstrate a taste for 'a short romance with plenty of incident and a central hero': *Middle English Romances of the Thirteenth and Fourteenth Centuries* (London, 1967), p. 58. Ad Putter stresses the importance of 'a sense of direction and a sense of narrative shape' in the tradition of Middle English popular romance: 'Story Line and Story Shape in *Sir Percyvell of Gales* and Chretien de Troyes's *Conte du Graal*', in *Pulp Fictions of Medieval England: Essays in Popular Romance*, ed. N. McDonald (Manchester, 2004), pp. 171–96 (p. 192).

[15] The English poem expands Charlemagne's brief demand (O, 740–2) into a detailed consideration of the dangers posed by the terrain and the Saracens (121–33).

'For he in word and werk greuyd vs neuer,
Nor sparid schewing of sheldis for non þat lyuyd euer;
For dred of dethe he hid neuer his hed,
With hym is worship euermor in ded:
Ther men may wyn worship for euer.' (lines 209–13)

As the Saracen forces gather to confront the Christians, the English text omits
the account in the French poem of all the Saracens arming for battle, and
instead transfers the motif to Roland, producing a new scene using the traditional topos of the arming of the hero, with appropriately richly decorated
equipment (lines 285–99), and again, the barons commend him as leader:

'It is fair, Roulond to follow in a braid:
He may boldly abid þat hathe siche a lord.' (lines 301–2)

Then, in a major rearrangement of source materials, the poem creates a 'new'
episode that now functions as the first engagement between the Peers and the
Saracens (lines 303–79), framed by two speeches in which Roland addresses
and encourages his fellows. In his opening speech, Roland gives a detailed
assessment of their situation, isolated in the hostile wilderness (a topic transferred to him from the narration, O, lines 814–15) and in danger of surprise
attack if Ganelon has betrayed them to the Sultan, and proposes a practical
plan in which Gauter takes a detachment to a vantage point, to see 'If eny
hethyn be þer to wirche vs wo' (line 318), while the rest will follow and
come to his help if need be (lines 319–21). Roland is presented here as a
wise leader in terms fitting the barons' praise of his good lordship, and paralleling the presentation of Charlemagne at the beginning of the episode (lines
121–33). Gauter's reconnaissance ends in a disastrous ambush which only he
survives to report, and the English poem then adds a speech in which Roland
(though equally moved) reasons with the sorrowful knights (lines 370–4) and
rallies them with fighting talk: 'let our hertis be hie and togedir rynn, / that no
hethyn hound of our men wyn' (lines 375–6). Again, Roland's central role as
good lord and inspiring leader is reinforced in this new, English reconfigura-
tion of the French material.

Several scattered scenes from the French corpus dealing with the calami-
tous encounter between Gualter de l'Hum and the Saracen king Almaris have
here been brought together and relocated, with new material and adapted
details, to make a single coherent episode. The relocated material derives
largely from the rhymed versions, which provide a narrative account of the
battle as well as the brief retrospective mention later on, found also in the
Oxford text.[16] The whole episode is given new and greater significance by

---

[16] Venice 7 version (Biblioteca Marciana, MS Fr. Z. 7), *laisses* 137–39, 203; Châteauroux version
(Bibliothèque municipale, MS 1), *laisses* 146–8, 213; Paris version (Bibliothèque nationale, fonds
français 860), *laisses* 46–8, 119; Oxford MS, *laisse* 152.

being configured as the first, albeit proxy, encounter between Roland and his opposing Saracen counterpart, the Sultan's nephew, for in the English poem, this personage is uniquely conflated with King Amaris. (In the French versions, the sultan's nephew Aelroth is named – if at all – only at the moment of his death at Roland's hands.) First introduced as 'of the soudan kyn' (line 266), Amaris later reminds the sultan: 'I am thy sister son' (line 474), using the same phrase 'sister son' that Charlemagne had pointedly used twice to address his nephew Roland as he tried to dissuade him from leading the rear-guard (lines 180, 186), so stressing the parallel between Amaris and Roland. To reinforce the narrative coherence of the episode, the English poem also transposes the moment when Roland sends Gauter forth with his men to the cliff (line 315), so that it now occurs not before, but after Amaris has made his request to the Sultan that he may lead the advance party, in the express hope that he may 'met with Roulond' (line 273). A clear progression is thus established between this preliminary encounter and the major battle that follows, in which Amaris finally does come face to face with Roland. In the light of this progression, a poignant foreshadowing of Roland's own ultimate fate may be felt in the details of the fierce fighting between the Saracen and Christian forces, the loss of all Gauter's men in the absence of any 'socour ne help' (line 345), and the wounded Gauter's laments. The whole, carefully reconstructed episode, with its unifying focus on Roland, his heroic status and his commanding role in the unfolding narrative, thus functions on several levels as an indicative prelude to the catastrophic events that follow, and contributes to a sense of the poem's plot as a single action with a central hero – characteristics precisely in line with the story's new context in the Middle English romance tradition.

Roland's pre-eminence as the heroic 'good lord' in this version runs somewhat counter to the proverbial twinning of Roland with Oliver, and it is notable that the passages which in the French *Chanson* most vividly express the relationship between the companions, centred on the famous epithets 'Rollant est proz e Oliver est sage; / ambedui unt merveillus vasselage' (lines 1093–4), are rendered very differently in the English poem. At the start of the build-up towards the climactic battle of Roncevaux, a new scene shows the Peers, in the aftermath of the massacre of Gauter's men, reflecting on what they should do:

> hou they rod togedur in counsall righte.
> som bad Roulond to blow aftur socour,
> and som bad hym bid of his blast lengour,
> and be redy to fight, for fle they nylle. (lines 434–7)

This scene does not replace the iconic dispute over blowing the horn between prudent Oliver and valiant Roland, but it sets the question in a wider context of consultation and debate peculiar to this poem. Then later, when Oliver, having seen the extent of the Saracen army, does ask Roland to blow for help (lines 526–33), the English poem replaces the *Chanson's* epic formula of repetition-with-variation with a simple but cogent exchange, as Roland convinces first Oliver and then all the Peers that they have no need of help – an argument that serves the important function of encouraging the troops:

> When they vndirstod hou he ne wold
> For to blow his horn for no socour bold,
> They tok hem comfort, and said full hye:
> 'now curssid be he that hens will flye.' (lines 568–71)

Oliver and all the Peers remind Roland of this a little later when he laments their imminent deaths on account of Ganelon's treachery, saying this is no time to lament, that it was his decision not to summon help with 'an horn blast', and reiterating their resolve: 'let on, prik out, and not to rid fast, / so shall they be fellid, yf they fendis wer' (lines 640–1). By reassigning speeches in this passage, the Middle English poet has changed the emphasis from a dispute between Roland and Oliver into a manifestation of corporate solidarity of purpose. As Barron observes, the spirit of this episode is significantly different from the focus in the *chanson de geste* on Roland's heroic *démesure*,[17] but it fits coherently with the different construction of Roland's role in the Middle English poem. The greater focus on Roland as the central figure is supported by the way in which other Peers are often mentioned alongside Oliver in the English poem, effectively reducing the impression of a pair of equal companions, and proposing instead the image of a single leader with his band of fellows.

The fellowship of the group is held up in the poem as an important ideal and a source of strength. Fervent speeches are reported from the Peers, volunteering to stay behind with Roland and expressing their loyalty to him and to each other: 'all they said atonys they will togedur hold' (line 207); 'they wold no furþer go ... / and leue lordis behind that they loued euer: / they will hold with them "till our hertis blede"' (lines 221–3). Roland correspondingly begins his first speech to the Peers with the words: 'we be fellos and frendis' (line 304), and when he grieves at the sight of the impossible odds they face, it is 'not for his own sak he soghed often, / but for his fellichip þat he most lovyden' (lines 600–1). As in the French texts, their allegiance to Charlemagne is one element of the bond that binds the fellows together: 'for our lordis loue, þat is god euer' (line 552); however, the emphasis throughout on Ganelon's treachery and the universal conviction that he has already sold the Peers to the Saracens effectively neutralises the good lord Charlemagne's power, and gives more than conventionally pious force to the speeches in which Roland and Archbishop Turpin offer to the others comfort and encouragement based on their confidence in Christ's protection and reward. At a

---

[17] Barron, p. 91; for discussion of this theme, see W. van Emden, *La Chanson de Roland* (London, 1995).

point where Roland believes they will all surely die, he urges them to think of themselves as a triumphant band of Christian warrior-martyrs:

> 'but euery knight be kene, & comfort other,
> ffor this day shall we dy, and go no further,
> but we shall supe ther seintis be many,
> and crist soulis fedithe, this is no nay.
> Think he suffrid for vs paynes sore,
> We shall wrek hem with wepins þer for.' (lines 623–8)

This inspirational vision is recalled in the knights' response to Oliver's exhortation: 'they went to sadly, and set þer dyntis / In the worship of hym that fedithe seintis' (lines 763–4), and in Roland's cry: 'crist, kep vs cristyn that ben here, / to serue your soper with seintis dere!' (lines 962–3). After the first major action in the battle, a scene is added in which Roland leads the knights in praise and thanksgiving to God for their apparently miraculous victory, and Turpin explicitly portrays them as vassals not of Charlemagne (as in the French texts)[18] but of Christ:

> 'lordingis', said Roulond, 'listynythe aright:
> we haue the formest feld to the ground,
> and yet is our host bothe hole and sound,
> and no man lost that we brought to place:
> we ought to worshippe god myche of his grace.'
> Then callithe furthe turpyn, & tellithe son:
> 'this lord that we serue louythe his own,
> that so few of his fellid so many.'
> euery man tok of his helme & lukyd on hie,
> lift vp ther hondis and thankid crist,
> that he sauf and sound defend hem hase. (lines 806–16)

It is not surprising that the enemies of the soldiers of Christ should be presented as false: the narration constantly epitomises the Saracens as a whole and individually as 'curssid' and 'fals' (lines 485–6, 514, 646, 825), pointing to their perceived theological situation as damned infidels, and characterises their military strategies as 'euyll' (lines 283, 645) or 'wickid' (line 439). Indeed, Roland's first encounter on the battlefield, in which he kills Amaris, is clearly figured as a stereotypical combat between Christian and heathen, which is not the case in the French tradition, where the issue is exclusively the honour of France and Charlemagne. Amaris challenges Roland as representative both of Charlemagne and of Christianity: 'wher art thou, Roulond, leder of charles? / thy lay is fals, and also thy lordes' (lines 655–6) and, having felled 'that fals kinge', Roland responds: 'thy soule … to satanas I beteche! / thou shalt neuer greve man þat to god will seche' (lines 663–4).

---

[18] 'Il est escrit en la Geste Francor / que bons vassals out nostre empereür' (O, lines 1443–4).

And fiercely partisan outbursts are presented in the voice of the narrator, as dramatic comments on the Saracens' preparations for attack: 'curse hym [Amaris], crist, that sittis in heuyn!' (line 506); 'And help Roulondes ost, he þat heuyn weldis!' (line 509).[19] The text also makes constant reference to 'fals' Ganelon and his treachery as the evil cause of the Peers' plight; in line with his reputation in late medieval culture, he is represented as known to be false 'long or þat tym' (line 175),[20] and inimical to all, not just towards Roland. There is an implied parity between his status and that of the Saracens, not only in common epithets but in details such as the indication given by the Sultan, instructing his men, that the Saracen strategy has been masterminded by Ganelon: 'tak ye no trewes, thoughe ye might, / for gift ne garison as gwynylon hight' (lines 261–2).

Roland and Ganelon are opposed in the Middle English poem as good and bad counsellors of Charlemagne. At the beginning of the fragment, in an episode augmented with material derived from the *Johannes Translation* of the *Pseudo-Turpin Chronicle* (lines 1–3, 28–30, 59–76), the English poem emphasises the peaceful outcome of Ganelon's supposed diplomacy (while still making abundantly clear to the reader or listener that all he promises is false). Ganelon says Charles need undertake 'no further fightinge' (line 19), he can enjoy the fruits of peace in 'playing' with noble ladies and drinking good wine (lines 28–30): there is no honour or advantage in fighting when peace is offered (line 32); and Charles's reply continues in the same positive vein, stressing the future friendship between himself and the soon-to-be Christian Sultan, for whom he plans lavish hospitality with gifts and feasting (lines 42–5). Charles's optimistic view of the future – 'For now I dred no day in all my lyf' (line 51) – informs the journey home as, only ten miles on their way, the army stops to enjoy a stately supper with plenty of wine; however, the narrator curses Ganelon for bringing it: 'euyll hym betid!'(line 69), since the knights, completely befuddled as a result, end up in bed with the Saracen ladies. The elaborate account of the way Ganelon's wine leads to confusion among the knights is carefully presented so as to excuse the knights, while heaping blame on the traitor, disparaged as 'þat vile':

> It [the wine] swymyd in ther hedis and mad hem to nap;
> they wist not what þey did, so þer wit failid.
> when they wer in bed and thought to a restid,
> they went to the women þat wer so hend,
> that wer sent fro saragos of sairsins kind.
> they synnyd so sore in þat ylk while
> that many men wept and cursid þat vile. (lines 70–6)

---

[19] For discussion of such conventional pious phrases in Middle English romances, see R. Dalrymple, *Language and Piety in Middle English Romance* (Cambridge, 2000).

[20] See M. Ailes, 'Ganelon in the Middle English *Fierabras* Romances', in *The Matter of Identity in Medieval Romance*, ed. P. Hardman (Cambridge, 2002), pp. 73–85 (p. 85).

Phillipa Hardman

Thus the sin which in the *Pseudo-Turpin Chronicle* served for a moralising justification of so many Christian deaths at Roncevaux ('quia ... fornicati sunt, mortem incurrerunt')[21] is here adapted to provide a striking example of the seductive power of Ganelon's treacherous Saracen deceptions.

The importance of Ganelon's role here as the counsellor whose advice guides the king's judgement is echoed in several passages added or altered in the Middle English poem that focus on the issue of counsel.[22] In the episode dealing with Charles's prophetic dreams, a brief detail found in the rhymed *Roland* tradition,[23] stating that Charles told his dreams on waking, is elaborated into a new scene in which the king seeks counsel on the interpretation of his dreams:

> he called the wissest men þen aright,
> and askid of his dreme hou it be might. (lines 107–8)

The poet has perhaps recalled scenes from Bible narratives such as Pharaoh's or Nebuchadnezzar's dreams; like theirs, Charles's consultation with his wise men produces inconclusive interpretations. However, the passage ends with an interesting display of properly informed Christian good counsel:

> throughe right resson, they said him till:
> 'now let god alone and do all his will.' (lines 119–20)

In fact, attention is drawn to the problem of getting wise counsel at each crucial stage of the story. When Charles asks who should stay behind to command the rear, he recognises that Ganelon's plausible argument proposing Roland is malevolent 'counsell' (line 149), but in a new scene he tries and fails to find any replacement for Roland among his barons, who fear death through Ganelon's known treachery (lines 134–79). Roland's willing acceptance of the charge is thus pointedly presented as an exemplum of loyal obedience by being phrased in classic terms of good counsel: 'when euery man hathe said, do ye the best' (line 160).[24]

Later on, when Charlemagne worries about the safety of the rearguard, the same fearful barons are presented as self-righteously censuring the king's response to advice:

> ye trist no trew men þat tellis you right;
> whoo tellis you soothe, gothe out of sight. (lines 396–7)[25]

---

[21] *Historia Karoli Magni.et Rotholandi ou Chronique du Pseudo-Turpin*, ed. C. Meredith-Jones (Paris, 1936), pp. 180, xix–xxii, and 181, xxi–xxiv.

[22] For further discussion and contextualisation of this important theme, see G. Barnes, *Counsel and Strategy in Middle English Romance* (Cambridge, 1993).

[23] Venice 7 MS, 1093–4/Châteauroux MS, 1065–6.

[24] For a compendium of traditional teaching on the proper role of counsel and the ruler's exercise of wisdom in good government, see Chaucer's *Tale of Melibee*, lines 1115–1231; see especially line 1208: 'And in all thise thynges thou shalt chese the beste' (*The Riverside Chaucer*, 3rd edn, ed. Larry D. Benson [Boston MA, 1987], p. 224).

[25] For an extended contemporary treatment of this conventional complaint about truth ignored, see *Mum and the Sothsegger*, ed. J. M. Dean (Kalamazoo, 2000), lines 165–78.

Their criticism is immediately silenced by Ganelon's menacing appearance and his formal challenge. This dramatic event is part of another carefully rearranged sequence of episodes. The Middle English poem brings forward the confrontation between the barons and Ganelon's kin from the end of the story (where it prefaces the concluding episode of Ganelon's trial and punishment), and enhances Ganelon's role by making him (rather than Pinabel) issue the challenge (lines 407–14). The transported scene is combined with a different relocated incident (taken from the later episode in the French texts when Charlemagne hears Roland's horn), in which Ganelon falsely reassures Charles that Roland delays because he is hunting, and the English poem adds the new detail that he will no doubt bring Charles a fat deer (lines 419–26) – like the courtly feast with ladies and wine, this is another of Ganelon's seductive images of peace-time normality. The English poet has taken some pains to prepare for the famous moment (not present in the fragmentary manuscript) when Roland finally blows his horn, with several oblique references to this well-known episode added throughout the text, thus creating enjoyable dramatic irony for those who know the story. First, Charles explicitly forbids any blowing of horns unless it be to summon his help against the Saracens (lines 236–42); then Ganelon's elaborate fiction about Roland's recreational hunting (lines 419–26) effectively pre-empts the knights' discussion of whether or not to blow for aid (lines 435–6, 526–77) by undermining Roland's credit if and when he ever should sound the horn.

These examples of rewriting and restructuring, besides showing a marked concern for narrative coherence, emphasise the depth of Ganelon's manipulative treachery,[26] and highlight the need for wise counsel – topics of particular interest in this as in other fifteenth-century texts representing fictional counterparts to contemporary political turbulence, such as Malory's *Morte Darthur*. Similar concerns may lie behind the focus on Roland and his ties with the Peers and other knights who accompany him. In the French *Chanson*, eleven Peers choose to stay behind with Roland; in the English poem, two separate named groups of twelve Peers pledge themselves to Roland (as noted above).[27] Possibly this increase relates to the same interest that Ralph Norris notes in Malory's addition of names to his sources, creating 'a large cast of minor knights, who in many cases end up allying themselves to one of the major characters', in a reflection of the support and patronage structures between great magnates and the gentry class in the fifteenth century.[28]

In a wider historical contextualisation, among the conventional expressions used to convey the great numbers of dead on both sides in the climactic battle, the English poem inserts a striking and largely original passage in

---

[26] Critics have often noted the lack of ambivalence in the representation of Ganelon in the Middle English text as compared with the *Chanson de Roland*: see Barron, p. 90; Smyser, p. 96.

[27] The first group is introduced as 'the princes xij', but actually comprises nine names 'and oþer iiij'.

[28] *Malory's Library: The Sources of the Morte Darthur* (Cambridge, 2008), p. 168.

the narrator's voice that takes a long chronological view, setting the carnage in a time-scale stretching back to two distant milestones of human history, documented in both biblical and classical record, God's giving the Law to Moses and the Siege of Troy:

> sithe god spek with mouthe on the montaigne,
> And taught moyses his men to preche,
> In so litill whille was neuer mo marrid, I you teche,
> As wer drof to dethe as the dais end;
> not in the battaille of troy, who so will trouthe find. (lines 840–4)

Moses' conversation with God on Mount Sinai in Exodus begins with a reminder of God's deeds in destroying the Egyptians (19.4). It was perhaps the thick cloud and fire from which God speaks (vv. 9, 18) that suggested to the English poet the other addition to his source here, the blood-red cloud that appears as a sign of the many dead (lines 859–62). These two events do both recall occasions of great loss of life (the overthrow of all Pharaoh's Egyptians and the destruction of Troy), but they are also significant originary moments, marking God's making a covenant with His people (Exodus 19.5–6) and the emergence from the ruins of Troy (according to their foundation myths) of Rome, Britain and other European nations. The added passage, with its allusions to the sources of both the religious and national identities of the audience, can be seen to show a sense of the larger historical context as contributing to the meaning of the story, alongside a more predictable impulse to reach after epic comparisons in response to the drama of the moment.[29] The new material here appears to have been developed from a detail found much later in the text of the rhymed *Chanson de Roland*, in the account of the battle in Spain between Charlemagne and Baligant. Whereas in the Oxford version the fighting is said to be uniquely fierce: 'ne fut si fort enceis ne puis cel tens' (O, 3382), in the Châteauroux/Venice 7 version its fierceness is measured back to the time of Moses: 'ne fu si forz des le tens Moÿsant' (C, 5591).[30] It seems highly likely that the English poet was prompted by a similar phrase, but developed the stock formula into a more significant instance of historical contextualisation by paralleling it with a reference to the fall of Troy.

Like the focus on a central hero, this restructuring of source material is by no means unusual in Middle English romance – indeed, the process by which discrete scenes are detached from their contexts in the sources and reconnected as a consecutive narrative bears obvious comparison with

---

[29] Shepherd notes the 'learned' and 'rhetorical' aspect of the references to Moses and Troy, adding to 'the air of heroic grandeur': 'I have gone for þi sak wonderfull wais', p. 235.

[30] This phrase, 'des le tens Moÿsant', is used three times in the C/V7 version (C, 4226, 5143, 5591) to express the idea 'since time immemorial'; there are also two periphrastic references to God as giver of the law to Moses (C, 4078, 5419).

Malory's treatment of his French sources.[31] However, this habit of extracting and rearranging material from discrete sites in the source texts raises an important question about the content of the missing conclusion of the Middle English *Roland* fragment – what would have been left at the end? The evidence shown here of the poet's pre-empting material from the later battle scene between Charlemagne and Baligant in order to enhance his account of Roland's battle at Roncevaux, together with the earlier relocation of the confrontation between Charlemagne and Ganelon that opens the last episode of the *Chanson*, strongly suggests that the Middle English poem as originally composed presented a radically abbreviated version of the story, focusing purely on Roland and omitting the subsequent accounts of Charlemagne's conquest of Saragossa and the punishment of Ganelon – material which would then have been available to be quarried for reuse elsewhere in the text. The earlier tradition of the *Chanson de Roland*, as represented in the Anglo-Norman Oxford version, MS Digby 23, preserves a leaner, less expansive narrative than that of the later continental rhymed versions, on which the Middle English poem also draws, where further episodes greatly extend the story beyond the death of Roland.[32] The English poem, in its selection and rearrangement of narrative material, demonstrates a marked preference for a pared-down, causally related sequence of incidents focused upon a single major action and a central hero, and it seems very unlikely that it would have incorporated the later episodes.

By comparison with the French epic tradition, both Roland as hero and Ganelon as villain are also presented in simplified, unambivalent terms,[33] again encouraging a wholly positive view of Roland and his actions.[34] In a very particular sense, then, it seems that the title *The Song of Roland* fits this text uniquely well, for the Middle English poem is shaped to display and celebrate the qualities of its central hero, a newly imagined, unambiguously exemplary Roland: a heroic lord beloved by his knights, a wise counsellor, and a Christian leader not only in his embracing the role of warrior-martyr, but in his pious devotion, contemplating Christ's suffering (627), and humbly

---

31 This process in Malory's adaptation of his sources is described in detail by Eugène Vinaver in the introduction to his edition, *The Works of Sir Thomas Malory*, 2nd edn, 3 vols. (Oxford, 1967), I, lxiv–lxxiii.

32 All the later versions include the episodes of Aude's history and of Ganelon's escapes; the Venice 4 version also includes the *Prise de Narbonne* episode – possibly inserted in response to the mention of Narbonne in the closely related Oxford version at this point (O, 3683) – in a text described as a 'compilation' from various manuscript sources, not unlike the ME *Roland* text.

33 For a summary of the diverse interpretations of Roland's moral status, both in medieval texts and in modern criticism, see Ailes, *Song of Roland*, pp. 26–8, and for Ganelon, pp. 49–50.

34 Interesting parallels may be seen in other English texts where heroic figures of ambiguous virtue in the French tradition are refashioned for their new Middle English romance context in accord with a similarly positive agenda: for example, Malory's Lancelot, or the hero of the English Gawain romances. I am indebted to Rhiannon Purdie for this suggestion.

giving thanks for victory (810).[35] It is only fitting that the poem would apparently not have extended far beyond the close of the hero's life.

The Middle English *Roland* fragment is thus not guilty as charged of being a 'somewhat superficial' (Barron, p. 92) 'translation of the *Chanson de Roland*' in which important features of the *chanson de geste* are 'sadly mishandled' and 'barely recognizable' (Smyser, pp. 95–6), but is a distinct, innovative treatment of the material, which depends for its full effect on the audience's familiarity with the story. Ganelon's proverbial treachery is knowledge shared by the characters within the narrative and the audience, who are thus also able to share in the poem's sense of fore-doomed tragedy and the opportunity for Roland to show heroic Christian self-sacrifice. Only readers and listeners who already know the story and the climactic incident of Roland's finally blowing his horn would pick up the significance of the proleptic allusions to this moment earlier in the text. But equally, the story has evidently been thoroughly remodelled to fit its new context in the tradition of Middle English romance, with its characteristic preference for clearly contrasted heroes and villains and its frequently pious tone. This version of the *Roland* legend can thus offer both the pleasure of recognition in the retelling of a familiar story, and the accompanying pleasure of difference, as the reader or listener becomes aware that new episodes and changed emphases are producing a fresh take on the story.

---

[35] For a discussion of the limited representation of Roland's Christian faith at comparable instances in the Oxford version, see van Emden, *La Chanson de Roland*, p. 47.

8

Romance Baptisms and Theological Contexts in *The King of Tars* and *Sir Ferumbras*[1]

SIOBHAIN BLY CALKIN

While romances may be secular narratives, they make frequent use of religion to entertain their audiences. Characters often engage in prayer or
pilgrimage, and masses, marriages and baptisms regularly appear. Although it
is not particularly helpful to sift romance depictions of religious ceremonies
for evidence about liturgical practices, it is intriguing to reverse the process
and consider the ways in which romances engage the cultural ideas of their
day. This essay examines how late medieval theological understandings of
baptism are taken up in two fourteenth-century English romances, *The King
of Tars* and *Sir Ferumbras*. Theological and romance depictions of baptism
both use the sacrament to reflect upon what makes a body Christian, or what
establishes Christian identity in a body.

Baptism, according to Thomas Aquinas, 'is called the *sacrament of faith*
because it involves a profession of faith and joins those who receive it to
the congregation of believers'.[2] It is the rite through which both newborns
and adult converts become Christian and manifest publicly their beliefs and
allegiances. As such, baptism is a moment in which to study the question of
what makes a Christian. Medieval thinkers, both theological and literary, used
this moment to contemplate what effects change in a person, how that change
can be perceived by others, and the respective roles of language and the body
in determining identity and belief. Indeed, one of the Gospels to be read at
baptism was John 1:1–14, the passage that opens 'In the beginning was the
Word, and the Word was with God, and the Word was God,'[3] and ends 'And
the Word was made flesh, and dwelt among us, (and we saw his glory, the

---

1 Research for this paper was made possible in part by funding from the Social Sciences and
Humanities Research Council of Canada.
2 Thomas Aquinas, *Summa theologiae: Latin Text and English Translation*. Vol. 57 *Baptism and
Confirmation (3a. 66–72)*, ed. and trans. J. J. Cunningham (Westminster, 1975). Hereafter cited as
ST. 3a, qu. 70, art. 1, responsio. Dicendum quod baptismus dicitur *sacramentum fidei*, inquantum
scilicet in baptismo fit quædam fidei professio, et per baptismum aggregatur homo congregationi
fidelium.
3 'In principio erat Verbum et Verbum erat apud Deum et Deus erat Verbum' (John. 1:1).

glory as it were of the only begotten of the Father,) full of grace and truth.'[4] The ceremony of baptism, both in what it purports to effect and in what it says about what is being done, demands consideration of how word and flesh, or language and the body, are related in effecting change. It is not surprising, then, to find that both theologians and romance redactors use baptism as an occasion to reflect on what makes a Christian.

For late medieval theologians, what makes a Christian is the pronunciation of a specific verbal formula over the body of the candidate as that body is washed with water. Aquinas states 'the integrity of baptism consists in the form of the words and in the use of water'.[5] The water as physical element is important, but it is the words that make the Christian, as Aquinas indicates:

> the sacrament is not conferred if the act of baptism is not expressed either as we do or as is the custom of the Greeks. So it is stated in the decretal of Alexander III, *If anyone plunge a child three times in the water in the name of the Father and of the Son and of the Holy Spirit Amen and does not say, I baptize you in the name of the Father and of the Son and of the Holy Spirit Amen, the child is not baptized.*
>
> [3.] The words which are uttered in the forms of the sacrament are not pronounced solely for the sake of signifying something but also for the purpose of effecting something inasmuch as they have their effectiveness from that Word *through whom all things were made.*[6]

The same concern with the words of baptism can be found in manuals for priests. For example, in his *Instructions for Parish Priests*, John Myrc explains that midwives must baptize any newborns in peril of dying, and that the priest must teach the midwives to

> ... sey þe wordes wel,
> And say the wordes alle on rowe
> As a-non I wole ȝow schowe;
> Say ryȝt thus and no more,
> ...
> I folowe the, or elles I crystene þe, in the nome of
> the fader & þe sone and the holy gost. Amen.
> Or elles thus, Ego baptizo te N. In nomine patris
> & filij & spiritus sancti. Amen.

---

4   'Et Verbum caro factum est et habitavit in nobis et vidimus gloriam eius gloriam quasi unigeniti a Patre plenum gratiae et veritatis' (John 1:14).
5   *ST*, 3a, qu. 67, art. 6, ad 3. Integritas baptismi consistit in forma verborum et in usu materiæ.
6   *ST*, 3a, qu. 66, art. 5, ad 2–3. Et ideo, si non exprimatur actus baptismi, vel per modum nostrum vel per modum Græcorum, non perficitur sacramentum: secundum illam decretalem Alexandri III, *Si quis puerum ter in aquam merserit in nomine Patris et Filii et Spiritus Sancti Amen, et non dixerit, Ego te baptizo in nomine Patris et Filii et Spiritus Sancti Amen, non est puer baptizatus.* [3] Ad tertium dicendum quod verba quæ proferuntur in formis sacramentorum, non pronuntiantur solum causa significandi, sed etiam causa efficiendi, inquantum habent efficaciam ab illo Verbo *per quod facta sunt omnia.*

Englysch or latyn, whether me seyþ,
Hyt suffyseth to the feyth,
So that þe wordes be seyde on rowe.[7]

Myrc's comments show both how important baptism is, and how its efficacy inheres in the words rather than the speaker. Priestly utterance may be desirable, but is not essential, as Aquinas also indicates when he states 'the non-baptized, whether Jews or pagans, can confer the sacrament of baptism as long as they baptize in the form of the Church'.[8] Myrc emphasizes the importance of the words again when instructing priests about their own performance of the sacrament. He states that if someone says the above formula, then the child is baptized, even if no name was given and even if only the first syllables of the words were pronounced correctly (lines 561–76). However, if the words were

… sayde a-mys,
Or þus In nomine filij & patris & spiritus sancti. Amen.
Or any oþer wey but þey set hem on rowe,
As þe fader & þe sone & þe holy gost,
In nomine patris & filij & spiritus sancti. Amen
3ef hyt be oþer weyes I-went,
Alle þe folghþe ys clene I-schent;
Þenne moste þou, to make hyt trewe,
Say þe serves alle a-newe. (lines 597–605)

Clearly, for late medieval theologians, the words of baptism translate the candidate from a state of sin into one of grace, and from outsider to Christian insider and member of the body of Christ.

While theologians emphasize the role of words in creating religious identity, romance writers seem to have had other ideas. In accordance with religious practice, both the washing of the body and the utterance of words are depicted, but the washing receives more attention, as do the physical rites of the ceremony, those acts that make it a spectacle for others to behold. Aquinas writes,

Necessary for the sacrament are the form which designates the principal cause of the sacrament [the words], the minister who is the instrumental cause [the one who says the words], and the use of matter, viz, washing with water, which designates the principal effect of the sacrament. The

---

7 J. Myrc, *Instructions for Parish Priests*, ed. E. Peacock, 2nd edn (London, 1902), lines 122–33. All subsequent quotations are from this edition and will be referenced by line numbers in the text.
8 *ST*, 3a, qu. 67, art. 5, responsio. … per Ecclesiam determinatum est quod non-baptizati, sive sint Judæi sive pagani, possunt sacramentum baptismi conferre, dummodo in forma Ecclesiæ baptizent.

other things which the Church observes in the baptismal rite all pertain to the solemnity of the sacrament ... [and are desirable, but] not essential.[9]

The presence of the priest and of the water remain in the romance baptisms studied here, but the words so emphasized by Aquinas and Myrc do not appear, while non-essential elements of the rite receive highly imaginative elaboration. Baptism becomes a ceremony that emphasizes the spectacle of the body. The romances suggest that physical acts, experiences and sights, not words, change religious identity.

This is most spectacularly the case in *The King of Tars*, which presents two baptism ceremonies that achieve striking post-baptism manifestations of Christian identity. In one, the lump of flesh conceived by parents of different religions is baptized and becomes a beautiful little boy. In the other, the lump-child's Saracen father, having seen the lump's miraculous formation, becomes Christian and, in the course of his baptism, finds his colour changed from black to white. These baptism ceremonies and the changed identities they produce emphasize the physical over the verbal construction of religious identity, but do so in ways that focus attention on the community the baptizand is to enter and on baptism's role as a ritual through which a group admits a new member.

If theological writings emphasize the minister of baptism and the candidate, *The King of Tars* reproduces this dyad in both its baptisms, but depicts the ceremony in such a way that it evokes the larger Christian community not present at the text's secret baptisms. The ceremonies are presented so as to focus on the physical elements that could be seen by onlookers.[10] The hallowing of the water and the ministry of the priest are emphasized rather than pronunciation of the full baptismal formula. The lump's baptism begins thus: 'Þe prest no leng nold abide; / A feir vessel he tok þat tide, / & hali water he gan make.'[11] Here the priest is present,[12] as is the holy water. But what is manifestly absent, even in the full description of the episode, are

---

[9] *ST*, 3a, qu. 66, art. 10, responsio and ad 4. De necessitate quidem sacramenti est et forma, quæ designat principalem causam sacramenti; et minister, qui est causa instrumentalis; et usus materiæ, scilicet ablutio in aqua, quæ designat principalem sacramenti effectum. Ceætera vero omnia quæ in ritu baptizandi observat Ecclesia magis pertinent ad quandam solemnitatem sacramenti; ... ea quæ pertinent ad solemnitatem sacramenti, etsi non sint de necessitate sacramenti, non tamen sunt superflua, quia sunt ad bene esse sacramenti.

[10] Regarding the public visibility of late medieval baptisms in England, see J. D. C. Fisher, *Christian Initiation: Baptism in the Medieval West, A Study in the Disintegration of the Primitive Rite of Initiation* (London, 1965), pp. 114–15, 155; J. G. Davies, *The Architectural Setting of Baptism* (London, 1962), pp. 52–3, 61–3, 76; P. Niles, 'Baptism and the Naming of Children in Late Medieval England', in *Studies on the Personal Name in Late Medieval England and Wales*, ed. D. Postles and J. T. Rosenthal (Kalamazoo, 2006), pp. 147–57 (pp. 149, 151, 153); L. Haas, 'Social Connections Between Parents and Godparents in Late Medieval Yorkshire', in the same volume, pp. 159–75 (pp. 173–4).

[11] *The King of Tars, edited from the Auchinleck MS, Advocates 19.2.1*, ed. J. Perryman (Heidelberg, 1980), lines 766–8. All subsequent quotations are from this edition and are referenced by line numbers in the text.

[12] *ST*, 3a, qu. 67, articles 1–5.

the specific words of baptism, the formative essence of the sacrament for theologians:

> Þe prest no leng nold abide;
> A feir vessel he tok þat tide,
> & hali water he gan make.
>
> At missomer tide þat ded was don
> Þurth help of God, þat sitt in trone,
> As y ȝou tel may.
> Þe prest toke þe flesche anon,
> & cleped it þe name of Ion
> In worþschip of þe day
> & when þat it cristned was
> It hadde liif & lim & fas,
> & crid wiþ gret deray.
> & hadde hide & flesche & fel,
> & alle þat ever þerto bifel. (lines 766–79)

The same is true of the Sultan's baptism:

> Amorwe when þe prest gan wake,
> A wel feir fessel he gan take
> Wiþ water clere & cold;
> & halwed it for the soudan sake,
> & his preier he gan make
> To Ihesu, þat Iudas sold,
> & to Marie his moder dere,
> Þo þat þe soudan cristned were,
> Þat was so stout & bold,
> He schuld ȝif him miȝt & space
> Þurth his vertu & his grace
> His Cristendom wele to hold.
>
> & when it was liȝt of day
> Þe riche soudan, þer he lay,
> Up bigan to arise.
> To þe prest he went his way,
> & halp him alle þat he may
> Þat fel to his servise.
> & when þe prest hadde þo
> Diȝt redi þat fel þerto
> In al maner wise,
> Þe soudan, wiþ gode wille anon,
> Dede of his cloþes everichon
> To reseyve his baptize.
>
> Þe Cristen prest hiȝt Cleophas;
> He cleped þe soudan of Damas
> After his owhen name.

ant bodyr:

Siobhain Bly Calkin

His hide, þat blac & loþely was,
Al white bicom, þurth Godes gras,
& clere wiþouten blame.
& when þe soudan seye þat siȝt
þan leved he wele on God almiȝt;
His care went to game.
& when þe prest hadde alle yseyd,
& haly water on him leyd,
To chaumber þai went ysame. (lines 901–36)

Here one finds again the ministry of the priest, the hallowing of the water (lines 902–4), and the laying on of the holy water (line 935), but no formative words. Instead, the words of the ritual are merely referenced in the lines 'He cleped þe soudan of Damas / After his owhen name' and 'when þe prest hadde alle yseyd' (lines 926–7, 934). The physical presence and acts of the priest at a baptism are depicted, but the identity-changing words are not reproduced. In short, the elements seen by attendees at a medieval baptism are present, but the full ceremonial speech-act is not.

Some spoken words do appear in the text's baptisms however – those naming the candidate. In the lump's case, the text states 'Þe prest toke þe flesche anon, / & cleped it þe name of Ion' (lines 772–3), while the Sultan is named for the priest himself (lines 925–7). Myrc's *Instructions* indicate that the baptismal formula includes the naming of the candidate.[13] Myrc, however, notes that baptism can be performed without naming (lines 564–8, 586–7), and gives two presentations of the verbal formula that do not specify the insertion of the baptizand's name (lines 127–8, 571–2). Naming thus appears a non-essential part of the formula, although one commonly present. Naming was, however, a key moment in the historical performance of baptisms, and often informed the choice of godparents in late medieval England, since children frequently took the name of a godparent.[14] Naming was thus a socially significant part of late medieval baptisms, and is the one specific utterance included in *The King of Tars*'s depictions of baptism. Through this inclusion, the romance emphasizes the role of the ceremony as a process by which a community gains a new member. The redactor retains the only verbal element of baptism essential for everyday life in the baptizand's community, his or her name, and thereby highlights the ceremony's production of social identity.

Although *The King of Tars* includes one of the verbal utterances of baptism, it focuses attention on visible, physical aspects of the ceremony. We are told that 'þe soudan, ... Dede of his cloþes everichon / To reseyve

[13] See Myrc, *Instructions*, lines 129–30 and 562–3; and Fisher, *Christian Initiation*, Appendix III, 'The Rite of Baptism in the Sarum Manual,' pp. 158–79, p. 174.
[14] On this point, see R. Dinn, 'Baptism, Spiritual Kinship, and Popular Religion in Late Medieval Bury St Edmunds', *Bulletin of the John Rylands University Library* 72.3 (1990), 93–106 (p. 103); M. Bennett, 'Spiritual Kinship and the Baptismal Name in Traditional European Society', in *Studies on the Personal Name*, pp. 115–46 (p. 135); Niles, 'Baptism and the Naming of Children', pp. 147–57 (pp. 147–8, 150–4).

110

his baptize' (lines 922–4). Although nude adult baptism was not the practice in late medieval England,[15] *The King of Tars* hearkens back to earlier Church traditions and has the Sultan strip naked, a visual spectacle repeated in other romance depictions of Saracen baptism that stresses baptism's role as the ritual that marks and produces new Christian bodies. Furthermore, these romance baptisms have physical effects that publicly manifest characters' changed identities. The lump, upon baptism, gains 'liif & lim & fas' as well as 'hide & flesche & fel' (lines 776, 778). A baptism that emphasizes physical presences and visible acts produces a physically changed Christian body. The same can be said of the Sultan's baptism and his miraculous change of skin colour. In both cases, the text suggests that baptism physically incorporates outsiders into the Christian community by making them look like other Christians, such as the beautiful Princess of Tars who is 'As white as feþer of swan' (line 12). The physical effects of baptism prove irrefutably that the lump and Sultan are Christian and should be accepted as such. Indeed, the text even states that the Princess knows well the Sultan has forsaken his Saracen beliefs 'For chaunged was his hewe' (line 945). In this text, baptism is a predominantly physical, visible process that effects physical, visible results to prove the veracity of the convert's new religious identity to the larger Christian community.

The physicality of the incorporation of both the lump and the Sultan into Christianity may surprise readers, but it is not incompatible with late medieval theological ideas about baptism. Theologians perceived baptism as a sacrament that physically incorporated individuals into the Christian community and occasionally had corporeal effects. Aquinas states, 'when [believing adults] are baptized, they are incorporated in a certain bodily way, namely, by the visible sacrament, [into Christ]'.[16] Aquinas also allows for the possibility of miraculous physical change or healing at baptism, stating that

> An indirect effect of baptism is something beyond the purpose of baptism which is effected miraculously by divine power … Such effects are not equally received by all the baptized, even if they approach with the same devotion; rather they are dispensed according to the determination of divine providence … [4] Bodily health is not an essential effect of baptism but a miraculous work of divine providence.[17]

---

[15] Infant baptism had long been the norm by the fourteenth century. See, for example, Fisher, *Christian Initiation*, pp. 82–7 and Davies, *Architectural Setting*, pp. 52–3, 72, 86.

[16] *ST*, 3a, qu. 69, art. 5, ad 1. … adulti prius credentes in Christum sunt ei incorporati mentaliter. Sed postmodum, cum baptizantur, incorporantur ei quodammodo corporaliter, scilicet per visibile sacramentum.

[17] *ST*, 3a, qu. 69, art. 8, responsio and ad 4. Effectus autem baptismi per accidens est ad quem baptismus non est ordinatus, sed divina virtus hoc in baptismo miraculose operatur … Et tales effectus non æqualiter suscipiuntur ab omnibus baptizatis, etiam si cum æquali devotione accedant: sed dispensantur hujusmodi effectus secundum ordinem providentiæ divinæ; … sanitas corporalis non est per se effectus baptismi, sed est quoddam miraculosum opus providentiæ divinæ.

Aquinas allows for the type of physical miracles seen at baptism in *The King of Tars*, but attributes these directly to God, and does not accord the sacrament itself such shaping power over the physical.

The King of Tars suggests that corporeal acts bring somebody into the Christian community, while the words of baptism are important only as an act of social naming. It further suggests that baptism produces physically miraculous effects. In this romance, the visible manifestations of baptism are important. These may not be entirely orthodox, but engage a community's desire to be assured of the inner beliefs of its newly joined members. In other romances, however, the consideration of how word and body interact in the establishment of a new Christian identity is somewhat different. While romances may privilege non-verbal elements of Christian identity formation, they do so in different ways, and to different ends. Baptism in *The King of Tars* is made through physical acts, and in turn makes even more stunning physical spectacles of change in religious identity. Baptism in *Sir Ferumbras* is also made through physical acts, but it makes and identifies a Christian body defined by subjection to infirmity and passion. What makes a body Christian in this text is its corporeal vulnerability, and what interests this romance redactor most are not the socially incorporative after-effects of baptism, but rather the physical experiences that precede baptism and influence the decision to convert.[18]

Sir Ferumbras presents two successful baptisms and one failed one. The successful baptisms are those of the eponymous hero and his sister Floripas. The unsuccessful one is that of the siblings' father, the Amiral Balan, who refuses baptism at the font itself and is beheaded by Ogier. In all cases, the romance presents a wealth of information about what makes, or fails to make, a character convert, and then depicts the baptism ceremony so as to encapsulate *in parvo* those concerns.

Ferumbras's conversion is the central event of the first 1100 lines. In these, Ferumbras challenges Charlemagne's Peers to single combat and ends up fighting a wounded Oliver. The relative health and wholeness of bodies are frequently referenced in these lines, and the text repeatedly identifies Christian bodies as damaged and wounded while Saracen bodies are overwhelmingly, even supernaturally, healthy and whole. As a result, it is not surprising that Ferumbras's conversion is a story of the progressive wounding

---

[18] *Sir Ferumbras* translates an earlier Old French *chanson de geste*, *Fierabras*, and some of the points made here hold true for some of the Old French versions. The other Middle English versions of this tale, however (*Firumbras*, *The Sultan of Babylon*, Caxton's 1485 *Lyf of the Noble and Crysten Prynce Charles the Grete*), differ noticeably from *Sir Ferumbras* and so points made about *Sir Ferumbras* are not necessarily true of those texts. This essay is not a study of the relations among different versions of the Ferumbras texts, but rather a consideration of the interplay between some theological and romance depictions of baptism, so I concentrate solely on *Sir Ferumbras* as it offers what I consider the most full and complex engagement of baptism among the Middle English versions of this narrative.

and making vulnerable of his body, a concentration on the physical body as constitutive of Christian identity that is replayed in his baptism.

Ferumbras is in full health when we meet him. He is lying relaxed on the ground and disdains to rise to face Oliver. When he eventually does, we are told

> ... huge was he of lengþe,
> Fifteuene fet hol & sound   & wonderliche muche of strengþe.
> ...
> Fyrumbras of Alysaundre   was a man of gret stature,
> & ful brod in þe scholdres was   & long man in forchure.
>
> (lines 547–51)[19]

If Ferumbras cuts an impressive, healthy figure, this is most certainly not true of his Christian opponent. Before he rides to meet Ferumbras, Oliver

> lokede oppon is syde,
> & saw is blod how [doun] it ran   out of is wonde wyde:
> Hys wounde was þo in yvel aray   & for Angwys gan to chyne.
>
> (lines 210–12)

This wound is repeatedly discussed in the French camp, and is the first thing Ferumbras notices when he looks at Oliver. Other Christian bodies, too, are presented as vulnerable. Ferumbras introduces himself to Oliver by describing his slaughter of the Pope and Cardinals at Rome and his subsequent capture of the relics of Christ's Passion (lines 366–9). The officers of Christian religious worship are thus linked to mortality and vulnerability, while the reference to Passion relics reminds readers of the mortal and vulnerable aspect of Christ himself.

The text uses Oliver's wound and Ferumbras's wholeness to explore the possibility of different assessments of health, or of what counts as 'hol & sounde', a phrase repeated throughout this encounter. Ferumbras, upon seeing Oliver's wound, offers to let the Christian use a magic ointment to make himself 'hol & sounde' (line 515). This healing balm, however, has rich religious significance since, as Ferumbras tells Oliver, it is the ointment 'þat ȝoure god was wiþ anoynt   wan he was ded & graved' (line 512). The balm that heals is thus linked to Christ's death and entombment, his human suffering and mortality. This relic suggests that what makes for ultimate wholeness and soundness in a Christian framework is not the physical health of this world valued so highly by Ferumbras. This is further implied

---

[19] All quotations of *Sir Ferumbras* are taken from *The English Charlemagne Romances Part 1: Sir Ferumbras, Edited from the Unique Manuscript Bodleian MS. Ashmole 33*, ed. S. J. Herrtage, EETS ES 34 (London, 1879, rep. 1966), and are referenced by line numbers within the text. Where Herrtage marks a caesura with an inverted semi-colon in imitation of the manuscript's punctuation, I have instead used the modern convention of a triple space.

when Oliver defiantly rejects Ferumbras's offer, telling him 'or we departye henne   al hool þou schalt me vynde' (line 522).[20] While Ferumbras treasures the balm for its literal healing powers rather than its contact with Christ's body, Oliver's refusal of the balm rejects the Saracen's pragmatic evaluation. The Christian knight's actions suggest that Ferumbras's understanding of the balm is inappropriate, and the words that terminate Oliver's refusal indicate that another understanding of wholeness is possible, one in which physical wholeness does not reign supreme.

This proves to be the case when the wounded Oliver strikes a blow that destroys the bottle of balm and disembowels Ferumbras. The text then states 'Of herte was [Ferumbras] hol & sound   & pleynede him þe ȝute no þyng, / Ac sone he knelede oppon þe grond   & þankede hevene kyng' (lines 750–1). Ferumbras follows his acknowledgement of the Christian God with an appeal for mercy and a request to be 'cristned' since the gods he trusted are clearly powerless and, as he says, 'þay moȝe no more do þan a ston   & þat y now auynde' (line 757). Ferumbras, wounded and separated from the healing balm, experiences what it is physically to be a Christian. This reveals to him the inefficacy of his gods and the puissance of a God who can ensure the victory of a sorely wounded Christian knight over a giant, healthy Saracen.

The emphasis on wounded Christian bodies in this romance foregrounds the wounded nature of Christ's body, an appropriate emphasis given that Middle English Charlemagne romances generally are concerned with relics of Christ's passion.[21] Intriguingly, the wound in the crucified Christ's side that led to an effusion of water and blood was particularly important in theological discussions of baptism. Aquinas writes:

> The water from Christ's side was a case of pure water miraculously coming forth from a dead body, as was true also of the blood, to prove the truth of the Lord's body, contrary to the error of the Manicheans. The water, one of the four elements, showed that the body of Christ was truly composed of the four elements; the blood showed that it was composed of the four humours.[22]

---

[20] This line with its placement of the 'hool' idea in non-rhyme position supports my decision to ascribe significance to the repeated references to 'hol & sounde'. This is not an empty metrical filler phrase, but one that has important connotations for the text, as this reading seeks to demonstrate. Roger Dalrymple enjoins us to read seeming tag lines in romances more seriously, according them greater import than has often heretofore been the case. R. Dalrymple, *Language and Piety in Middle English Romance* (Cambridge, 2000), pp. 1–34. The 'hol & sounde' references in *Sir Ferumbras* seem to me a solid example of the ways in which romance tag phrases that are not explicitly religious can also convey significant literary import.

[21] See J. M. Cowen, 'The English Charlemagne Romances', in *Roland and Charlemagne in Europe: Essays on the Reception and Transformation of a Legend*, ed. K. Pratt (London, 1996), pp. 149–68, pp. 150, 153. Marianne Ailes also notes that relics are a central feature of the Old French *Fierabras* narratives. M. Ailes, 'Faith in *Fierabras*', in *Charlemagne in the North: Proceedings of the Twelfth International Conference of the Société Rencesvals, Edinburgh, 4–11 August 1991*, ed. P Bennett, A. Cobby and G. Runnalls (Edinburgh, 1993), pp. 125–33 (pp. 127–9).

[22] *ST*, 3a, qu. 66, art. 4, ad 3. Fuit autem aqua pura miraculose egrediens a corpore mortuo, sicut et sanguis, ad comprobandam veritatem Dominici corporis, contra Manichæorum errorem: ut

The water of baptism thus testified to Christ's physical humanity, his corporeal likeness to medieval Christians as God's word made flesh. The baptismal Gospel reading from John (1:1–14) reminded medieval Christians of this aspect of God, so it is not theologically inappropriate that Ferumbras's route to the baptismal font be through experiencing physical wounds and the fleshly frailty so central to Christian belief.

If it is through wounding that Ferumbras becomes Christian, however, it is also through his wound that he publicly displays his new Christian status. No longer the whole Saracen of the opening, Ferumbras collapses after acknowledging his desire for baptism. Oliver then '[pul[ls] is bowels in ageyn   & is goffanoun he gan to berste; / To make a bond he was ful feyn   & bond hem in wel feste' (lines 774–5). Oliver's binding of Ferumbras's wound echoes his earlier binding of his own wound:

> Olyuer tok his mantel of say   gold peynt hit was wel fyne,
> & rent hit al to peces smal   & þer wiþ is wonde he diȝte,
> & stoppede is wounde þer wyþ al   & bond hure as he miȝte.
>
> (lines 213–15)

These mirrored bandagings establish a similarity between Oliver and his new brother, while the fact that this bandaging literally dresses Ferumbras in Oliver's colours signals the change of allegiance that has taken place. Oliver's act of pulling in the bowels also suggests that he makes Ferumbras Christian from the inside out. In other words, Ferumbras's voiced desire to become Christian leads to a Christian reconstitution of his innards.

In case this reading may seem to stress unduly the physical remaking of Ferumbras as a Christian, it is helpful to consider how the convert's baptism ceremony itself plays out since it, too, stresses the idea that Christian identity is a physical identity, physically made. When Charlemagne comes upon the wounded Ferumbras, Ferumbras tells him

> … y schal euere fro þys day   þe heþene lay for-sake
> And beleue in cristene fay   & folloht to me take.
> y suffrie ynow of sorwe & pyn   my syde ys al to-tore. (lines 1046–8)

His words express his physical resemblance to the crucified Christ, and connect his desire for baptism with suffering and pain. It is also Ferumbras's wounded body that leads Charlemagne to baptize him. After Charlemagne and his knights carry Ferumbras back to camp, they unarm him, 'auyse[ ] is schap echon' (line 1071), and determine that 'A wel fair kniȝt was Firumbras   ounarmid wan he lay' (line 1078), even though 'ys Fysage al discol-

---

scilicet per aquam, quæ est unum quatuor elementorum, ostenderetur corpus Christi vere fuisse compositum ex quatuor elementis; per sanguinem vero ostenderetur esse compositum ex quatuor humoribus.

ourid was   for is blod was gon away' (line 1079). The act of seeing and
appraising Ferumbras's body, even as it swoons and bleeds, precedes Charlemagne's decision to baptize him, suggesting that it is the state of Ferumbras's
body that determines Charlemagne's course of action. Ferumbras's wounded
body proclaims his appropriateness for baptism, and it is when Charlemagne
takes 'pite of þat siȝt' (line 1082) that he calls an archbishop to perform the
ceremony. Unsurprisingly, the physical elements of the ceremony are high-
lighted: Charlemagne commands the archbishop

> … to blessy þe holy fanston,
> þat [Ferumbras] were fulled þat ilke niȝt   & ymad cristenmon.
> þe prelat dide al so he hiȝt   & plungede him sone þer-on.
>
> (line 1083–5)

The baptism ceremony is reduced to the priestly presence, the physical
hallowing of water, and Ferumbras's immersion in the font. Ferumbras's bodily
experiences make him Christian both on the battlefield and in the baptism.
The redactor does describe one verbal element of baptism, the renaming of
Ferumbras, only to show how inefficacious this verbal baptism is:

> ys name ther y-chaunged was   & was ihote Florens,
> ac þoȝ me tornde þar ys name   as þe manere was,
> Evere ȝut after a baar þe same   & men cliped him Firumbras.
>
> (lines 1087–9)

Renaming does not make one Christian in *Sir Ferumbras*, physical remaking
does.

The inefficacy of words in effecting religious change is made clear when
the text later describes the failed baptism of Ferumbras's father Balan. During
the final Christian–Saracen battle in the text, Balan receives various offers
to save his wealth and realm by converting to Christianity. These culminate
in a scene in which Charlemagne calls an archbishop to fill a vat with water
and pray over it because Charlemagne 'wolde fully ther-on / þan Amyral þat
was þere' (lines 5697–8). Again the physical elements of priestly presence,
hallowed water, and baptismal font are present. To these the text adds the
physical spectacle of Balan being forcibly stripped for immersion in the font:

> [Charlemagne] het anon …
>   Dispoily hym by-fore þe ston.
> Wan þay by-gunne ys cloþys of-do Myche strif made þe Amerel tho,
>   And tornde & wende faste,
> Ac Roland and Olyuer hulde hym so, That whather he wolde oþer no,
>   ys cloþys of thay caste. (lines 5713–18)

What follows, however, is not a forcible immersion, but rather repeated verbal
attempts to convert him. These include promises of land and wealth as well
as a twenty-line summary of Christian tenets spoken by Charlemagne himself

(lines 5723–45). This verbal attempt at conversion proves unsuccessful, but, as if to drive the point home, the romance depicts one last verbal appeal to Balan to convert, this time from his son. Ferumbras seems to succeed until the bishop tells the Amiral what he must say:

> … if þou wilt ben a crysteman,
>   Mahoun þou most for-sake,
> Aller-ferst by-fore ous here. (lines 5791–3)

This speech comes much closer to the words of the full baptismal ceremony when the priest asks the baptizand to renounce Satan and all his works.[23] In *Sir Ferumbras*, however, these words lead Balan to punch the bishop and spit in the font. They provoke his most vehement refusal of Christianity. Words, however, are not yet abandoned. Ferumbras again implores Balan to believe in Christ, to which Balan replies

> … By Mahoun þou art a nycy man
>   þat þou dost me rede
> To by-lyve on such a mon þat was on a croys y-don,
>   for ys owe mysdede. (lines 5843–6)

Repeated words are ineffective because, for Balan, the fundamental truth of Christianity is a body 'on a croys y-don / for ys owe mysdede'. His perception of a wounded body and what it represents is such that no words will change it. The body is what decides Balan's final religious identity and concomitant beheading. All the words in the world prove ineffective in producing religious change.

The privileged site of the physical body as the decisive venue for religious conversion is reaffirmed in the final baptism of *Sir Ferumbras*, that of Floripas. Her successful baptism immediately follows her father's failed one, and concludes the Ashmole romance as we have it. It also concludes a narrative of conversion that, like her brother's, emphasizes physical vulnerability as the path to Christian identity. In Floripas's case, physical vulnerability does not consist of physical wounds, but rather the body's physical frailty, its subjection to desire, hunger, and violation. As Floripas experiences these, she finds repeatedly that Christianity, in the form of Christian knights, can satisfy her desire, assuage her hunger, and preserve her body from violation. It is thus no surprise that she decides to become Christian.

Like her brother, Floripas is converted by a display of Christian prowess and the physical vulnerability it awakens in her. In her case, however, the vulnerability is romantic rather than martial. She tells us in lines 2073–87 that she saw one of Charles's knights, Guy of Borgoyne, strike a particularly effective blow against the Saracen Lucafer in the battle for Rome. 'Riȝt

---

[23] Fisher, *Christian Initiation*, pp. 172–3.

fro þat day in-to þis myn herte haþ [Guy] y-raft. / ... / Wolde he be my worldly make & wedde me to wyue, / For his loue wold y take cristendom þanne blyue' (lines 2084–7). Floripas's decision to become Christian is thus born initially of her body's desire. Other physical experiences reinforce her decision. When she and the Peers are starving because of a siege, Floripas insists that they all pray to the Saracen gods to assuage their hunger. The Peers use the occasion to demonstrate not only that these gods cannot fulfil her desire for food, but that they are so weak the Peers can dash them to pieces (lines 2525–86). Moreover, that same destructive Christian prowess enables the Peers to do what the Saracen gods cannot – feed Floripas (lines 2593–818, 3115–60). This further encourages Floripas's commitment to Christianity, a commitment strengthened when Floripas is almost raped by a Saracen thief. This thief has 'hur legges oundo' (line 2439) when Guy rushes onto the scene, slices the thief in two and preserves her virginal body intact. Floripas's experiences throughout the narrative indicate the vulnerability of the body as well as the ability of Christian knights to help her overcome this vulnerability. Christian prowess works with experiences of physical frailty to convince Floripas to convert.

Floripas's baptism emphasizes the physical needs and desires that led her to convert. The ceremony also reminds readers that the larger Christian community is just as vulnerable to those needs and desires. The baptism scene begins when Floripas comes forward to negotiate for Guy's hand in marriage. Charlemagne grants her this, and Floripas strips for her immersion, an act that leads to a twelve-line excursus on her body and its powerful effect on others:

> Þe Damesele dispoilled hure þanne anon, Hyr skyn was as whyt so þe melkis fom,
> fairer was non on molde:
> Wiþ eȝene graye, and browes bent, And ȝealwe traces, & fayre y-trent,
> Ech her semede of gold.
> Hure vysage was fair & tretys, Hure body iantil and pure fetys,
> & semblych of stature.
> In al þe werld ne miȝt be non fayrer wymman of flesch & bon,
> þan was þat creature.
> Wan þys lordes had seyȝen hur naked, In alle manere wyse weel y-maked,
> On hure þay toke lekynge.
> Was non of hem þat ys flechs ne-raas, Noþer kyng, ne baroun, ne non þat was,
> Sche was so fair a þynge. (lines 5879–90)

The text breaks off at this point because of manuscript damage, but enough of the baptism is preserved to signal what issues the ceremony is being used to emphasize. First, the reference to the marriage negotiations for Guy communicates the physical desire that led Floripas to become Christian, a desire she ensures will be satisfied before she takes the final step of baptism. This focus on physical desire as part of Christian experience is emphasized by the redactor's depiction of masculine desire. Floripas's adult baptismal nakedness, a spectacular evocation of historical rather than contemporary fourteenth-century practices, becomes an occasion for the manifestation of physical desire in the observing Christian community. The undressing also provides the occasion for a blazon of Floripas's body, a minute examination of its parts not unlike the 'avysement' that Ferumbras undergoes before his baptism. In this case, too, the judgement is positive. The virginal body earlier preserved by Guy's martial prowess is carefully studied, and Floripas is deemed the fairest 'wymman of flesch & bon', a judgement which signals her worthiness to be part of the Christian family that highly values virginity in its members.

Sir Ferumbras certainly uses Floripas's baptism as an occasion for titillation and the satisfaction of various physical desires – both hers and those of the men watching her. In so doing, it again emphasizes the fleshly, mortal aspect of Christian identity, the body's vulnerability not just to wounds but also to sins. These, of course, were the consequences of mortality, and baptism, theologians agreed, could not render the mortal immortal, only free the soul. Aquinas writes, 'those who are baptized are renewed in spirit through baptism, while the body remains subjected to the old state of sin'.[24] Floripas's baptism emphasizes this aspect of the Christian body – its mortal and moral frailty. What makes a body Christian in her case is precisely its vulnerability to desire and passion, its human frailty, and this is encapsulated in the text's depiction of her baptism.

To conclude, romances are known for their artistic ability to translate emotional and mental states into physical actions and thus it is not surprising that romances also explore the ways in which religious identity might be etched on, and manifested through, the body. Too often in the case of romances about Saracens and Christians, the bodily manifestation of religious identity is believed to consist solely of opposition in battle. Romances, however, do offer richer and much more subtle reflections on the body's role in the making and manifestation of religious identity. Juxtaposing theological and romance presentations of baptism suggests that romances, like theological writings, can use sacraments as occasions to explore extremely complex ideas about what makes a body Christian, what translates it from one religious state to another, and what the respective roles of language and the body are in effecting such changes and determining identity and belief.

---

[24] *ST*, 3a, qu. 68, art. 1, ad 2. Illi qui baptizantur, renovantur per baptismum secundum spiritum, corpus tamen remanet subjectum vetustati peccati.

9

Modern and Medieval Views on Swooning: the Literary and Medical Contexts of Fainting in Romance

JUDITH WEISS

The most famous literary swoon in insular literature is probably Troilus's, in Chaucer's *Troilus and Criseyde*. Although I do not wish to make this swoon the principal focus of my look at fainting in romances, it is instructive to start with it, because recent reactions to it have been polarised and as a result might perhaps skew our attitudes to other fainting men and women in medieval literature. In my necessarily incomplete investigation of when and why medieval fictional people faint, and who do so, I have primarily used examples from insular romances in Anglo-Norman and English, and have sought to widen their context by referring to medieval medical views on syncope (still the word for fainting today). The latters' objective accounts and explanations of the phenomenon provide a welcome antidote to some of the twentieth- and twenty-first-century approaches adopted in recent studies of Chaucer's masterpiece.

In Book III of *Troilus* the hero swoons during his first night with Criseyde and has to be revived by his beloved and Pandarus. Many critics of the last twenty years have characterised Troilus's faint in disparaging terms: he is unmanly, even emasculated, impotent, helpless and passive. In other words he is supposedly behaving like a woman, or at least like a stereotypical one.[1] Two important studies by Jill Mann and Gretchen Mieszkowski have rebutted these charges, approaching them from different directions.[2] Mieszkowski has alerted us to the way our outlook has been influenced by attitudes to fainting observable in the narratives of the eighteenth and subsequent centuries, when

---

[1] I am very grateful to Gretchen Mieszkowski for alerting me to many of the articles expressing these views and also for drawing my attention to recent work on how gender is constructed.

[2] G. Mieszkowski, 'Revisiting Troilus's Faint', in *Men and Masculinities in Chaucer's Troilus and Criseyde*, ed. Tison Pugh and M. Smith Marzec (Cambridge, 2008), pp. 8–106; J. Mann, 'Troilus' Swoon', *Chaucer Review* 14 (1980), 319–35, reprinted in *Critical Essays on Chaucer's Troilus and Criseyde*, ed. C. D. Benson (Milton Keynes, 1991), pp. 149–63. Mann returned to the fray in the Preface to her *Feminizing Chaucer* (Cambridge, 2002).

'women became the swooners' and men rarely faint and are ridiculed if they do.[3] Taking the historical long view, she shows us that medieval romances depict both men and women fainting from various strong emotions but never regard the action as effeminate or question the heroes' manliness.[4] Mann likewise observes that some modern critics 'rely on traditional gender stereotyping'[5] and that Troilus is very similar to famous romance lovers such as Lancelot and Tristan, whose manliness is not usually questioned. She too analyses his faint as a noble reaction to 'an irresolvable disorder in the outside world', and she seeks to redeem his 'feminine' responses: vulnerability, compassion and sensitivity of feeling, far from being weak and futile, are presented as superior and positive reactions.[6] The feminine is firmly separated from the effeminate; Troilus is described in terms of female experience, yes, but that experience is attractive and good.

Why Troilus should be so disparaged in the strand of feminist criticism challenged by Mann and Mieszkowski[7] is not entirely clear, though it may have something to do with such criticism's wish to reduce male heroes in general, a wish which accompanies the concentration, as Caroline Bynum has remarked, 'on the negative stereotyping of woman's sexuality and on women's lack of worldly power'.[8] At any rate it has the unfortunate effect of blocking out other views of fainting, and of not taking swoons by women into account: precisely because they are thought an action so characteristic of women, they can be ignored. It is important to de-gender the medieval swoon, to disconnect it from being associated purely with love, and to study the large range of responses to it, which embrace the approving, the disapproving and the merely neutral.[9]

Fainting heroes are not thick on the ground in early *chansons de geste*, nor are fainting heroines especially common. But though infrequent, the swoon

---

[3] Mieszkowski, 'Revisiting', pp. 92–4.

[4] She also usefully reminds us that medieval allegorical narratives use swoons to depict 'great moments of spiritual vision' (p. 91).

[5] Mann, *Feminizing Chaucer*, p. xii.

[6] 'Troilus' Swoon', p. 157; *Feminizing Chaucer*, pp. 129–31. Mann's argument is far more subtle than I have summarised it here; one of the central claims of her book is that 'Chaucer complicates the binary opposition between active and passive, traditionally associated with the male/female binary' (p. xv).

[7] And also challenged by others: see for example, though not specifically on the scene of the swoon, D. Brewer, 'Troilus's "Gentil Manhood"', in *Masculinities in Chaucer: Approaches to Maleness in The Canterbury Tales and Troilus and Criseyde*, ed. P. Beidler (Cambridge, 1998), pp. 237–52.

[8] C. Walker Bynum, *Holy Feast and Holy Fast* (Berkeley, 1987), p. 29. Bynum's books have been very influential on recent criticism, especially, for our purposes, her observation of the 'feminization' of religious language, from the twelfth century onwards, used by male writers describing religious experience, though this does not seem to reflect 'an increased respect for actual women by men': C. Walker Bynum, *Jesus as Mother* (Berkeley, Los Angeles and London, 1982), pp. 138, 143.

[9] See Mieszkowski, 'Revisiting', p. 85: 'In the Middle Ages ... fainting was not gendered either male or female.' Like her, I discuss French narratives before Chaucer's time, but while hers are Continental, I have mostly confined myself to those written in, or copied and widely available in, England.

does not appear to be a gendered action in French epic, and it is mostly approved. Though Geoffrey of Anjou rebukes Charlemagne in the *Chanson de Roland* for showing overmuch grief – the emperor has just fainted twice over Roland's dead body[10] – twenty thousand Franks share his sorrow and 's'en pasment cuntre tere' ('swoon to the ground', line 2932). A stiff upper lip is not shown by William of Orange either, as he faints at the sight of his dying nephew Vivien.[11] The formidable and feisty Floripas faints as she announces her conversion to Christianity, and when she learns of her beloved Gui's capture by Saracens, while her enemies swoon at the death of Clarion at the hands of the French.[12] Swooning is never a symptom of weakness or effeminacy: rather, where it is not a sign of religious ecstasy it is a recognised response to overwhelming grief or physical pain, sympathetically received; it is closely associated with death, which on occasion is mistaken for it.[13]

From the twelfth century onwards, there appears to be a rise in approved emotional behaviour, in both secular and religious contexts: for example, Linda Georgianna, introducing her study of the *Ancrene Wisse*, charts 'the cult of tears' and the importance of 'a tender conscience' and points out how many depictions there were, post St Bernard, of Mary's *compassio*, weeping and fainting at the foot of the Cross.[14] Amy Neff, remarking that the imagery of the swoon begins to flourish in this period, points out how what might be regarded as a weakness becomes, on the contrary, a sign of huge strength: the Virgin, by fainting at the foot of the Cross, shares Christ's suffering and death; it is like a labour which 'gives birth to the eternal Church'.[15] If, then, we look at those early Anglo-Norman hybrids of epic form and a romance-influenced content, *Horn*, *Boeve de Haumtone* and *Le Roman d'Alixandre*, all from the twelfth century, we might expect some infusion of emotionalism, indicated through swoons.[16] But in fact there is not very much; certainly little that has anything to do with love. In *Alixandre*, only the hero swoons and then in the understandable context of exhaustion from commanding troops and

---

10 *La Chanson de Roland*, ed. F. Whitehead, revised T. D. Hemming (London, 1993), lines 2880, 2891, 2946.
11 *Aliscans*, ed. F. Guessard and A. de Montaiglon (Paris, 1870) in extracts from *Le Cycle de Guillaume d'Orange*, ed. D. Boutet (Paris, 1996), p. 336, lines 715–21, 806.
12 *Fierabras*, ed. M. Le Person (Paris, 2003), lines 3308–10, 3479–93, 4382.
13 See Aude's end on hearing of Roland's death: *Alde la bele est a sa fin alee./ Quidet li reis que el se seit pasmee* ('The beautiful Aude met her end/ The king thought she had fainted': *La Chanson de Roland*, lines 3723–4).
14 L. Georgianna, *The Solitary Self: Individuality in the Ancrene Wisse* (London and Cambridge, Mass., 1981), pp. 91ff. Frank considered the rise of the *roman courtois* 'undoubtedly encouraged the cultivation of sentiment and sentimentalism': R. Worth Frank, Jr, *Chaucer and the Legend of Good Women* (Cambridge, 1972), pp. 94–5. See also the influential work of Caroline Walker Bynum (n. 8).
15 A. Neff, 'The Pain of *Compassio*: Mary's Labor at the Foot of the Cross', *Art Bulletin* 80 (1998), 254–73 (p. 265).
16 For a slightly different view of the blending of epic and romance elements in these texts, see the essay by Ailes, 'What's in a Name?', in the present volume.

crossing the Tigris.[17] The hero and the heroine in *Boeve*, and their assorted allies, all occasionally faint, the men from grief, Boeve once from fear lest Josiane is dead (he is recalled to his senses by his horse).[18] Josiane faints twice, once at the report of Boeve's supposed marriage, once when Boeve rejects her advances.[19] The first swoon is from shock and is of course allied to her love for him, but the second has much more to do with fury: she 'taint cum carboun' ('she turned the colour of charcoal', line 693), the traditional colour of outrage. In none of these cases do swoons attract disapproval. But in *Horn*, earliest of the three (by 1170), and the work of a strongly moralistic poet, the situation is different: there is a closer connection between fainting and love, and in one case it would be more precise to label it lust, which attracts marked disapproval. The hero never faints, but women do, reacting strongly to his handsome looks:

> Dame ne.l poet veer ke n'en seit esragée,
> U pres est del murir, u del tut es pasméé.[20]
>
> ['No lady could see him without being distraught; either they
> were close to dying or they swooned away.']

We are much closer to traditional misogynistic stereotyping of women here: swooning is linked to a temporary loss of rationality and self-control, as when the otherwise formidable heroine, Rigmel, faints as Horn departs for Ireland, because 'sis sens fu esperduz' ('she was distraught', lines 2014–15). At its most cynical, this attitude is expressed in a proverb: 'de fole pansee vient fole paumee' ('from a crazy thought comes a crazy fainting woman').[21]

With the appearance of the *romans antiques*, the earlier two contemporary with *Horn* (*Le Roman de Thèbes* and *Le Roman d'Enéas* are both c.1160), the phenomenon of fainting by both men and women is well established and is clearly meant to denote an accepted response to strong emotion. In *Thèbes*, this emotion is still primarily grief, and with the men it is grief for their wounded or slain fellows, for their friends, lords and followers, as we might expect in a genre still strongly influenced by the contemporary, homosocial *chanson de geste*. The knights of the slain Athon:

> de devant lui ne se remuent,
> aincois se pasment et se tuent
> et leur seignor regretent fort …
> Pasmez gisent el pavement.[22]

---

[17] Thomas of Kent, *The Anglo-Norman Alexander (Le Roman de Toute Chevalerie)*, ed. B. Foster with I. Short, ANTS 29–33, 2 vols. (London, 1976–77 [for 1971–75]), vol. 1, lines 2786–9.

[18] *Der Anglonormannische Boeve de Haumtone*, ed. A. Stimming (Halle, 1899), lines 1686–90.

[19] *Boeve*, lines 1419–20 and 693–4.

[20] Thomas, *The Romance of Horn*, ed. M. K. Pope, ANTS 9–10 and 12–13, 2 vols. (Oxford, 1955, 1964): vol. 1, lines 861–2.

[21] J. Morawski, *Proverbes français antérieurs au XVe siècle* (Paris, 1925), no. 489.

[22] *Le Roman de Thèbes*, ed. G. R. de Lage, 2 vols. (Paris, 1966–68), lines 6003–7.

['did not stir from in front of him but swooned and killed themselves and deeply lamented their lord ... They lay swooning on
the paving stones.'][23]

Women likewise faint from grief: Ysmeine, at the sight of her lover Athon's
body, utters loud cries associated with loss of rationality ('comme desvee crie
e bret', 'she cries and wails like a madwoman', line 5922) and her swoon is
a kind of death in which she loses heat and breath.

In the *Roman d'Enéas*, fainting has for the first time a close association
with love and with women, while continuing its connection with death. Dido's
symptoms of infatuation add swooning to the other, better-known ones, such
as tossing and turning all night: she faints when trying to utter Eneas's name
to Anna and appears 'almost dead'.[24] Dido's repeated faints at watching the
departure of the Trojans lead to physical coldness and so her waiting women
anticipate death even before she commits suicide.[25] The love affair of Eneas
and Lavine of course has a happier outcome, but Lavine's canny mother
early on makes the by now expected and paradoxical connection of love and
sorrow, which involves fainting:

> Ris et joie vient de plorer,
> Grant deport vienent de pasmer.
>
> ['Laughter and joy come from weeping, great delight from
> fainting': *Enéas,* lines 7961–2]

Though Eneas's love-symptoms also include fainting, female faints in this
poem far outnumber the male: after one conversation with her mother on the
subject of love, Lavine swoons seven times. But if, in this romance at least,
this physical demonstration of strong emotion seems especially characteristic
of women, there is no suggestion that it marks inferiority.

In the *lais* of Marie de France, it is once more the women who outnumber
the men in fainting by three to one. Again, joy, grief and love are closely mixed
as the causes. In *Yonec* in particular, a swoon presages death by mimicking it:
the lady faints over her wounded lover on his bier, later faints on his tomb,
then dies. These early romances or *lais*, then, take swooning seriously. But
not all twelfth-century poets did. It is not surprising to find in the romances
of Chrétien some scenes where swoons are depicted with tongue in cheek.
While men faint as often as women, for grief, love, or a mixture of both,
two scenes in *Yvain* suggest that this is an exaggerated reaction. The first

---

23 As Mieszkowski remarks about heroes in later English romances: 'These men are not feminized
by their suffering; they are merely suffering': 'Revisiting Troilus's Faint', p. 84.
24 *Le Roman d'Enéas*, ed. A. Petit (Paris, 1997), lines 1278 and 1325.
25 Galen discusses fainting spells and chilling of the body in connection with widows and their
retention of 'semen': see R. E. Siegel, *Galen on the Affected Parts (De Locis Affectis)* (Basel,
1976), p. 190. See further below, pp. 130–1.

concerns the behaviour of the widowed Laudine, accompanying the corpse of her recently murdered husband:

> Mes de duel feire estoit si fole,
> Qu'a po qu'ele ne s'ocioit.
> A la foiiee s'escrioit
> Si haut, qu'ele ne pooit plus,
> Et recheoit pasmee jus.
> Et quant ele estoit relevee,
> Aussi come fame desvee
> Se comançoit a descirer
> Et ses chevos a detirer.
> Ses chevos tire et ront ses dras,
> Si se repasme a chascun pas,
> Ne riens ne la puet conforter.[26]

['But she was so crazed with grief as to be close to taking her own life. From time to time she would cry out at the top of her voice and then fall down in a faint. Then, when she had got up again, just like a madwoman, she would begin to rend her clothes and tear her hair. She tears her hair and rips her clothing, swooning again at every step, and nothing can comfort her.']

But when all her retinue has departed, Laudine is left alone:

> Mes cele i remaint tote sole,
> Qui sovent se prant a la gole,
> Et tort ses poinz et bat ses paumes,
> Et list an un sautier ses saumes,
> Anluminé a letres d'or.

['But she stays there quite alone, and often clutches at her throat and wrings her hands and slaps her palms, and reads her psalms in a psalter illuminated with gold lettering': lines 1411–15].

In the light of her subsequent rapid capitulation to Yvain, the widow's traditional mourning behaviour comes across as excessive, as if primarily for public consumption, and when she is in private, the remaining gestures of grief are oddly discrepant with her calm reading of the psalms and the whole line devoted to her richly decorated book.

The second scene shows Yvain returning to the fountain under the pine, and fainting when he recollects this is the place which led to his meeting Laudine, now his wife, from whom he is estranged. As he faints, his sword

---

[26] Chrétien de Troyes, *Yvain*, ed. T. B. W. Reid (Manchester, 1942), lines 1150–61. The translation used here and for the next quotation is by D. D. R. Owen, *Chrétien de Troyes, Arthurian Romances* (London, 1991).

cuts him and he loses blood. His faithful lion thinks his lord is dead and in distress attempts to commit suicide with the same sword (lines 3492–525). I am not alone in thinking this episode verges on comedy.[27] The animal's mistaking a swoon for death of course resembles the mistake made by humans, as we have seen, but the deliberate absurdity of its attempt to mimic human action is perhaps a way of poking fun at Yvain's excessive reaction to painful memory.

An equally tongue-in-cheek insular writer, Hue de Rotelande, author of *Ipomédon*, probably followed Chretien's cue here. In *Ipomédon*'s sequel, *Protheselaus*, Hue has fun with the improbable idea of love between Ipomedon's son and Medea, someone who loved his father – in other words between a young man and a woman around twenty years older. The love has no substance to it at all (it only just makes it to consummation after repeated postponements), and Medea's reactions to it are always excessive: when she first sees Protheselaus she nearly faints because of his resemblance to his father; she swoons when discovering his identity; swoons on hearing he loves her; swoons again on hearing he must leave her.[28] It is not so much the swoon which is ridiculed here as exploiting it to indicate a deliberately unconvincing emotion.

This parodic tendency, in Anglo-Norman at any rate, unfortunately did not continue after Hue de Rotelande: the expectation that swooning was the way serious heroes and heroines behaved is obvious in the very popular *Amadas et Ydoine* (end of the twelfth century: the story, and possibly this version of it, was well known in England). *Amadas* had a particularly strong influence on *Gui de Warewic* (about a decade later) in this respect: the whole early pattern of the hero repeatedly returning to his mistress to declare his love, repeatedly being rejected and repeatedly fainting was transferred wholesale to the later romance. The hero's faints in *Amadas* do, however, finally produce a result: when Ydoine fears the last one is actually death, not a swoon, her pity for Amadas leads to love. The poet supplies an arch comment, which is nevertheless based on medical views:

> Vous savés bien que dou baisier
> A icel point eut grant mestier
> Quant hom est pasmés par tristrece,
> Par vanité u par feblece,
> Se on le baise auques sovent
> Par bon corage doucement.[29]

['You are well aware that he was very much in need of kisses at that moment. When a man has swooned out of grief, vanity

---

27 See T. Hunt, *Chrétien de Troyes, Yvain (Le Chevalier au Lion)* (London, 1986), p. 75.

28 Hue de Rotelande, *Protheselaus*, ed. A. J. Holden, ANTS 47–49, 3 vols. (London, 1991, 1993), lines 2565–7, 3123–6, 3599–601, 3776–90. See J. Weiss, 'A Reappraisal of Hue de Rotelande's *Protheselaus*', *Medium Aevum* 52 (1983), 104–11 (pp. 106–7).

29 *Amadas et Ydoine*, ed. J. R. Reinhard (Paris, 1926; repr. 1998), lines 1155–61.

or weakness, if one kisses him very often, gently and sincerely,
he will quickly revive from a faint.']

Ydoine's kisses bring Amadas round, as Criseyde's will Troilus.[30]

In *Gui de Warewic*, however, fainting has no effect on the hero's obdurate
beloved, Felice, and thus Gui has to leave for foreign parts in order to win
fame and, ultimately, her hand. At this juncture fainting for love stops, and
female fainting is likewise sparse. Men do most of the swooning, and they
swoon for grief, joy, and upon recognition of their fellow men. It is a mark of
their emotional refinement that they feel so intensely for each other. This is
especially marked in the second part of the romance when Gui has abandoned
his wife and family and fights three formidable opponents in order to help
his male friends and his king. The moments of reunion, when those helped
at last realise who it is that has helped them, are affecting. Deep feeling
again manifests itself through faints; in particular, it is compassion or *pité*
which Gui and Terri feel, that sign of true nobility which in turn can affect
any bystander for the better. This is explicitly pointed out during the scene
when Terri at last recognises that it is Gui who has saved his life. Words are
redundant: they are replaced by signs, above all that of the swoon.

> Quant Terri le vit enmi le vis,
> Un mot ne sonast pur tut Paris;
> Pasmé chet del mul a tere,
> Tel duel ne veissez home mes faire ...
> La plure e fait dolur mult grant,
> *Suz ciel n'est home vivant,*
> *Ja de si dur corage ne fust,*
> *Qui de li grant pité n'en eust.*
> Gui ad al quor tel doel e ire,
> A peine pout un sul mot dire.
> Entre ses braz l'ad sus levé,
> La se sunt dunc entrebaisé;
> Amdui cheent a tere pasmé,
> Chascun ad d'altre si grant pité.[31]

['When Terri studied his face, he could not, for all Paris,
utter a word. He fell swooning from the mule to the ground;
you never saw a man grieve so much.... There he wept and
mourned bitterly; there is no one alive under heaven, however
hard-hearted he might be, who would not have had great pity
on him. Gui had such sorrow and anguish in his heart that he

---

[30] Mieszkowski, 'Revisiting Troilus's Faint', p. 86: she cites similar scenes (pp. 90–1) in a thirteenth-century Continental romance, *Claris et Laris*, and the fifteenth-century Middle English
Generydes. This belief is also established in medical thought by the fourteenth century: see
further below, p. 133.

[31] *Gui de Warewic: Roman du XIIIe Siècle*, ed. A. Ewert, 2 vols. (Paris, 1933), lines 10673–6,
10699–708 (my italics).

could hardly utter a single word. He raised him up in his arms
and then they kissed each other. Each felt such great pity for
the other that both fell fainting to the ground.']

The swoon in early medieval literature, therefore, often has the function of
both exhibiting and inspiring fine feeling. It is not associated with passivity,
subjection and surrender. These terms, used by Mann to describe positively
Troilus's behaviour towards Criseyde,[32] are negatively used by other critics,
as in this quotation from Elaine Hansen: 'The courtly, aristocratic, male lover
in the very act of falling in love is, by convention and by rhetoric, rendered
to some degree passive and submissive ... the courtly model of aristocratic
behaviour feminizes the male lover – rendering him subservient, weakened,
infantilized.'[33] Mann may have been influenced by descriptions of *amor heros*
(or *heroes*) or 'heroic love';[34] Hansen certainly has been, above all in the
work of an important critic, Mary Wack, which came to fruition in her book,
Lovesickness in the Middle Ages.[35]

Wack traces the idea of *eros* as illness back to ancient times and points
out the early confusion between *herus* (lord), *eros* and *heros* (hero) (p. 60),
so that the phrase mutated into *amor heroicus* and was 'class-specific', 'the
sufferer was typically thought to be a noble man' (pp. xi–xii). A good example
of this belief was the influential work of Arnald de Villanova in his *Epistola
de amore qui dicitur heroicus* (1276–86): he glossed *amor heroicus* as *quasi
dominalis* because this love especially affects lords, dominates man's mind
and heart, and pushes lovers to behave towards the desired object as subjects
do towards their lord.[36] An earlier writer on lovesickness, Constantine the
African (died c.1087) described symptoms still familiar to us from medieval and Renaissance texts: frequent sighing, slow and uneven pulse, feverish
breathing when hearing something pleasing, melancholia or madness, sleep-
lessness.[37] But these symptoms do not include fainting.

---

[32] 'Troilus' Swoon', pp. 157, 160: Troilus's swoon demonstrates 'his subjection to Criseyde ... [it] is not a piece of behaviour designed to show his ineffectuality ... but a demonstration of surrender ... dictated by a deeply-felt emotion.'

[33] E. Tuttle Hansen, *Chaucer and the Fictions of Gender* (Berkeley, 1992), pp. 17, 20; see also pp. 148–50.

[34] See J. Livingston Lowes, '"The Loveres Malady of Hereos"', *Modern Philology* 11 (1913–14), 491–546.

[35] M. F. Wack, *Lovesickness in the Middle Ages* (Philadelphia, 1990). Her chapter on Peter of Spain first appeared in *Viator* 17 (1986), 173–96, and is cited by Hansen, *Chaucer and the Fictions of Gender*, n. 12, p. 149. McInerney's article, cited by Mieszkowski, also cites Wack in a disparaging reference to Troilus's faint: M. Burnett McInerney, '"Is this a mannes herte?"': Unman-
ning Troilus through Ovidian Allusion', in *Masculinities in Chaucer*, ed. Beidler, pp. 221–35 (p. 223). Wack's influence often feeds indirectly through other articles which are then in turn much cited, such as V. L. Bullough, 'On Being a Male in the Middle Ages', in *Medieval Masculinities: Regarding Men in the Middle Ages*, ed. C. A. Lees (Minneapolis and London, 1994), pp. 149–68.

[36] Quoted in D. Jacquart and C. Thomasset, 'L'amour "héroïque" à travers le traité d'Arnaud de Villeneuve', in *La Folie et le Corps*, ed. J. Céard (Paris, 1985), pp. 143–58 (pp. 143, 150–2).

[37] Quoted from Constantine the African, *Treatise on the Viaticum*, extracted and translated in Wack, *Lovesickness*, pp. 255–7.

Gerard of Berry (last quarter of the twelfth century) wrote the earliest surviving commentary upon Constantine's *Viaticum*. He too argued that the wealth and leisure of the nobility made 'heroic' love a likely hazard, and like Constantine he prescribed sexual intercourse as a cure for it. Berry added an extra observation: the lover is uncomprehending and unmoved except when hearing about his beloved.[38]

While not wanting to disparage the excellent work done by Wack, it is worth noting that she glosses the observations she finds in Gerard and interprets them in a manner not in the original extracts she cites. 'The lover's helplessness and inarticulateness seem those of an infant, *in-fans*, the one who cannot speak … Gerard's addition of the symptom, then, obliquely indicates that *amor heros* is incompatible with conventions of masculine adult social behaviour' (p. 64). But this is oblique indeed, since Gerard has not said that the lover is either helpless or inarticulate. According to Wack, when Gerard synthesises the comments of earlier writers such as Avicenna and Constantine the African the symptoms he describes '*essentially* feminise the male lover': 'the passivity *inherent in being a patient*, with the helplessness and vulnerability *that it implies … connote* traits *customarily associated with* the feminine in medieval culture' (p. 65). In a later chapter she sums up the writings of several physicians including Gerard: 'the symptoms of the disease "unman" the lover. As a patient he is passive, helpless and vulnerable. The signs of lovesickness, as shown in chapter three [on Gerard] connote feminine and infantile behaviour', and she cites Freud and Caroline Walker Bynum in support (p. 151). I have italicised some of these phrases because they seem to me to demonstrate unsubstantiated deductions from the medical texts (which are more objective in their observations), which later seem to harden into certainties, and it is these unquestioned certainties which appear to have been adopted by some critics.

At any rate, as far as I can see, the symptoms of *amor heros* in these and other medical authors do not include fainting. Burton's *Anatomy of Melancholy* (1621), which mentions this kind of love in his survey, does list one example of a swoon, but it is a sign of 'windy Hypochondriacal Melancholy', not love.[39] So one must look elsewhere in medical texts written or used in the Middle Ages for non-literary ideas about fainting. Almost every investigation of medieval medical conditions must go back to Galen (c.130–215 AD), the greatest doctor of the post-Classical world, whose ideas survived for centuries. Galen inherited from Plato, Hippocrates, Pliny and Soranus a belief in 'hysteria' in both men and women, whose symptoms included fainting, and which was attributed to retained secretions, superfluous residues like menses and semen, which could be harmful to the body and indicated an

38 Gerard of Berry, *Glosses on the Viaticum*, quoted in Wack, *Lovesickness*, pp. 203, 201.
39 R. Burton, *Anatomy of Melancholy*, ed. T. C. Faulkner, N. K. Kiessling and R. L. Blair, 3 vols. (Oxford, 1989–94), I, 411.

inadequate sexual life.[40] In the case of women, Plato thought this resulted in the 'wandering womb': when the womb remained unfertilised for a long time, it became angry and moved all over the body; if it touched the diaphragm, it interfered with respiration.[41] Galen rejected the idea of the wandering womb, though it remained popular for centuries afterwards, and attributed *hysterike pnyx* or 'uterine suffocation' to harmful retentions, including female semen, flowing from the ovaries to the uterus:

> It is generally agreed upon that this disease [uterine suffocation] mostly affects widows and particularly those who have previously menstruated regularly, had been pregnant and were eager to have intercourse, but were now deprived of all this ... [He attributes it to] retention of menstrual flow or of semen ... by which some women become apnoic, suffocated or spastic.[42]

Galen believed in female as well as male semen, and claimed male hysteria was likewise caused by retention of sperm.[43]

Soranus (second century AD, also sceptical about the wandering womb) had described the symptoms of *hysterike pnyx*: obstructed respiration, inability to speak, 'seizure of the senses', a very small or non-existent pulse,[44] not unlike some of the symptoms of *amor heros*. This reappears in Ibn al-Jazzar's *Viaticum*, which was translated from the Arabic by Constantine the African: corrupted semen or menses are turned into a 'cold fumosity', ascending to parts close to the lungs and heart and other organs of the voice, producing 'an impediment of speaking'.[45] Galen, meanwhile, pointed out that syncope, common to both sexes, could also be caused by pain as a result of a terrible fright or extreme joy; this came from a sudden loss of innate heat in the left ventricle of the heart. Those who suffered frequent faints were likely to die suddenly.[46]

The twelfth-century Salernitan corpus of medical writings about women's health, known as the *Trotula*, continued to peddle these ideas. It conveys 'the general medical assumption throughout most of the medieval period that women needed regular sexual activity in order to remain healthy',[47] so the women most prone to uterine suffocation were, as we have seen in Galen, widows and virgins of marriageable age: 'certain girls seem as if they are suffering from the falling sickness, which comes about from uterine suffoca-

---

[40] P. Brain, *Galen on Bloodletting* (Cambridge, 1986), p. 13; Siegel, *Affected Parts*, p. 4.

[41] Siegel, *Affected Parts*, p. 187. See also Bullough, 'On Being a Male', citing Hippocrates: if a woman were not kept moist by intercourse, the uterus would rise towards the hypochondrium, impeding the flow of breath (p. 39).

[42] Galen, *De Locis Affectis*, quoted in Siegel, *Affected Parts*, p. 184.

[43] Siegel, *Affected Parts*, p. 13.

[44] M. H. Green, *The Trotula: A Medieval Compendium of Women's Medicine* (Philadelphia, 2001), p. 23.

[45] Quoted in Green, *The Trotula*, p. 25. Ibn al-Jazzar died AD 979.

[46] Siegel, *Affected Parts*, pp. 137–8.

[47] Green, *The Trotula*, p. 26.

tion compressing the respiratory organs'.[48] Gilbertus Anglicus, whose work, the *Compendium Medicinae* (c.1240) is referred to by Chaucer,[49] conveyed both of Galen's ideas on fainting, the first that it is due to 'suffocacioun of the moder [uterus]':

> Prolonged retention of menstrua affects women so gravely that they appear to be dead. For the vapour, long closed in, rises to the spiritual members, affects the brain, oppresses the noble members and all those in the breast ... and they lose consciousness and cannot speak. Their pulse is slow and weak and sometimes so faint that they appear to be dead.[50]

the second, that it is due to 'the grevaunce of the spirits of the hert':

> [when] the herte hath mo than he sholde kyndly haue, as it hapneth whan a man fallith from a sodeyn gladness into a sodeyn sorewe, either fallith from a grete hete into a grete colde ... whan a mannes spiritis [vital breath] goon sodeynly oute of his herte and ben y-sparplid abrode in al the body, as it happneth when a man fallith into a sodden ioy aftir his sorowe, either into a grete hete aftir a grete cold.[51]

Much the same ideas recur in extended form in Bartholomaeus Anglicus's *De Proprietatibus Rerum* (1230s), translated by Trevisa in the fourteenth century:

> Also of defaute of the herte and febilnesse of spiritis cometh swownynge that hatte comenlich *spasmacio*, and that cometh somtyme of accidentis of the soule, as of drede that closith the herte swithe, somtyme of grete ioye other of wrathe that openeth the herte to swithe, and so spiritis passith out by euaporaciuns, exsolaciouns, and schedinge. Somtyme it cometh of accidentis of the body, as of euel complexioun, of grete replecioun of mete and of drinke, of gret abstinence, of stoppynge of veynes and of pressinge and wryngynge of spiritis, and somtyme of to grete swetynge. And of this swownynge som dieth sodaynly ... And somtyme it cometh of grete pressinge of the ful stomak or of gret pressinge of the modir [uterus].[52]

Doctors knew how to treat faints: as in *Amadas et Ydoine*, so in Gilbertus Anglicus, one had to 'bynde [a man's] fyngris with thongis and his toon also,

---

[48] *De Curis Mulierum* (*On Treatments for Women*), chapter 203, reproduced and translated in Green, *The Trotula*, pp. 148–9.

[49] E. M. Liggins, 'The lovers' swoons in *Troilus and Criseyde*', *Parergon* 3 (1985), 93–106 (p. 96).

[50] Gilbertus Anglicus, *Compendium Medicinae*, quoted in C. H. Talbot, *Medicine in Medieval England* (London, 1967), p. 81.

[51] *Healing and Society in Medieval England: a Middle English Translation of the Pharmaceutical Writings of Gilbertus Anglicus*, ed. with introduction and notes by F. M. Getz (Madison, 1991), chapter xi, Part 2, p. 149.

[52] Bartholomaeus Anglicus, *De Proprietatibus Rerum*, trans. John Trevisa as *On the Properties of Things*, ed. M. C. Seymour, 2 vols. (Oxford, 1975), vol. 1, Book 7, p. 378.

that the spiritis and the blode moun drawe outeward from the herte', 'wring him wel by the nose', pull the hair on his head, kiss him tenderly and rub his hands.[53]

It is not unexpected that medieval medical texts should consider the causes of fainting in both men and women to be due, not to their heightened, refined sensitivities, as fictional narratives suggest, but to strong emotional disturbance, causing loss of blood and heat and the temporary departure of the vital breath ('spirits'),[54] and to the deprivation of a good sex life. While medieval literature – and modern critics – concur with the first cause,[55] the second cause may appear foreign to it. Yet it is possible that the doctors influenced the poets more than we realise: in romances, heroes and heroines may swoon from this most basic of medical reasons. Certainly Amadas and Gui's repeated early faints could have as much to do with lack of sexual activity as with idealistic attachment; so could those of Eneas and Lancelot; so could those of the virginal Josiane (in *Boeve*) and Rigmel (in *Horn*), hard beset by their lovers' testing of their chastity; of Ysmeine (in *Thèbes*), so keen to sleep with Athon; and of the widowed Dido, without a husband for a long time and then cruelly deserted by her new lover (*Enéas*). These and the other faints I have mentioned can obviously all be attributed to the impact of intense emotions like grief and shock as well, but there is no reason to suppose the writers and audiences of medieval fictions were unaware that intense emotion could frequently go hand in hand with acute privation.[56]

Does Troilus swoon in part because of an as-yet unfulfilled sexual life? To suggest this may lay me open to the same charge of coarsening and misunderstanding him that I am happy to lay at the doors of others. It is certainly true that Chaucer's description of his faint, as Liggins has pointed out, is in complete and precise concordance with medical views of the time: Troilus's heart, centre of vital heat, where the blood vessels arise which carry blood and nourishment around the body, is 'shette' by sorrow and constricted by violent emotion, so that 'every spirit his vigour in knette',[57] his vital energy

---

53 Getz, *Healing and Society*, p. 150; see also Liggins, 'The lovers' swoons', pp. 98–9, quoting Bernard of Gordon and drawing attention to the similar treatment after Troilus's swoon. Mieszkowski observes the analogous treatment given to Boccaccio's fainting Troilo, not in the bedchamber but when hearing of the proposed exchange of Antenor and Criseida (p. 86).

54 For the widespread belief that the spirit could temporarily leave the body see Liggins, 'The lovers' swoons', pp. 96–7.

55 Like Mieszkowski, I think some critics interpret 'emotional disturbance' too far: Aers suggests Troilus faints from fear of being impotent. See 'Revisiting', p. 84.

56 Chaucer, for one, 'had an intimate acquaintance with certain of the prevailing medical views of his day' (Lowes, 'The Loveres Malady', p. 528). In the General Prologue to the *Canterbury Tales* he cites an impressive list of medical authors known to the Doctor of Physik, including Galen and Gilbertus Anglicus (lines 429–34); in the *Book of the Duchess* he gives the physical effects of a faint (lines 488–91).

57 This line (1088) is variously glossed: the *Riverside Chaucer* interprets this as 'each vital spirit contracted in force'; Liggins, 'The lovers' swoons', refers to the 'spirit' as being much the same as the soul but also points out the medical belief that man's body was controlled by three 'virtues' or spirits, located in heart, liver and brain (p. 97). Trevisa and the translation of Gilbertus Anglicus seem to use 'spirit' to mean breath and vital essence. The *MED* glosses 'vigour' as vital essence,

or essence restrained (or contracted or oppressed) every breath (lines 1069–92). The weakened body fails in sensation 'and from that comes syncope'.[58] It has nothing to do with effeminacy, emasculation, impotence (or fear of it). Its 'remedy' is carried out scrupulously by Criseyde and Pandarus, and the comedy the latter brings to the scene does not undermine the seriousness of an aristocratic hero's proper reaction to his own emotions of shock, guilt and compassion for Criseyde's tears. The precision of Chaucer's medical references may well have also reminded his audience to bring to the scene their own knowledge of one of the sources of swoons. If they did so, and he intended that they should, it enriches rather than coarsens the episode by adding to the complexity of a multi-signifying act. To take Troilus's swoon out of its medieval medical and literary contexts is to risk simplifying Chaucer at best, and at worst, to wholly misinterpret him. The same applies generally to the swooning heroes and heroines of medieval romance. This example illustrates how easy it is to unwittingly apply a modern cultural context to a medieval text in which it has no place.

energy. Wimsatt argues that Chaucer was borrowing closely from Machaut's *Remède de Fortune* at this point, where Amant describes his swoon as resulting from being 'desvoiez' ('led astray, distracted') from feeling, strength and 'toute autre vigour': J. L. Wimsatt, 'Guillaume de Machaut and Chaucer's *Troilus and Criseyde*', *Medium Aevum* 45 (1976), 277–93 (p. 281).

[58] Liggins, 'The lovers' swoons' (p. 97), quoting Gilbertus Anglicus, *Compendium Medicinae.*

10

Walking (between) the Lines:
Romance as Itinerary/Map

ROBERT ROUSE

'What can we know of the world? What quantity of space can our eyes hope to take in between our birth and our death? How many square centimetres of Planet Earth will the soles of our feet have touched?'[1]

A s Georges Perec observes, our personal experience of the world is lamentably finite. As much – or as little – as one seeks to travel, one will never experience the entire world. The only way we can know the world outside of our personal experience is necessarily at a remove. Our geographical knowledge of the overwhelming majority of the world is thus mediated through text, image, narrative. No less true for the modern age, this was particularly the case during the medieval period, where the geographical radii of peoples' lives, as well as their exposure to geographical media, were commonly more restricted than today. However, just as we today experience the world through National Geographic, travel shows and the aspirational reading of Lonely Planet guidebooks, the people of the medieval period also revelled in travel narratives. In the Auchinleck manuscript narrative of *Guy of Warwick*, the eponymous protagonist travels throughout Europe, from Warwick to Normandy, through Spain, Germany, Lombardy and thence onwards to more exotic locales such as Constantinople, Jerusalem, Bethlehem and Alexandria. His travels chart his development as first a chivalric and later a Christian hero, transforming him from an ideal lover-knight into the embodiment of the pious martial pilgrim.[2] But these places are not simply an arbitrary series of stages through which the romance hero moves. They represent real places, more or less familiar to the text's audience. As much as it is a narrative of the development of the ideal knight, the romance also participates in the articulation of geographical knowledge. For the medieval

---

[1] G. Perec, *Species of Spaces and Other Pieces*, translated by J. Sturrock (London, 1999), p. 78.
[2] For an extended analysis of this process, see R. Rouse, 'An Exemplary Life: Guy of Warwick as Medieval Culture Hero', in *Guy of Warwick: Icon and Ancestor*, ed. A. Wiggins and R. Field (Cambridge, 2007), pp. 94–109.

audience of these romances, what did these places represent? What did the act of journeying to them or through them signify? How were these distant and dimly-known cities and lands given meaning by the texts in which they were narrated? Through an analysis of the way in which geography is deployed in *Guy of Warwick*, I hope to frame both a series of questions and a methodological approach through which to explore the important role that medieval romance plays within the medieval English geographical imagination.

Medieval romance has often been accused of having a geographical vagueness that has been seen to be largely characteristic of the genre as a whole. Locations in many romances have been viewed as being ill-defined, or as having names that do not correspond to cities and countries in the 'real' historical medieval world, or when they do, as representing them in an entirely unrealistic fashion. However, such traditional criticisms are in fact grounded upon a lack of understanding as to the nature of medieval geography. That the medieval geographical sensibility is not concerned with an accurate one-to-one representation of the real world becomes self-evident when one examines an object such as the Hereford Map. This wondrous *mappa mundi*, produced around 1300, presents a cosmological understanding of the medieval Christian world in the well-known T-O map form (i.e. a circular map in which the three continents are arranged such that Asia forms the top half and Europe and Africa the lower two quarters, forming a T-shape), highlighting in both image and text the chief sites and places of biblical and legendary history. The map, as Naomi Kline and Scott Westrem have convincingly demonstrated, was compiled through the process of selecting those places and narratives that the map-maker deemed to be central to his ideological purpose.[3] The Hereford Map highlights, as do many such medieval maps, the centrality of Christ's Passion to the Christian world, but also includes narratives such as those of Alexander the Great's walling up of the tribes of Gog and Magog, and the marginal presence of the monstrous Marvels of the East. In the light of the geographical nature of an artefact such as the Hereford Map, we should not then be surprised by the highly *selective* use of geography within the romances. It is in fact this *geographical selectivity* that casts the romances as the textual equivalents of works such as the Hereford Map. Like the *mappa mundi*, romance constructs an image of the world that emphasises the narrative and ideological discourse of the text. In doing so, romances engage in a process of 'writing the world'. This construction of the world may not be the mimetic representation of geography that a modern reader may expect, but this illuminates more our own preconceptions about the nature of geographical knowledge than it highlights any lack in medieval representations of the world.

Why should we be interested in the way in which geography is articulated

---

3   N. Kline, *Maps of Medieval Thought: The Hereford Paradigm* (Woodbridge, 2001); S. D. Westrem, *The Hereford Map: A Transcription and Translation of the Legends with Commentary*, Terrarum orbis I (Turnhout, 2001).

in romance? An understanding of the nature of geography within romance is essential in order to assess the role that the genre plays in a number of current debates within medieval scholarship. Primary among these is the strong connection that has been postulated between romance and nationalism in the medieval period. The connection between a people and their land is one of the central tenets of theories of national identity: Homi Bhabha has termed landscape a metaphor for the 'inscape of national identity', posting a sign as to its importance that has become a concern for many recent critics.[4] Geography is one of the primary signifiers of the Other within the identity politics of the medieval period: we live *here*, they live *there*. However, this binary only maintains an undiluted signification when populations remain in stasis, obligingly occupying their assigned places within the world. On the contrary, much medieval romance is concerned with the movement of the narrative's protagonists through the world, constituting in itself an early form of travel literature: such peripatetic romances operate both to define and to problematise notions of geographically-based identity. If we are to fully appreciate the complexities of the deployment of geographical place within the discourses of romance, including but not limited to the rhetoric of national identity, then a more complete understanding of the nature of romance geography and landscape is required.

The Geographical Knowledge of the Romance Audience

How much did the audience of medieval romance know of the world? Before assessing how the reading of romance might impact upon the medieval geographical consciousness, one must first consider the nature and extent of medieval geographical knowledge. The learned tradition of geographical knowledge in the medieval period derived from the works of the classical world, such as Pliny's *Natural History*, and was incorporated into numerous histories and encyclopaedic works.[5] This learned tradition was slowly modified as the medieval period progressed, through the impact of the Crusades, early travellers such as John of Plano Carpini and William of Rubruck, and innovations such as *portolan* maps with their focus on information for sailors.

---

4   Studies such as N. Lozovsky's *The Earth is our Book: Geographical Knowledge in the Latin West ca. 400–1000* (Ann Arbor, 2001) have assessed the state of learned geographical knowledge in the Middle Ages. We have also seen in recent years a movement towards the study of narrative geographies. Collections of essays such as S. Gilles's *Text and Territory: Geographical Imagination in the European Middle Ages* (Philadelphia, 1998), and B. Hanawalt and M. Kobialka's *Medieval Practices of Space* (Minneapolis, 2000) have reflected this growing interest, foregrounding the appearance of more prolonged engagements with the cultural role of medieval geography such as K. Lavezzo's *Angels on the Edge of the World: Geography, Literature, and English Community, 1000–1534* (New York, 2006).
5   For a discussion of the classical influence on the medieval knowledge of geography, and the changes the learned tradition underwent, see J. Verdon, *Travel in the Middle Ages*, trans. G. Holoch (Notre Dame, 2003), pp. 127–40.

However, the situation for the unlearned majority of the medieval population was rather different. Their geographical knowledge was limited to that which they had experienced themselves, or that narrated in stories they had read or heard. This is the context in which we need to consider the geographical work performed by medieval romance.

While the audience of medieval romance is notoriously a polymorphous and many-headed beast, only a small section of this audience would have been personally familiar with some of the places to which these romance protagonists travel: for the overwhelming majority they would have been far off and mysterious locales. Helen Cooper notes the general paucity of geographical knowledge among the medieval populace, due in part to the widespread practical limitations on personal travel:

> Those Englishmen whose professional functions required them to travel – merchants, messengers, friars, the king himself, and all levels of his house-hold from the cooks to the highest barons – were familiar with some of the main roads of England, and perhaps a few of those of mainland Europe. Such people were far outnumbered, however, by those whose horizons were limited by the nearest market town, or by the literal horizon seen from their own village.[6]

The majority of the audience of *Guy of Warwick* would not then have been personally familiar with the range of places to which Guy travels. But what about that other source of geographical information, stories read or heard? If we consider the list of major places that Guy visits – Warwick, Normandy, Spain, Germany, Lombardy, Constantinople, Jerusalem, Bethlehem and Alexandria – we can immediately see that certain places would have been already replete with meaning in the minds of the audience. We can be fairly well assured that for most of the audience Jerusalem and Bethlehem would have brought to mind Christ's birth and passion, appropriately enough for the role that these places play in Guy's own journey of Christian transformation. The different European regions would have brought to mind stereotypes of foreign cultures – as they still do today – variously in the context of war or trade, depending on the historical moment.[7] Constantinople, that wondrously liminal city at the edge of Christendom, was – not only to the readers of romance – simultaneously both bulwark against the threatening heathen world and the home of the treacherously-hybridised Orthodox Greeks themselves.[8]

The pre-existing horizons of geographical expectation within the audience

---

[6] H. Cooper, *The English Romance in Time: Transforming Motifs from Geoffrey of Monmouth to the Death of Shakespeare* (Oxford, 2004), p. 68.

[7] These stereotypes were no doubt as complex and as contradictory as they are in today's world, with the figure of the Lombard of special importance in other Auchinleck romances such as *Bevis of Hampton*. See further D. Pearsall, 'Strangers in Late-Fourteenth-Century London', in *The Stranger in Medieval Society*, ed. F. R. P. Akehurst and S. Cain Van D'Elden (Minneapolis, 1997), pp. 46–62 (p. 53).

[8] M. Barber, 'Western Attitudes to Frankish Greece', in *Latins and Greeks in the Eastern Mediterranean after 1204*, ed. B. Hamilton et al. (London, 1989), pp. 111–28.

of romance illustrate the context through which we can begin to analyse the role that the deployment of place plays in romance. A given romance engages with such pre-existing geographical connotations to use a form of semantic shorthand – a geographical grammar perhaps – by which to convey meaning to the audience. Events that occur in one place may carry a very different meaning than the same event occurring elsewhere: treachery in England, for example, might point towards exceptional and individual transgression of the chivalric and political norm, whereas a similar moment of treachery occurring in Alexandria might simply reinforce the accepted and expected – by the English audience, at least – invidious nature of the place and its inhabitants.

However, this process of narrative spatial pre-conception is not unidirectional. At the same time as romances operate within a background of narratives that provide meaning to the world, they also contribute to this body of narrative. If the audience's geographical imagination is composed of the narratives that they have encountered, then each new romance that they read, each new story that they hear, adds to this accretive and palimpsestic model of geographical knowledge. In this way romance not only articulates the world of its audience, but also actively participates in its construction in a vicariously experiential manner.

Romance as Itinerary, Romance as Writing the World

Cooper describes the correspondence between romance narrative and travel: that 'travel was experienced as linear, however wandering a line it might follow, makes sense of a great deal of what at first appears strange about the journeyings of a questing knight. The story, like an itinerary, focuses on specific foci along the line of travel …'.[9] This form of depicting geography is far from unique to medieval romance, and the itinerary form was the preeminent mode for the dissemination of geographical knowledge in the medieval period. P. D. A. Harley observes that 'the itinerary map seems to have been better understood in medieval Europe than some other kinds of cartography'.[10] Furthermore, not only do narratives such as romance encode spatial itineraries – and thus geographical knowledge – they also permit a form of vicarious travel through the process of experiencing the text. Cooper tells us that 'journeying beyond an area personally known to you required a guide';[11] here I want to extend Cooper's observation by suggesting that romances themselves have the *potential* to act in the form of such a guide,

---

9   Cooper, *English Romance in Time*, p. 70.
10 *Cartography in Prehistoric, Ancient, and Medieval Europe and the Mediterranean*, ed. J. B. Harley and D. Woodward: Volume 1 of *The History of Cartography* (Chicago and London, 1987), pp. 495–6.
11 Cooper, *English Romance in Time*, p. 68.

leading the reader through the textualised world of the narrative – and, in the case of many romances, through the wider 'real' medieval world itself.

So, given that some romances might be thought of as providing a guide for their cartographically-challenged audiences, what kind of world do they lead through? What kind of space do they produce for their audience? Of course, some romances operate within other worlds – Arthurian, Celtic, sometimes too anonymous to identify – which nonetheless often bear a shadowy resemblance to the world of their audience.[12] Other romances – for example those of the so-called Matter of England group – present us with a much more concrete engagement with the 'real' world of medieval England, Europe and beyond. To get a sense of how romance might contribute to the 'writing of the world' I shall examine the construction and articulation of the geography of *Guy of Warwick*.

Guy of Warwick as Exemplar of Romance Geography

The Auchinleck *Guy of Warwick* is a narrative that encompasses a wide geographical reach, with its protagonist travelling extensively throughout Europe and lands of the eastern Mediterranean, and as such it represents a useful case study of the nature of romance geographies. From the sequence of places listed above, we can construct an itinerary that takes us in a series of helical movements from the centre of the romance – Warwick – outwards and back again. I term these movements helical rather than circular as Guy returns from these journeys changed: elevated in reputation and – later – in spiritual standing. The first series of helical journeys involves his attempts to prove himself to his paramour Felice. She sends him first to Normandy, and then on each successive return sends him on a progressively more distant and impressive chivalric journey. This series of movements eventually ends near the beginning of the second – stanzaic – portion of the romance, when she finally agrees to marry him. His marriage, curiously enough, initiates a new form of wandering for our protagonist. Realising that he has spent his life pursuing worldly love, Guy now devotes his life to Christ, and leaves his newly pregnant wife and embarks on a pilgrimage that will occupy the remainder of the romance (*Stanzaic Guy of Warwick*, 241–64).[13] What interests me most about these categories of geographical movements is not so much the places to which Guy travels, but rather the causes of such movement through the world. What *produces* geography in the romance? What propels the protagonist, narrative and audience through the text and the world? What motivates movement in these texts, and thus produces geographical experience and space? Why, rather than how, is this romance geography constructed?

Guy's motivation for travel within the text can be read as falling into two

[12] Cooper terms these romances as being set '*somewhere else*' (*English Romance in Time*, p. 71).
[13] *The Stanzaic Guy of Warwick*, ed. A. Wiggins (Kalamazoo, 2004).

broad categories. His first motivation – to construct, through feats of arms, a superlative chivalric identity in order to win the love of Felice – prompts his travels to Normandy, Spain, Germany, and Lombardy, and eventually the Emperor's court. After this he travels to Constantinople where he completes his secular chivalric maturation. The primary motivation for this section of the romance is the demands of the chivalric maturation romance, allied here – as it often is – to the demands of the game of courtly love. The second movement in the narrative follows Guy's post-nuptial epiphany which moves us into a pilgrimage mode of travel in which Guy visits first – and briefly – Bethlehem and Jerusalem, before travelling onwards throughout the East. The motivation here is clear:

> For mani a bern and knight hardi
> Ich have ysleyn sikerly
> > And strued cites fale
> And for ich have destrued mankin
> Y schal walk for mi sinne
> > Barfot bi doun and dale.
> That ich have with mi bodi wrought,
> With mi bodi it schal be bought
> > To bote me of that bale. (*Stanzaic Guy of Warwick*, 340–8)

Guy's movement here is motivated by a desire for penitential pilgrimage in order to redeem his soul from the perceived sins of his previous chivalric life. These two contrasting motivations for Guy's travel, and the different views of the world that they represent, alert the curious reader to the presence of multiple ideological conceptions of spatial meaning within the text – and within the wider medieval geographical imagination. Geography is not just about charting the physical places of the world, but rather it is a discourse about the significations that these places carry.[14] This is true of geography in all temporal and cultural moments, and this sense of the meaning of the world can be clearly seen in medieval geographies.

Types of Space in *Guy of Warwick*

The movement inherent in these two phases of the narrative of Guy's life produces two types of space: chivalric and religious. In the first part of the romance – up until his religious epiphany – Guy explores the world motivated by his need to perform chivalric deeds. This period of movement 'maps' the world in terms of its relationship to the chivalric programme: Normandy,

14 The work of cultural geographers exemplified by figures such as Yi-Fu Tuan provides an important theorising of the meaning(s) of space and place within human culture (for a discussion see Y-F. Tuan, 'Introduction', in his *Space and Place: The Perspective of Experience* (Minneapolis, 1977), pp. 3–7).

Germany and Spain are sites where chivalry is performed, where suitable opponents are to be found. Once Guy has proved himself superior to the opponents he finds in these parts of Europe, he returns to Warwick, to recount his deeds and seek the approval of Felice. By doing so, Guy inscribes these places with a meaning that becomes a part of his burgeoning reputation. The motivation behind these chivalric journeys is voiced in the condition Felice places upon his suit to her:

> 'Er þou perles holden be
> & best doand in þis cuntre,
> Þat nowhar bi lond no w[e]ter
> No be founde þi beter;
> & when þou art hold best doinde
> In armes þat animan mai finde,
> Þat vnder heuen þi beter no be,
> Mi loue ichil þan graunti þe.'
>
> (Auchinleck *Guy of Warwick*, 1153–60)[15]

The meaning inscribed upon these places by the romance is determined by Guy's need to become *perles*, and takes the form of the subjugation of foreign knights – and foreign chivalry – to his prowess. Worthy opponents may be found in these places, but not as worthy as Guy, the exemplar of English chivalry.

This chivalric understanding of movement – and thus geographical experience, or 'mapping', by the protagonist and for the audience – as a process regulated by chivalric endeavour and success lies at the heart of chivalric romance. Let us consider, as an example, the stock romance trope of a knight and a guarded bridge. On a very basic level, a knight moves through the world of romance via feats of prowess: he defeats knights who guard bridges; he wins access to new places and realms via feats of arms. Knights move outwards from a court – in *Guy* the court of Warwick, embodied in Felice – discovering, or textually-speaking constructing, space. They then return to court – or paramour – and narrate stories of these new places and their occupants, and the symbolic or literal conquest of these new places. Thus the narratives told as part of the chivalric system of exploit and memorialisation act to narrate an expanding and reinscribed world. This manner of theorising how space is revealed – or perhaps constructed – subjugates physical and geographical space to chivalric exploit, and to the needs and desires of the chivalric classes. The world is understood in terms of its hierarchical relationship to the protagonist: he is superior to knights from *there*, charting the nature of the world through a chivalric lens.

However, after Guy's redirection of motivation following his wedding, the world suddenly becomes a very different place for both our hero and

---

15 *Guy of Warwick, Edited from the Auchinleck MS. in the Advocates' Library, Edinburgh, and from MS. 107 in Caius College, Cambridge*, ed. J. Zupitza, EETS ES 42, 49, 59 (London, 1883–91).

his audience. Guy's 'road to Damascus' moment transforms his – and our – understanding of the world from a theatre of chivalric glory into a stage for Christian sin and redemption. This reinscribing of the world in terms of Christian religious space – what Henri Lefebvre has termed 'cryptic space' – presents the audience with a view of the world familiar to us – and them – from cosmological representations of religious space such as the Hereford Map. Guy now visits those places familiar from pilgrimage itineraries – Bethlehem and Jerusalem – presenting the reader with a simplified yet no less spiritually-resonant journey to the heart of the Christ's passion. For the Christian audience, a pilgrimage to the sites of the Holy Land was a transtemporal undertaking, as much a movement through the geography of the passion story as that of the contemporary Levant. To visit such places was to encounter Christ's passion in the most intimate way possible, proving an affective experience unrivalled in the practice of medieval Christian worship. The geography of this second half of the romance takes on Christian meaning in some surprising ways: Guy's defeat of the giant Amoraunt near Alexandria, for example, has the effect of opening up the Holy Land 'That Cristen men schul comen and gon / To her owhen wille in wold' (*Stanzaic Guy of Warwick*, 1052–3). Guy's exploits provide access to the holy places of the East for Christians, both those 'Cristen men' of the romance and those Christian men of his audience. Having delineated, with deliberately broad brushstrokes, a bipartite system of spatial significance in *Guy of Warwick*, I now want to further complicate this reading. Despite the apparent dominance of these two modes of spatial production within the text, this dichotomy is not always as clear and unproblematic as it at first seems, and in certain interstitial episodes of the romance there are more complex motivations for spatial construction to be found.

Interstitial Interruption: Guy's Journey to Constantinople Reconsidered

One of the most memorable narrative movements in *Guy of Warwick* occurs when Guy travels from the court of Emperor Reyner to help defend the city of Constantinople from the onrushing Saracen hordes. This episode produces Guy's first encounter with the East – and the Saracen other – and cements his status as the best knight in Christendom and thus his acceptance by the ever-demanding Felice. It also – notably – is one of his last chivalric deeds before his marriage and religious revelation.[16] The motivation that underlies this episode has been the subject of much comment, as it marks something

---

[16] He does, of course, also then go on to defeat an Irish Dragon in Northumbria, but Constantinople stands as the apex of the quest-and-return sequence of chivalric testing that structures much of the maturation section of the romance.

of a turning point for the narrative.[17] In my 2007 article on the role that the episode plays in Guy's development as a symbolic culture-hero, I argued that while 'this "aventure" has a markedly different tone to those that Guy has undertaken thus far', we should be wary of an 'optimistic reading of the motivations that lie behind Guy's exploits [which] would lead us to view him as already developing into the role of the *milites Christi*'.[18] Instead, I suggested that '[r]ather than casting Guy in the role of a pious *milites Christi*, the romance presents him as the more troubling figure of a crusading knight motivated not by God, but by his own continuing quest for chivalric glory'.[19] However, further analysis of the motivations that underlie the geographical movement of the 'troubling figure' of Guy in the Constantinople episode reveals the complex issues of spatial construction that this episode encodes. While Guy's apparent motivation may perhaps be chivalric exploit, the text seems to posit an alternative catalyst for his actions.

Guy's journey from the Court of the German Emperor Reyner to Constantinople begins in following way:

> On a day as he cam fram hunting
> A dromond he seye ariueing
> Þider-ward sir Gij is y-gon,
> & gret þe marchandes euerichon.
> 'Lordinges, whennes com ye,
> Þat in þis river arived be?
> Bi your semblant y se, y-wisse,
> Þat ye ledde gret richesse.'
> Among hem alle þer spac on,
> Þat couþe speke for hem euerichon:
> 'Fram Costentine þe noble y-comen we be:
> Lond of peys þan seche we.
> Marchandes we ben of þat lond,
> & out y-driuen wiþ michel wrong:
>
> (Auchinleck *Guy of Warwick*, 2801–14)

The merchants make complaint to Guy that they have been wrongfully ejected from the lands of Constantinople, whence they were accustomed to trade:

> Fowe & griis anouy lade we,
> Gold and siluer, & riche stones,
> Þat vertu bere mani for þe nones,

---

17 Guy's motivation, and the possible resonances for the audience, are discussed in R. Wilcox, 'Romancing the East: Greeks and Saracens in *Guy of Warwick*', in *Pulp Fictions of Medieval England: Essays in Popular Romance*, ed. N. McDonald (Manchester, 2004), pp. 217–40, and in Rouse, 'An Exemplary Life'.

18 Rouse, 'An Exemplary Life', p. 98.

19 Rouse, 'An Exemplary Life', p. 99.

Gode cloþes of sikelatoun & Alisaundrinis,
Peloure of Matre, & pu[r]per & biis
(Auchinleck *Guy of Warwick*, 2833–7)

This mercantile complaint, along with the catalogue of luxury goods of which Western trade has now been deprived, presents us with a challenging alternative reading of Guy's motivations for immediately raising a force and departing for Constantinople: that of mercantile interest. This possibility has a number of intriguing implications, not the least of which is the conception of geography. What from a chivalric reading of Guy's motivations might be seen as a mapping of Constantinople as the pre-eminent place in which a Christian knight can seek to prove himself against the cultural Other of the Saracen world, is transformed through a mercantile reading into a depiction of Constantinople's pivotal role in the trade networks of the Eastern Mediterranean. Is Guy charting for the audience a city that stands as bulwark against the heathen and perfidious East, or a city that acts as a permeable trading port? Is he projecting English (and Christian) military power to defend Christendom, or placing his sword at the behest of dangerously liminal eastern merchants?

Trading Spaces: The Mercantile Production of Space

Henri Lefebvre, in his influential study *The Production of Space*, charts – in his typical grand narrative style – the dominant systems of medieval spatial production.[20] Beginning somewhat arbitrarily with the year 1000, Lefebvre characterises medieval Europe as predominantly a 'cryptic' space, comprising a primarily agrarian landscape punctuated with churches, shrines and the pilgrimage routes that ran between them.[21] This is, of course, a simplistic view of the nature of the early medieval world, but one that is nonetheless recognisable as expressive of the Christian ideological view of the world witnessed in texts such as that of the Hereford Map, with its emphasis upon biblical place and narrative.

However, as the medieval period progresses Lefebvre reads a transition from the dominance of this cryptic space through the rise of the medieval town, in which he sees the marketplace as replacing the cathedral as the dominant urban spatial signifier: the increasing complexity and importance of the new urban economies has, for Lefebvre, important consequences for our understanding of medieval spatial production: 'Money and commodities, still *in statu nascendi*, were destined to bring with them not only a "culture", but also a space. The uniqueness of the marketplace, doubtless on account of the splendour of religious and political structure, has tended to be

---

20 H. Lefebvre, *The Production of Space*, trans. D. Nicholson-Smith (London, 1991).
21 Lefebvre, *Production of Space*, p. 254.

overlooked.'[22] Furthermore, the rise of the marketplace had implications well beyond the walls of the *urbis*: 'The medieval revolution brought commerce inside the town and lodged it at the centre of a transformed urban space. The marketplace ... opened up on every side onto the surrounding territory – the territory the town dominated and exploited – and into the countryside's network of roads and lanes.'[23] 'This space which established itself during the Middle Ages ... was by definition a space of exchange and communications, and therefore of networks. What networks? In the first place, networks of overland routes: those of traders, and those of pilgrims and crusaders.'[24]

If we use Lefebvre's conception of the changing nature of medieval space to examine the alternative possible readings of Constantinople in *Guy of Warwick*, it is possible to read a tension between competing ideological discourses that might be seen to be motivating Guy's actions, and the different spatial meaning that these alternatives might produce. So, how do we read this episode? Is Guy motivated by crusading zeal, chivalric glory, or a desire to maintain the trade routes of Christian Europe? Fortunately, we do not have to choose: 'Social space', Lefebvre tells us, 'is multifaceted ... Religious space did not disappear with the advent of commercial space ... Alongside religious space, and even within it, there were places, there was room, for other spaces – for the space of exchange, for the space of power. Representations of space and representational spaces diverged, yet the unity of the whole was not shattered.'[25] Space exists for both chivalric and mercantile understandings of Guy's actions, and of the world that they produce.

This multifaceted reading of the episode perhaps highlights something of the widespread appeal of the Guy narrative, especially if we take into account that the Auchinleck version represents only a minor embellishment of the Anglo-Norman version of the romance. There too we find Gui motivated by a similar tale of mercantile woe. A narrative that can appeal – with essentially the same story – to the baronial audience of the Anglo-Norman version, to the more socially-mixed audience of the Auchinleck manuscript, and to the increasingly popular audiences of its later reception history, must be one upon which a multiplicity of readings can be inscribed.

New Readers, New Readings

One of the implications of this reading of the geography of *Guy of Warwick* is a reminder of the increasing connection between the mercantile classes and the reading of romance that we encounter in late-medieval England. *Guy of Warwick* is an important romance both within the context of the Auchin-

---

[22] Lefebvre, *Production of Space*, p. 265.
[23] Lefebvre, *Production of Space*, p. 265.
[24] Lefebvre, *Production of Space*, p. 266.
[25] Lefebvre, *Production of Space*, p. 266.

leck manuscript and within wider fourteenth-century English culture. Representative of the type of romance that was becoming the reading matter of the expanding gentry and mercantile classes, the narrative can be seen as being increasingly subject to new modes of reading. Melissa Furrow, in her *Expectations of Medieval Romance*, reminds us that '[h]orizons of expectation change as readers change':[26] thus, with new audience expectations and preconceptions of geographical meaning, an episode such as that of Guy's defence of Constantinople, and of romance geographies more generally, can 'write the world' in new and challenging ways.

---

[26] M. Furrow, *Expectations of Romance: The Reception of a Genre in Medieval England* (Cambridge, 2009), p. 58.

11

Romances of Continuity in the English Rous Roll

YIN LIU

Both romance and genealogy depend on the idea of continuity: romance because it is narrative, obviously, and genealogy because its function is to connect the present with the past, to make links and trace lineage. In both romance and genealogy, continuity – fictive or historical – may be constructed or foregrounded when issues of identity or inheritance are at stake. In late medieval England, especially, the interests of chivalric romance and of genealogy converged powerfully;[1] certainly they did so in the work of a fifteenth-century Warwickshire chantry priest, John Rous, whose armorial rolls pressed both romance and genealogy into the service of his patrons, the earls of Warwick. I begin this discussion by exploring briefly a genealogical conundrum related to Warwick's influential local romance, that of Guy of Warwick, to raise the question of whether Rous was writing romance or history – or both.

One theory about the origins of the Anglo-Norman romance *Gui de Warewic*, the poem on which subsequent medieval versions, including the Middle English *Guy of Warwick*, were based, is complicated by a small genealogical problem. Here is the theory.[2] It has been noticed that the Anglo-Norman *Gui* is at great pains to imply that the lords of Wallingford were hereditary stewards of the earls of Warwick. Now Wallingford had been held before the Conquest by Wigot (Wigod), whose name might be rendered in Anglo-Norman as Gwido and thus as Gui; Wigot's daughter Ealdgyth married a Norman, Robert d'Oilly, who may have been a sheriff of Warwick and who held lands in Warwickshire from Thurkil of Arden, one of only

---

[1] For the European context, see R. H. Bloch, *Etymologies and Genealogies: A Literary Anthropology of the French Middle Ages* (Chicago, 1983), and R. L. Radulescu and E. D. Kennedy, eds., *Broken Lines: Genealogical Literature in Medieval Britain and France* (Turnhout, 2008), especially the essay by M. Fisher, 'Genealogy Rewritten: Inheriting the Legendary in Insular Historiography', pp. 123–41.

[2] E. Mason, 'Legends of the Beauchamps' Ancestors: The Use of Baronial Propaganda in Medieval England', *Journal of Medieval History* 10 (1984), 25–40 (pp. 30–2); see also D. Crouch, 'The Local Influence of the Earls of Warwick, 1088–1242: A Study in Decline and Resourcefulness', *Midland History* 21 (1996), 1–22, who also discusses the genealogical problem (p. 20).

three or four Englishmen who still had substantial property at the time of the Domesday survey. When the earldom of Warwick was formed in 1088 and granted to Henry de Beaumont (sometimes styled de Newburgh), a large portion of those lands had belonged to Thurkil, who probably then held them from the new earl as his tenant. Thurkil's descendants continued to be prominent local figures, serving at least twice as stewards to the Beaumont earls of Warwick between 1153 and 1204.[3] Now one important character in the Guy of Warwick story is Guy's foster-father Herhaud of Arderne (Herault de Ardenne), who gives Guy his initial chivalric training and spends much of his later life trying to rescue Guy's son Reinbrun. We thus have a romance in which characters with names that recall historical persons enact close ties between the descendants of Wigot of Wallingford, the earls of Warwick, and the Arden family.

When might such ties have existed? David Crouch has pointed out that the relationship of the Ardens to the Warwick earls became much weaker after 1204, so an earlier date is more likely. Indeed, we find that the d'Oilly family was linked to the Beaumont earls of Warwick by marriage in the twelfth century. The usual version of the genealogy at that point, described in the *Complete Peerage*,[4] is this:

Figure 1. D'Oilly/Beaumont Relations: common version

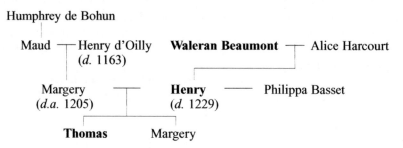

The key relationship here is the marriage of Margery d'Oilly to Earl Henry Beaumont II, and the theory is that *Gui de Warewic* was composed to celebrate that union. Here, however, the genealogical problems begin. When Earl Waleran died in 1204, his heir, Henry, was still a minor, and his wardship was purchased by Thomas Basset. For her part, Margery d'Oilly would have

---

3   Crouch, 'Local Influence', pp. 21–2. D. J. Conlon, ed., *Le Rommant de Guy de Warwik et de Herolt d'Ardenne* (Chapel Hill, 1971), pp. 42–3, notes that Thurkil may have had a daughter named Felicia, whose name is that of the heroine of the romance. For the Arden family, see A. Williams, 'A Vice-Comital Family in Pre-Conquest Warwickshire', in *Anglo-Norman Studies XI: Proceedings of the Battle Conference 1988*, ed. R. A. Brown (Woodbridge, 1989), pp. 279–95.

4   *The Complete Peerage of England, Scotland, Ireland, Great Britain and the United Kingdom*, ed. G. E. Cokayne, rev. ed. V. Gibbs, XII/2 (Tracton to Zouche), ed. G. H. White (Gloucester, 1982), pp. 364–5.

been at least in her forties. The genealogy presented here thus requires us to believe that Henry fathered two children on a woman in her forties before he himself reached his teens, a situation that might be most kindly described as an improbability.

A recent correction to the genealogy, however, solves our problems and also happens to be corroborated by some independent documentary evidence.[5] The corrected genealogy looks like this:

Figure 2. D'Oilly/Beaumont Relations: corrected version

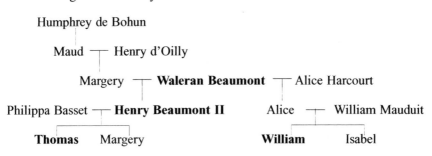

The main change is that Margery d'Oilly married not Henry Beaumont II, but his father, Waleran. To suggest that the Anglo-Norman *Gui* was created to celebrate *that* union now makes sense, and gives us a date before 1204 for the composition of the poem. It also supports the idea that the romance of Guy of Warwick was originally meant to be a topical, even a political text, using family legend to enhance the reputations of historical people.

The mistaken genealogy that made it into the *Complete Peerage* and continued to mystify scholars comes ultimately from a fifteenth-century source, an armorial roll produced by John Rous, chaplain of Guyscliff, Warwick. Rous's surviving works are his Latin history of England, *Historia regum Angliae* (British Library, Cotton Vespasian MS A. XII), and his two armorial rolls, the Latin Roll (College of Arms MS Warwick Roll) probably serving as the basis for the English version, British Library Additional MS 48976.[6] I will focus my discussion here on the English Rous Roll, and will explore especially its uses of romance.

Rous has a dubious reputation among modern historians. They are grateful for his valuable list of depopulated Warwickshire villages, which Rous included in the *Historia* to show the dire effects of fifteenth-century enclo-

5   R. Bevan, 'A Realignment of the 12th and 13th Century Pedigree of the Earls of Warwick – Complete Peerage Correction', *Foundations* 1.3 (2004), 194–7.

6   An inscription on the dorse of the English Roll attributes its production to 'Master John Rows of Warrewyk', and Rous can probably be identified with Scribe C, who is responsible for the genealogies and corrections in the English Roll, and for the entire text of the Latin Roll. See C. E. Wright, 'The Rous Roll: The English Version', *British Museum Quarterly* 20 (1957), 78–9; and K. L. Scott, *Later Gothic Manuscripts 1390–1490*, II (London, 1996), p. 361.

sures, but also accuse him of narrow-mindedness and parochialism. He is also charged with being a time-server and turncoat. Both Rous Rolls, which were made during the reign of Richard III, were originally complimentary to that king; the English Roll in particular names Richard's son Edward of Middleham as Prince of Wales (which means that the Roll was finished between 8 September 1483 and 9 April 1484) and presents a blandly positive picture of Richard III, saying that he punished extortioners, ruled commendably, and was universally praised. The Latin Roll must have included a similar encomium, but after the death of Richard III and the accession of Henry VII in 1485, the now-despised Yorkist king was physically cut out of the Latin Roll and other changes were performed to make it less Yorkist. Even more obviously, Rous's *Historia*, finished in 1486 and dedicated to the new King Henry, savages Richard's reputation, repeating rumours that the former monarch had been born with all his teeth after a gestation of two years, describing him as a deformed and merciless tyrant, and comparing him to Antichrist.[7]

But the most persistent complaint about Rous is what modern historians often regard as his regrettable credulity. Commentators acknowledge that Rous took pains to consult practically every source a fifteenth-century scholar could be expected to know: Cicero, Aristotle, Seneca, Augustine, Gregory, Isidore of Seville, Albertus Magnus, Nicholas of Lyra, Bernard de Breydenbach, Caesarius of Heisterbach, Martinus Polonus, Vincent of Beauvais, Petrus Berchorius, Gildas, Gerald of Wales, Gervase of Tilbury, Ranulf Higden, Geoffrey of Monmouth, Bede, John of Worcester, William of Malmesbury, Henry of Huntingdon, Ralph Diceto, William of Newburgh, Roger of Howden, Matthew Paris, Nicholas Trevet, John Harding, Mandeville's *Travels*, the *Brut*, Domesday Book, and monastic chronicles in Evesham, Osney, Winchester, and Wales.[8] Such a man was obviously no ignoramus, but at the same time Rous is accused of being utterly undiscriminating, accepting legend and history with equal facility. This charge may be true, but it is also unfair, as an examination of the English Rous Roll will show.

The English Rous Roll presents four different kinds of narrative. Most of the text consists of the brief biographical descriptions that accompany each figure in the Roll. Above them are pen-and-ink portraits of the persons thus described, usually in armour if male, robed if female, and surrounded by or holding symbolic objects, such as churches they built. Above each portrait is the person's complete coat of arms, in colour. Between the portraits are genealogical charts, sometimes very elaborate, not always accurate, showing the relationships of the earls of Warwick to the royal line and to other prom-

---

7   See the discussion by A. Gransden, *Historical Writing in England*, II (London, 1982), p. 316. The passage from the *Historia* that describes the life of Richard III can be found in the print edition by T. Hearne (Oxford, 1716), pp. 212–18, and an English translation (from the MS) by A. Hanham, *Richard III and His Early Historians, 1483–1535* (Oxford, 1975), pp. 118–24.

8   Most of these are listed by Gransden, *Historical Writing*, pp. 321–2. I have added a few to her list.

inent noble families. Monarchs are marked with little gold crowns above their roundels. These four forms of narrative, mutually supporting, project a sense of continuity through the Roll, so that figure follows figure in unbroken succession. The accretion of legend in the Roll is most obvious at its beginning, which gives an account of the origins of the earldom of Warwick. We are told that the city of Warwick was founded by King Guthelin, who originally called it Caerleon.[9] Guthelin was an invention of Geoffrey of Monmouth, who hardly mentions Warwick at all, but, by identifying Warwick with Caerleon, Rous manages to work his beloved hometown right into the middle of the Galfridian master narrative.[10] The bear and ragged staff on the badge of Warwick are also given fictitious origins. Rous claims that the bear is a punning reference to Arthgall or Artegal, a Welsh earl of Warwick (Welsh *arth* meaning 'bear'),[11] and that the ragged staff alludes to a fight between Gwayr, another pre-Saxon lord of Warwick and cousin of King Arthur, and a giant who carried a stripped tree trunk as a club.[12]

These origin legends all appear in the first part of the Roll, which is primarily a list of kings and other notable figures who contributed to the prosperity of Warwick in some way. This is followed by the main sequence of the Roll, a chronological list of the earls of Warwick. The series begins with Enyas, the Knight of the Swan, here explicitly described as an ancestor of the Warwick earls. The next figure is his descendant Rohaud, the Earl of Warwick in the Guy romance. He is followed by his daughter Felice, Guy's wife, and then by the legendary Guy himself, who gets two sections that describe his martial prowess, his disguise as a pilgrim, his defeat of the giant Colbrond, and his saintly death at Guyscliff. Predictably, the next figure in the sequence is Guy's son Reinbrun. He is followed by a series of Saxons of doubtful historicity – Wegeat, Ufa, Wolgeat, Wygod – and a real Saxon, Ailwyn (Æthelwine) and his son, the historical Thurkil of Arden, here promoted to Earl of Warwick, whose daughter Margaret, says Rous, married Henry of Newburgh (i.e. Henry Beaumont), the first Norman earl. At this point, says Kendrick,

---

9   Rous Roll, item 1: 'kyng guthelyne or kenelyn holekyng of grete Brytayn ... made thys borow abowte the byrthe of kyng Alysaunder the grete conquerowr on of the ix worthy and named hyt Caerleon.' Quotations from the English Rous Roll are from my transcription. Numbering of the items in the Roll follows W. Courthope, ed., *The Rous Roll* (Gloucester, 1980; originally published 1645). Courthope's edition prints the text of the Roll and reproduces (in line drawings) the images, but omits the genealogies.

10 Geoffrey of Monmouth, *The History of the Kings of Britain*, ed. M. D. Reeve, trans. N. Wright (Woodbridge, 2007), pp. 60–1 (Book 3, §47). Geoffrey makes no connection between Guthelin and Warwick.

11 Rous Roll, item 7. Geoffrey of Monmouth mentions 'Arthgal Cargueirensis, quae nunc Warwic appellatur', who is present at Arthur's coronation (Book 9, §156, pp. 210–11).

12 Rous Roll, item 5. The story of the giant is not in Geoffrey. Of Geoffrey's fictitious British place name, J. S. P. Tatlock, *The Legendary History of Britain: Geoffrey of Monmouth's Historia Regum Britanniae and its Early Vernacular Versions* (Berkeley, 1950), notes that it is a 'good but unprecedented British name': 'Caer-gueir, a natural enough alteration of Warewic, would mean Hay-town, natural enough in such a country, and would show Geoffrey's knowledge of Welsh' (p. 28).

'it is with a sense of refreshment and thanksgiving that we turn from Rous's medieval vision of his country's ancient history to his work as a practical antiquary'.[13] In other words, at this point the legends end and the real history begins.

Of course, Rous would not have seen it that way. What we moderns see as a sharp divide between fiction and history, he did not see at all. In the parts of the Roll that deal with the historical earls of Warwick, he has no trouble telling us that it was during the tenure of Earl Guy Beauchamp (who was, incidentally, probably named after the legendary Guy of romance) that the famous outlaws Robin Hood and Little John lived, and, says Rous, 'hit is maruel that no chroniclar writis of hem'. In the same section, he tells us that the greatest crime of Piers Gaveston was that 'he solde also owt of the land the round table of siluer that was kyng arthurs'.[14] Rous, always meticulous in his scholarship, could produce hard evidence for his early history of Warwick, the part modern historians dismiss as legend. For figures such as Guthelin or Arthgall he could cite that influential authority Geoffrey of Monmouth. For Gwayr he appeals to some mysterious chronicles that he found in Wales. For Enyas he produces an actual artefact. According to the legend, Enyas's enchanted siblings are able to control their transformations into swans by means of golden necklaces, one of which, unfortunately, is melted down to make a cup. This golden cup, says Rous, is in the treasury at Warwick Castle, and he himself has drunk from it.[15] The mysterious Saxon earls that Rous lists show how he collected his information. At some point he visited Evesham Abbey, where he was able to consult a chronicle, probably Thomas of Marlborough's thirteenth-century history of the abbey. Thomas records that 'In the year *Anno Domini* 973 Ufa "the Huuede", earl of Warwick, gave to the church of St Mary and St Ecgwine, with the assent of King Edgar, Wixford and Grafton Minor'.[16] This information, which Rous quotes very closely, appears to be based on an Evesham charter, dated 962,[17] which Rous may also have seen. Rous could not be expected to know that the charter was

13 T. D. Kendrick, *British Antiquity* (London, 1950), p. 27.
14 Rous Roll, item 46. I have been unable to trace the origin of the story about Gaveston. Rous's reference to the Round Table is to the fourteenth-century table in the Great Hall at Winchester; see M. Biddle, *King Arthur's Round Table: An Archaeological Investigation* (Woodbridge, 2000). Rous may have been speculating on the basis of the well-known story that Gaveston had stolen the crown jewels.
15 The cup was acquired sometime before 1400 by the Beauchamp earls of Warwick, who enthusiastically collected such artefacts; they also acquired Guy of Warwick's sword and armour. These items are listed in the will of Earl Thomas Beauchamp (d. 1401), 1 April 1400: see *Testamenta vetusta*, I, ed. N. H. Nicolas (London, 1826), p. 154.
16 'Anno ab incarnatione Domini nongentesimo septuagesimo tercio Huue þe Huuede, come Warewikie, dedit ecclesie beate Marie et beati Ecgwini, consentiente rege Eadgaro, Witlakesforde et Greftone Minorem.' Thomas of Marlborough, *History of the Abbey of Evesham*, ed. and trans. J. Sayers and L. Watkiss (Oxford, 2003), pp. 134–5.
17 British Library, Harley MS 3763, fol. 64r (s. xii). Listed in P. H. Sawyer, *Anglo-Saxon Charters: An Annotated List and Bibliography* (London, 1968) as no. 1214; in C. R. Hart, *The Early Charters of Northern England and the North Midlands* (Leicester, 1975) as no. 56.

a forgery.[18] The point is that, from Rous's perspective, all this early history of Warwick could be documented, from sources that he, at any rate, had no reason to doubt.

One feature of the Rous Rolls would have been difficult to substantiate from early sources – the heraldic arms for any figure before the twelfth century. Still, it was common to assign armorial bearings to Arthurian knights and other fictional persons, and so Rous was not unusual in assuming that heraldry had somehow always existed. Nevertheless, what is significant in the English Rous Roll is the extent to which heraldry reinforces the main narrative and covers any potentially embarrassing gaps. Thus Rous has no evidence, and therefore cannot say outright, that his Saxon earls are direct descendants of Guy of Warwick's son Reinbrun; but the device of the ragged staff, which in the Roll is first adopted by the giant-killer Gwayr, is displayed not only by Reinbrun but also by all the Saxon earls, making the line of descent obvious. Even more ingeniously, Rous claims that the first to bear the Beauchamp arms of the earls of Warwick were the descendants of Enyas, who by this device were commemorating the episode in the romance where an angel presents the young Enyas with a magical shield on which is blazoned a golden cross; in combat, fire springs from the cross and blinds the Swan Knight's opponent. The shield of Enyas thus becomes the basis of the Beauchamp arms: *gules, a fess or between six cross crosslets or*. Furthermore, the first figure in the Roll to bear the arms of the Beaumont/Newburgh earls of Warwick is not a Beaumont, but the romance hero Guy of Warwick, whose descendants up to the first Beauchamp earl also include in their arms an image of Guy's famous adversary, the giant Colbrond. The heraldry of the English Rous Roll therefore presents a visual narrative of continuity that makes explicit the direct connections between the romance figures Enyas and Guy and the historical earls of Warwick. The Beauchamp and Beaumont arms are well attested in thirteenth-century heraldic manuscripts – in fact, Earl Waleran Beaumont's use of a chequered shield on his seals in the twelfth century is one of the first instances we have of a systematic use of heraldry in England[19] – but in the Rous Roll those arms extend backward in time to an origin in the founding legends of Warwick.

Thus, rather than presenting us with the modern dichotomy between legend and history, Rous constructs a narrative of continuity based on genealogy, on lineal descent. The Welsh chronicles that Rous consulted, he informs us, trace the ancestry of Gwayr 'from hym to our formast fader Adam'.[20] Rous deals with the potentially embarrassing disunity of pre-Conquest England by assuring us that intermarriage between the Saxon kings meant that anyone

[18] Sayers and Watkiss note that it 'was probably forged at Evesham between 1097 and 1104' (p. 135 n. 5); see also Hart, no. 56.
[19] D. Crouch, 'The Historian, Lineage and Heraldry 1050–1250', in *Heraldry, Pageantry and Social Display in Medieval England*, ed. P. Coss and M. Keen (Woodbridge, 2002), pp. 29–33; also discussed in Crouch, *The Beaumont Twins* (Cambridge, 1986), pp. 10–12, 211–12.
[20] Rous Roll, item 5.

descended from one king was descended from them all[21] – as if the multi-plicity of kingdoms should concentrate rather than disperse the royal blood. Earl Rohaud, from whom Guy of Warwick inherits the kingdom, is 'lyneally descendid' of the 'Saxon blode' of the Swan Knight.[22] Guy himself may be the son of a lowly baron of Wallingford, but his mother is 'of the noblest blode' of Italy.[23] Henry, the first Norman earl, is described as being closely related to both Edward the Confessor and William the Conqueror. He was a rela-tion, albeit a distant one.[24] Where the line of descent is hazy – for example, Rous admits that he does not know the names of the Saxon earls between Enyas and Rohaud, and does not explicitly say that Rohaud had children – the heraldic narrative assures us that the succession continues unbroken. Between the portraits on the Roll, genealogical charts, sometimes very elabo-rate and not always accurate, illustrate the relationships between the Warwick line and other notable families of the kingdom, including the royal family. Along the way, Rous manages to connect the earls of Warwick to two of the Nine Worthies, Arthur and Godfrey of Bouillon.[25] The Warwick line thus unrolls in ever-increasing splendour, accumulating illustrious names, until Queen Anne, the daughter of Earl Richard Neville, the Kingmaker, can be described as 'borne of the ryall blode of dyuers realmes lenyally descendying from pryncis kyngys emperowris & mony gloryous seyntys'.[26]

This linear series of invariably praiseworthy nobles, the reconstructed heraldry, the effervescent genealogical diagrams, the very physical form of this roll – a strip of parchment seven metres long – smooth over a messier reality. Take, for example, the way in which Rous bridges that quintessen-tial discontinuity, the Norman Conquest. The earldom of Warwick was in fact created in 1088 for the Norman lord Henry de Beaumont, possibly as a reward for supporting William Rufus against the rebellion of that year. Henry's father Roger had received a small Warwickshire estate after the Conquest, and to this were added some lands from Henry's brother Robert, Count of Meulan and later Earl of Leicester, and also the lands of the Englishman Thurkil of Arden.[27] That Thurkil exchanged his status as one of the few

---

21 Rous Roll, item 11: 'And soo the kynges were cosyns ech to odur and who euer com lyneally of on com of all bothe of kynges Quenys and grete lordys and ladies and cosyns of blode to many holy and Glorius Seyntys.'

22 Rous Roll, item 19.

23 Rous Roll, item 21.

24 Henry's great-grandfather had married a sister of Edward's grandmother, who had married William's great-grandfather. This hardly makes Earl Henry a 'ner cosyn' to either king, as Rous claims (item 31).

25 Constantine (item 4) is Arthur's grandfather, and Gwayr (item 5) his 'ny cosyn'. William Beau-mont (d. 1184), according to Rous, married the sister of the wife of the son of Godfrey of Bouillon. Rous is quite wrong; William's first wife was Matilda de Percy, whose sister Agnes (d. c.1202) married Joscelin de Louvain (d. 1180). Joscelin was not the son of the legendary Crusader but of the later Godefroi duke of Brabant (Lower Lotharingia) and count of Louvain (d. 1140).

26 Rous Roll, item 62.

27 *Complete Peerage*, XII/2, p. 358, citing Orderic Vitalis; Crouch, 'Local Influence', *passim*; on Thurkil of Arden see Williams, 'Vice-Comital Family', p. 291.

remaining English landowners of any stature for a subservient position as the Earl of Warwick's tenant has not endeared him to modern historians, who have called him, among other things, a 'Conquest quisling'.[28] Rous deals with this uncomfortable episode of political expediency by a genealogical sleight of hand. He first makes Thurkil the last Saxon earl of Warwick. Then he has Thurkil's daughter Margaret marry Henry Beaumont, the first Norman earl. Thus the earldom passes smoothly by marriage from Saxon to Norman, and the great cultural and political divide is neatly bridged. However, this genealogy is patently false. We have no record of a daughter of Thurkil named Margaret, and the Margaret that Henry actually married was a Norman lady, the daughter of Geoffrey, Count of Perche and Mortagne.[29] All the same, it was necessary for Rous's project that there be no break in the links that bound the fifteenth-century earls of Warwick to their illustrious ancestors, particularly to such eminent figures as Enyas and Guy. To inherit Warwick was necessarily to inherit its glorious past.

It remains for us to ask what Rous's project was, and what point there may have been to his genealogical shenanigans. Certainly we must believe that Rous had a personal and scholarly interest in the local history of Warwick – particularly in the history of Guyscliff, his own chantry – and in the family history of his patrons, the Warwick earls. It has often been suggested that Rous probably had political motives as well as personal ones: specifically, that the two Rous Rolls and a related manuscript, the Beauchamp Pageant (probably not by Rous but probably known by him), were produced to urge the Crown to restore the Warwick inheritance to the dowager Countess Anne, the widow of Earl Richard Neville, the Kingmaker.[30]

The English Rous Roll, completed in the first year of Richard III's troubled reign, also came into being at a period of crisis in the earldom itself. Upon the deaths of the last Beauchamp lord of Warwick, Duke Henry, and his young daughter Anne, the Warwick inheritance passed by right of Henry's sister Anne Beauchamp to her husband, Richard Neville, over vigorous objections from Anne's half-sisters. Richard Neville's death in 1471 launched a bitter dispute between his two sons-in-law, George Duke of Clarence and Richard Duke of Gloucester, over the Warwick inheritance. The settlement that gave George the earldom of Warwick in 1474 treated the dowager Countess Anne – who, as the Croyland Chronicler noted, had a better claim than either of

---

28 The words are those of P. Coss, *Lordship, Knighthood and Locality* (Cambridge, 1991), p. 46.

29 *Complete Peerage*, XII/2, p. 360, citing Orderic; David Crouch, 'Oddities in the Early History of the Marcher Lordship of Gower, 1107–1166', *Bulletin of the Board of Celtic Studies* 31 (1984), 133–41, citing Orderic and Robert of Torigny (p. 133).

30 For this view see M. Lowry, 'John Rous and the Survival of the Neville Circle', *Viator* 19 (1988), 327–38 (especially pp. 336–7); and M. W. Driver, '"In her owne persone semly and bewteus": Representing Women in Stories of Guy of Warwick', in *Guy of Warwick: Icon and Ancestor*, ed. A. Wiggins and R. Field (Cambridge, 2007), pp. 133–53 (especially pp. 151–3). For the Beauchamp Pageant, see the edition by A. Sinclair, *The Beauchamp Pageant* (Donington, 2003), and the discussion by Scott, *Later Gothic Manuscripts*, II, pp. 355–9.

her sons-in-law – as if she were dead. Her rights were not restored until 1486, under the new Tudor king.[31]

The English Rous Roll in particular contains some pointed lessons on preserving the Warwick inheritance intact and ensuring an orderly succession. For example, Rous is our only source for a highly unlikely story that William, one of the Beaumont earls, returned from crusade after 1184 to challenge his brother Waleran, who had succeeded as earl on the assumption that William was dead. By selling bits of the Warwick estates to finance their campaigns and win supporters, William and Waleran, Rous says, 'made of a ryche and notable Eorldam but a pore thyng to the grete hurt of there successurs'.[32] The less exciting reality was that the twelfth-century Beaumont earls had frittered away their resources through bad management, but Rous's apocryphal story of the dispute between brothers surely invited comparison to the wrangles over the Warwick inheritance in the 1470s.

It is also worth noting that in the main narrative line of the English Rous Roll, the sequence of earls of Warwick, Rous includes every woman through which the succession passed. For example, another threat to the continuity of the earldom had occurred in the thirteenth century, when the Beaumonts ran out of male heirs. When Earl Thomas died in 1242, the female heir, the recently widowed Margery, was married by the king's command to John de Plessis – probably against her will, as rumours of a previous betrothal suggest. The doubtful legitimacy of this forced marriage meant that the earldom reverted to the Beaumont line after John de Plessis's death – specifically, to William Mauduit, the son of Alice Beaumont.[33] When he died without issue, the inheritance passed through his sister Isabel to her son, William Beauchamp, the first of the Beauchamp earls. Thus the transfer of the earldom from one family to the other was made possible when the next earl inherited by right of his wife – in other words, when the succession passed through a woman. Let us recall that before describing the shift from Beaumont to Beauchamp earls in the thirteenth century, Rous had already presented us with the same pattern in the transfer of the Warwick estates from the Saxon earls to the Norman, through the marriage of the allegedly Saxon Margaret, daughter of Thurkil of Arden, to a Norman lord. Of course, the precedent for this pattern is found in the romance of Guy of Warwick, who inherits the earldom by right of his wife Felice. From Felice, who is Countess of Warwick while her husband is wandering about Europe disguised as a pilgrim, to the compli-

---

[31] A detailed discussion of this affair can be found in M. A. Hicks, 'Descent, Partition and Extinction: The "Warwick Inheritance"', *Bulletin of the Institute of Historical Research* 52 (1979), 116–28.

[32] Rous Roll, item 33. E. Mason argues that there may be a substratum of truth to the story about William and Waleran, although she acknowledges that no direct evidence can be found: 'Fact and Fiction in the English Crusading Tradition: The Earls of Warwick in the Twelfth Century', *Journal of Medieval History* 14 (1988), 81–95.

[33] E. Mason, *The Beauchamp Cartulary: Charters 1100–1268* (London, 1980), p. xl; P. Coss, *The Lady in Medieval England 1000–1500* (Mechanicsburg, 1998), pp. 121–3.

cations of the thirteenth century from which the Beauchamps benefited so richly, the earldom of Warwick continues, according to the narrative in the Roll, because it is inherited by a woman. It takes little effort to extend the precedent to the case of the dispossessed Countess Anne, who is, says Rous, 'by trew enheritans countas of Warrewik'.[34]

Our modern distinction between romance and history has meant that many medieval forms of narrative fall into the gap between. Literary scholars may pass over something like the English Rous Roll because it is the territory of historians, but historians dismiss much of the material in the Roll because it is the stuff of romance. The generous dose of legend in the English Rous Roll may be an embarrassment to historians, but can be of great interest to literary scholars. It reminds us, first, that in the late fifteenth century the fictionality of incendiary shields from heaven, tree-wielding giants, pilgrim-knights recognised only on their deathbeds, or – for that matter – Saxon earls bearing Norman coats of arms, would not have been obvious even to a scholar like John Rous, who had, after all, authorities like Geoffrey of Monmouth and artefacts like the Cup of the Swan to back him up. Secondly, this equivalence of romance and history meant that romance in the fifteenth century was not necessarily an escapist genre but was directly relevant to immediate social and political concerns. It is possible that the original Guy of Warwick romance, inspired by the marriage of Margery d'Oilly to Earl Waleran, was intended to promote the reputation of the d'Oilly, Arden, and Beaumont families. Almost three centuries later, the self-justifying nexus of land, lineage, and lady that forms the ideological basis of the medieval English romance was perpetrated again by the English Rous Roll, this time possibly to restore the Warwick inheritance to the unfortunate Countess Anne by drawing attention to her glorious ancestry.

Rous was only one figure in a long history of Warwick self-promotion, albeit one who was a major source for William Dugdale's seventeenth-century classic of local history, *The Antiquities of Warwickshire*, and whose genealogical mistakes appear in the *Complete Peerage*. Relics of Guy of Warwick, including such items as a rib of the Dun Cow and Guy's horse armour, were on display at the castle through the nineteenth century, and 'Guy of Warwick's sword' is still visible there today. Warwick Castle is now a subsidiary of Merlin Entertainments. For a fee, the modern tourist can visit 'Britain's Ultimate Castle' and, as one advertisement says, 'experience the legend and live the adventure'. We cannot know what John Rous would have thought of this transformation of his local castle into a medieval theme park, but his own work shows that one of the persistent features of romance is its striking adaptability to new contexts.

---

[34] Rous Roll, item 56. See also the discussion by Driver, '"In her owne persone"', pp. 151–3.

12

'Ex Libris domini duncani / Campbell de glenwrquhay/ miles': *The Buik of King Alexander the Conquerour* in the household of Sir Duncan Campbell, seventh laird of Glenorchy

EMILY WINGFIELD

*T*he Buik of King Alexander the Conquerour* (hereafter *BKA*) is one of two surviving Older Scots Alexander romances.[1] In a little over nineteen thousand lines, this romance offers a full biography of Alexander's career, conquests and death. It supplements its main source, the second recension of the Latin *Historia de Preliis*, by drawing not only upon the Old French *Roman d'Alexandre*, and interpolations to it such as the *Voeux du Paon* and *Voyage au Paradis*,[2] but also upon the pseudo-Aristotelian *Secreta Secretorum* and several pieces of otherwise-independent Older Scots conduct literature.[3]

BKA is extant in British Library Additional MS 40732 (MS A) and National Archives of Scotland MS GD 112/71/9 (MS B). In both, the poem is acephalous. We thus lack its prologue and are forced to rely on the enigmatic final lines (19311–69) for information about its composition.[4] These final lines are not composed by the poem's author, nor simply by a scribe. They are instead written by a redactor, who claims to have rewritten and in the process 'mendit' the 'faltis' of the 'noble buike' (line 19343). He reports that he began this task in the May of 1499 and completed it in August of that year (lines

---

[1]   *The Buik of King Alexander the Conquerour by Sir Gilbert Hay*, ed. J. Cartwright, 2 vols, STS, 4th series, 16, 18 (Edinburgh, 1986; Aberdeen, 1990). All subsequent citations from this edition. The other Older Scots Alexander romance is the 1438 octosyllabic *Buik of Alexander*. See *The Buik of Alexander*, ed. R. L. Graeme Ritchie, 4 vols, STS, 2nd series, 12, 17, 21, 25 (Edinburgh, 1921–29).

[2]   J. Cartwright, 'Sir Gilbert Hay and the *Alexander* Tradition', in *Scottish Language and Literature, Medieval and Renaissance: Fourth International Conference 1984 Proceedings*, ed. D. Strauss and H. W. Drescher (Frankfurt, 1986), pp. 229–38; J. Cartwright, 'Sir Gilbert Hay's *Alexander*: A Study in Transformations', *Medium Aevum* 60 (1991), 61–72.

[3]   S. Mapstone, 'The Scots *Buke of Phisnomy* and Sir Gilbert Hay', in *The Renaissance in Scotland: Studies in Literature, Religion, History and Culture Offered to John Durkan*, ed. A. A. MacDonald, M. Lynch and I. B. Cowan (Leiden, 1994), pp. 1–44.

[4]   The missing 'Prolog' is referred to at line 19294.

19354–5). He also provides details of the poem's genesis, informing us that it was 'translaittit' 'out of the Frensche leid' 'At þe instance off Lord Erskein, be S*chir* Gilbert þe Hay' (lines 19319–20, 19334). Most scholars accept this attribution of *BKA* to Hay whilst recognising that the surviving version of the romance is at some remove from his original composition written c.1460 for Thomas, second Lord Erskine (d. c.1493).[5]

Studies of *BKA* made over the last thirty years have focused on either the poem's sources or themes, particularly kingship and good governance.[6] By contrast, the manuscript's two surviving witnesses have received little attention, although they have much to reveal about the activities of the scribes and readers of romance in sixteenth-century Scotland. Manuscripts A and B were both owned in the late sixteenth century by Sir Duncan Campbell, 7th laird of Glenorchy (1551×4–1631). It is not at all difficult to understand why he desired a copy of Hay's tale of Alexander's conquests since during the fifteenth and sixteenth centuries – and particularly under the leadership of Duncan Campbell and his father Colin Campbell, 6th laird (1499–1583) – the Glenorchy Campbells engaged in a phenomenal phase of territorial expansion throughout the central highlands.[7] They rose to a position of dominance via their deft exploitation of feudal rights and bonds of manrent,[8] a series of successful marriage alliances with Lowland families, and tenure of important positions at court. They strengthened their increasing territorial base with a policy of castle building and land development, and this, coupled with their support of the reformed religion and patronage of both Gaelic learned orders and Lowland professionals, ensured that the Glenorchy Campbells became one of sixteenth-century Scotland's most important and influential families.

In the first half of this chapter, I thus return to the late sixteenth-century manuscript contexts of Hay's *BKA*, focusing on the numerous flyleaf signatures and inscriptions which illustrate the lively literary community in which *BKA* was read.[9] The second half of the chapter situates Duncan Campbell's ownership of *BKA* within the context of his wider literary collection.

---

5   For further details of Hay's career, see S. Mapstone, 'The Advice to Princes Tradition in Scottish Literature, 1450–1500', unpublished D.Phil. thesis (Oxford, 1986), pp. 48–53. M. P. McDiarmid argues against Hay's authorship of *BKA* in 'Concerning Sir Gilbert Hay, the Authorship of *Alexander the Conquerour* and *The Buik of Alexander*', *Studies in Scottish Literature* 28 (1993), 28–54 (30–3).

6   Most recently, J. Martin, *Kingship and Love in Scottish Poetry, 1424–1540* (Aldershot, 2008), pp. 61–78.

7   Rev. W. A. Gillies, *In Famed Breadalbane: The Stories of the Antiquities, Lands, and People of a Highland District* (Perth, 1938), pp. 114–42; M. MacGregor, 'A Political History of the MacGregors before 1571', unpublished Ph.D thesis (Edinburgh, 1989), pp. 96–197.

8   J. Wormald, *Lords and Men in Scotland: Bonds of Manrent, 1442–1603* (Edinburgh, 1985), esp. pp. 101–2.

9   Detailed palaeographical descriptions of the two manuscripts are provided in my Oxford D.Phil. thesis, 'The Manuscript and Print Contexts of Older Scots Romance' (2010), Chap 2.

Scribes, Owners and Readers: The Flyleaf Evidence

Over the last ten years, bibliographical scholarship has paid increasing attention to the annotations and inscriptions found on the margins and flyleaves
of manuscripts and early printed books.[10] These provide valuable indications
of how late medieval and early modern readers responded to their texts and
also allow scholars to compile information about literary and book-owning
communities. The signatures and inscriptions on the two surviving witnesses
of *BKA* are no exception.

MS A Front Flyleaf I (recto)
This flyleaf contains the following signature at its centre: 'duncan Campbell
of glenvrquhie/ This buik pertenis onto him *etc*./ 1579'. It is repeated below
with the dates 1581, 1582, and 'the iiij of maii', and further signatures and
initials of Duncan Campbell surround it, as well as an unidentified notarial
sign manual.[11] MS A was thus in Duncan Campbell's possession by 1579 –
before he succeeded his father as laird of Glenorchy in 1583 – and was read
again by him at intervals over the following three years.

Front flyleaf I also contains several vernacular inscriptions, some of which
are now illegible. Those which can be read include 'The man is blist yat hes
nocht ben[t?]'. This incomplete sentence recalls the opening line of the first
Psalm as it appears in *The Forme of Prayers ... with the whole Psalmes of
David in English meter*: 'The man is blest that hath not bent to wicked rede
his eare'. The *Forme of Prayers*, otherwise known as *The Book of Common
Order*, was first published by the Edinburgh printer Robert Lekpreuik in 1564
(STC 16577) and derived from the Anglo-Genevan Psalter of 1556 (and the
later 1561 edition).[12] The inclusion of this inscription here points towards
the devotional household context in which the manuscript was read since the
Campbells of Glenorchy and their relatives, the Campbell earls of Argyll,
were staunch supporters of the reformed religion.[13]

Below this psalm quotation, and also upside down at the bottom of the
page, are the beginnings of the 'In my defence god me defend' prayer (NIMEV
1509), which frequently occurs on the flyleaves and margins of Older Scots

---

[10] Most recently, W. H. Sherman, *Used Books: Marking Readers in Renaissance England* (Philadelphia, 2008); A. Wiggins, 'What Did Renaissance Readers Write in their Printed Copies of
Chaucer?', *The Library* 9 (2008), 3–36.

[11] I suspect that this belongs to the Alexander Levingstoun who signed back flyleaf IV. See below.

[12] M. Patrick, *Four Centuries of Scottish Psalmody* (London, 1949), pp. 45–55.

[13] J. Dawson, 'Clan, kin, and Kirk: the Campbells and the Scottish Reformation', in *The Education
of a Christian Society: Humanism and Reformation in Britain and the Netherlands*, ed. N. Scott
Amos, A. Pettegree and H. van Nierop (Aldershot, 1999), pp. 211–42; and her 'The Protestant
Earl and Godly Gael: The Fifth Earl of Argyll (c.1538–73) and the Scottish Reformation', in *Life
and Thought in the Northern Church c.1100–1700. Essays in Honour of Claire Cross*, ed. D.
Wood, Studies in Church History, Subsidia, 12 (Oxford, 1999), pp. 337–63.

manuscripts.[14] A third inscription reads, 'he yat stallis yas buk fro me/ Nor he be hangit on ane trei/ W^t my hand at ye pain', written inside a crudely drawn box. Variations on the latter inscription found in English manuscripts have been detailed by Rossell Hope Robbins.[15] He labels them as Book Plate verses, but they are more specifically ownership-anathemata, generalised curses designed to be affixed to books by their owner with an accompanying signature or name.[16] Scottish examples include 'This booke is mine he that steles this booke frome me shaal be hanged on a tre', in a sixteenth-century medical book now in the Royal College of Physicians, Edinburgh (RCP K 1.39),[17] and '… he yat stelis yis Buyk fra me, god gif he be hangit one ane tre, amen for me amen for the amen for all gud timpany [*sic*]', which interestingly appears on the last page of the volume (now Cambridge University Library Inc.3.E.1.4 [2787]) containing a copy of the *Historia Alexandri* owned c.1475 by Henry Barry, rector of Collace, and afterwards gifted by him to the Blackfriars monastery in Dundee.[18]

MS A Front Flyleaf II (recto)
MS A's second flyleaf contains the poem's title, written twice. 'The Buike of King Alexander the Conqueroure' is written in pencil by a modern hand; 'Alexr the greats life', written in an earlier hand, has since been ruled through. There are also two early shelfmarks on this page: 'Shelf 28 Number 1' and 'pr: 6 sh:2 No. 36'. Shelfmarks in this style are found on the other books owned by the Campbells of Glenorchy which I discuss below.

MS A Back Flyleaf III (verso)
This flyleaf contains a large number of pentrials, all written in the same hand. It also contains a signature, 'Be me wre m^{c}illchreist', i.e. Walter McGillchreist. Several individuals of this surname are listed as Duncan Campbell of Glenorchy's tenants and servants, although I have found no exact match.[19]

---

14 See, P. Bawcutt, 'A First Line Index of Early Scottish Verse', *Studies in Scottish Literature* 26 (1991), 254–70 (263); and her 'The Commonplace Book of John Maxwell', in *A Day Estivall: Essays on the Music, Poetry and History of Scotland and England & poems previously unpublished in honour of Helena Mennie Shire*, ed. A. Gardner-Medwin and J. Hadley Williams (Aberdeen, 1990), pp. 59–68 (64).

15 *Secular Lyrics of the XIVth and XVth Centuries* (Oxford, 1952), p. 85, No. 89, and notes on pp. 255–6.

16 See further, M. Drogin, *Anathema! Medieval Scribes and the History of Book Curses* (Totowa NJ, 1983).

17 D. T. Bird, *A Catalogue of Sixteenth-Century Medical Books in Edinburgh Libraries* (Edinburgh, 1982), p. 172, no. 1805.

18 See (A. H. Millar), 'An Old Dundee Book: Relics of Blackfriars Monastery Dundee', *Dundee Advertiser* (Thursday 20 Dec. 1906), 3; F. J. H. Jenkinson, 'Note on a Volume from the Library of the Dominicans of Dundee', *Publications of the Edinburgh Bibliographical Society* 6 (1906), 181–4; J. C. T. Oates, *A Catalogue of the Fifteenth-Century Printed Books in the University Library Cambridge* (Cambridge, 1954), pp. 558, 613, nos. 3311, 3312 and 3686; J. Durkan and A. Ross, *Early Scottish Libraries* (Glasgow, 1961), p. 75.

19 C. Innes, ed., *The Black Book of Taymouth with Other Papers from the Breadalbane Charter Room*, Bannatyne Club, 106 (Edinburgh, 1855), pp. 258, 317, 366, 368, 373, 399, 401, 402

The pentrials consist of numerous variations on the phrase 'Be me'/ 'Be me Johne' and 'finis amen'. The same hand has also written 'Be me Duncan Campbell/ of glenvrquhay knicht/ Heritabill propriat^r of/ the king*is* of Scottland', 'Johne Campbell', 'Johne gentilman', and (upside down) 'Robert Campbell'. He has also repeated Walter McGillchreist's name, using the spelling variation 'McLechrist'. It is thus impossible to ascertain which of these names, if any, apply to the writer, although 'Johne gentilman' most likely refers to the man of that name who witnessed a charter to Duncan Campbell of Glenorchy on 28 June 1597.[20]

MS A Back Flyleaf IV (recto)
MS A's final flyleaf is the most full and contains pentrials, inscriptions and signatures written by several hands. The notarial sign manual which appeared on front flyleaf I also appears again here, as does 'This bwik pertenis to ane honorabill man/ Duncan Campbell of glenvrquhay/ Amen 1579'. The initials 'DC', presumably standing for Duncan Campbell, are written several times alongside this, as well as the initials 'MT' and 'BC'. I have been unable to identify the former, but 'BC' might conceivably stand for Beatrix Campbell, the eldest daughter of Colin Campbell, 6th laird of Glenorchy, who married Sir John Campbell of Laweris c.1559. Sir John Campbell of Laweris appears frequently throughout the Breadalbane muniments as both a party and witness to bonds or instruments involving Duncan Campbell. Professional and familial associations might thus account for the presence of the initials 'BC' on MS A.

An Alexander Levingstoun also signs back flyleaf IV, and a man of this name is occasionally found accompanying Sir John Campbell of Laweris or his son Colin as a witness to instruments involving Sir Duncan Campbell.[21] He appears upwards of thirty times in the Breadalbane muniments during the 1580s and 1590s and is described therein as a servitor first to Colin Campbell of Ardbeith and then to Duncan Campbell of Glenorchy. Martin MacGregor lists Alexander Levingstoun as one of several non-indigenous (i.e. non-Gaelic) individuals introduced as servitors of the Campbells of Glenorchy under the sixth and seventh lairds and he notes that such 'incomers often held the most important posts, as notaries and legal and financial agents'.[22] Alexander Levingstoun appears also to have worked as a scribe. The British Library catalogue entry for MS A suggests that Alexander Levingstoun be

and 403. See also, NAS MSS GD 112/2/7/4, 112/2/147/3(3), 112/10/1/1(36), 112/10/1/1(47), 112/10/1/1(48), and 112/26/16.
[20] NAS MS GD 112/1/347. MacGregor lists John Gentilman as one of Duncan's servitors, 'Political History', Appendix III, p. 319.
[21] See for instance, *Register of the Privy Council of Scotland*, vol. V 1592–99, ed. D. Masson (Edinburgh, 1882), p. 736.
[22] MacGregor, 'Political History', p. 176; Appendix III, p. 318.

identified with the third scribe of MS A,[23] and I agree since the letter forms
that appear in Alexander Levingstoun's flyleaf inscription all correspond to
those occurring in Scribe 3's stint from fols 265r–282r. Levingstoun/Scribe
3 also copied the *Florimond*-fragment (NAS MS GD 112/22/2), which I
discuss in more detail below. Levingstoun writes the same humorous inscription – 'Finis amen quod the dog' – on the flyleaf of this manuscript and on
MS A. He may, finally, also be associated with NAS MS GD 112/71/2, a late
sixteenth-/early seventeenth-century manuscript copy of the 'Practicks' of Sir
James Balfour of Pittendreich. The last folio is inscribed 'Finis per me quod
Livingstone' and although this manuscript's hand does not in fact resemble
that of the final pages of *BKA* MS A or the *Florimond*-fragment, one does
find on the remaining stub of its back flyleaf traces of an inscription associated in MS A with Alexander Levingstoun. When Levingstoun wrote his
name on the back flyleaf IV of MS A he appended it to the following verse,
'Amor vincit om*ni*a/ Mentiris quod pecunia'. The beginnings of the same
verse appear on the flyleaf stub of GD 112/71/2. The latter manuscript may
therefore be associated with Levingstoun even if it was not written by him.
He accordingly deserves to be added to the ever-increasing list of known
fifteenth- and sixteenth-century Scottish scribes.[24]

The first half of Levingstoun's inscription, 'Amor vincit om*ni*a/ Mentiris
quod pecunia', ultimately derives from Virgil's tenth *Eclogue*, although the
complete verse is also recorded as a medieval Latin proverb.[25] In addition, it
is given as the title of Lydgate's *Eche man folwith his owne fantasye*[26] in three
manuscripts written by or associated with John Shirley.[27] This is interesting
for two reasons. Firstly, Lydgate's poem speaks of Alexander the Great and
his love for Candace (lines 62–3). Secondly, the Campbells of Glenorchy are
also known to have read and owned Lydgate texts. As I discuss below, they
owned a copy of Lydgate's *Siege of Thebes* (Boston Public Library MS f.
med. 94) and they are also connected to the Scots-Gaelic *Book of the Dean
of Lismore* (NLS Adv. MS 72.1.37) which contains (p. 184) fragments from
Lydgate's *Fall of Princes* (Book I, lines 6371–7 and 6441–7).[28] It is thus

---

23   *The British Museum Catalogue of Additions to the Manuscripts 1921–5* (London, 1950), pp.
     154–5 (155). MS A is written by three scribes: Scribe 1 (fols 1r–45r), Scribe 2 (fols 45r–264r)
     and Scribe 3 (fols 265r–282r).
24   J. MacQueen, 'The Literature of Fifteenth-Century Scotland', *Scottish Society in the Fifteenth
     Century*, ed. J. M. Brown (London, 1977), pp. 184–208 (200–3).
25   *Proverbia sententiaeque Latinitatis Medii Aevi: Lateinische Sprichwörter und Sentenzen des
     Mittelalters in alphabetischer Anordnung*, ed. H. Walther, 6 vols, Carmina Medii Aevi Posterioris
     Latina, 2 (Göttingen, 1963–69), vol. I, p. 117, No. 98.
26   *The Minor Poems of John Lydgate*, ed. H. Noble MacCracken, 2 vols, EETS OS 192 and ES 107
     (London, 1911, 1934; repr. 1961, 1962), vol. II, pp. 744–9.
27   British Library MSS Harley 2251 (fols 46v–48v), Additional 29729 (fols 124v–126r); Oxford,
     Bodleian Library MS Ashmole 59 (fols 41r–43r).
28   See R. H. Robbins, 'A new Lydgate fragment', *English Language Notes* 5 (1968), 243–7 (244); A.
     S. G. Edwards, 'Selections from Lydgate's Fall of Princes: A Checklist', *The Library*, 5th Series,
     26 (1971), 337–42 (342). Also, J. MacKechnie, *Catalogue of Gaelic Manuscripts in Selected
     Libraries in Great Britain*, 2 vols (Boston, Mass., 1973), vol. I, pp. 179–89 (p. 186, No. 193)

possible that Lydgate's poem was circulating in Scotland with the title given to it in Shirley's manuscripts, and consequently that Alexander Levingstoun was recalling it in his inscription.[29]

Two inscriptions in MS A remain to be discussed. The first is: 'Quha will persew I will defend/ My lyef and hono^r to ye end', which occurs twice on this back flyleaf. The same proverbial phrase occurs in an almost identical form on fol. 5r of the Maxwell Commonplace Book (EUL MS Laing III.467). It is also recorded as a motto accompanied by the date 1552 on a broadsword belonging to the Kincaid family.[30]

The final inscription is the autograph signature of one Issobell MacKonoschie, written twice on this flyleaf, and also on back flyleaf III. Although I have been unable to identify this woman, the NAS online manuscript catalogue does record correspondence from c.1705 between a Lillian Campbell, lady McConochie, and John Campbell of Glenorchy, 1st earl of Breadalbane.[31] Issobell MacKonoschie may therefore have been Lillian's ancestor, but even if not, the presence of her name within MS A suggests that *BKA* appealed to both male and female readers. The romance certainly contains some strong female characters, notably Alexander's mother (Olimpias), his wife (Roxanne), his lover (Candace) and the Amazon leader (Pallissida) with whom he exchanges a series of letters.[32] Sir Gilbert Hay also himself emphasised the role of women by interpolating within his translation an adapted version of a mid fifteenth-century female advice poem, *The Thewis of Gudwomen*.[33]

MS B flyleaves

In contrast to MS A, the flyleaves of MS B contain relatively few inscriptions and signatures. The first front flyleaf contains the inscription used as this chapter's title quotation, 'Ex Libris domini duncani/ Campbell be [*sic*] Glenwrquhay/ miles',[34] as well as the phrases 'Finis Amen' and 'Be me/ Johne'

---

where the extract is confused with an extract from Henryson's *Troilus and Criseyde* which appears elsewhere in the manuscript. See S. Mapstone, '*The Testament of Cresseid*, lines 561–7: a new manuscript witness', *Notes & Queries* 230 (1985), 307–10.

29 For further details on the circulation of Lydgate in Scotland, see W. H. E. Sweet, 'Lydgate and Scottish Lydgateans', unpublished D.Phil. thesis (University of Oxford, 2009).

30 A. Nisbet, *A System of Heraldry* (Edinburgh, 1722), p. 421. W. Nimmo, *The History of Stirlingshire*, 2 vols, 3rd edn (London and Glasgow, 1880), vol. II, p. 100; J. Fergusson, *Lowland Lairds* (London, 1949), p. 59.

31 NAS MSS GD 112/39/197/14; 112/39/197/20; 112/39/200/8; 112/39/203/16; 112/39/203/17; 112/39/203/19; 112/39/203/20.

32 See M. Gosman, 'L'élément feminin dans le *Roman d'Alexandre*: Olimpias et Candace', in *Court and Poet: Selected Proceedings of the Third Congress of the International Courtly Literature Society*, ed. G. S. Burgess (Liverpool, 1980), pp. 167–76.

33 K. Saldanha, '*The Thewis of Gudwomen*: Middle Scots Moral Advice with European Connections?', in *The European Sun: Proceedings of the Seventh International Conference on Medieval and Renaissance Scottish Language and Literature*, ed. G. D. Caie, R. J. Lyall, S. Mapstone and K. Simpson (East Linton, 2001), pp. 288–99.

34 The word 'miles' is an addition to the original inscription, most likely added after Duncan Campbell was knighted in 1590.

which appear on the back flyleaf of MS A, and also on a flyleaf of Leving-stoun's *Florimond* manuscript (NAS MS GD 112/22/2). The second front flyleaf contains older shelfmarks in the same style as those in MS A. Finally, the last flyleaf contains a 'Memorandu*m*' dated 1597 about the breeding of horses owned by Duncan Campbell.[35] MS B was thus in Duncan Campbell's possession by this date.

Whatever MS B lacks in terms of inscriptions it gains from the inclusion upside down at the back of the volume (pp. 458–68) of *Duncan Laideus alias Macgregouris Testament* (*DLT*), and the short poems which accompany it: 'Off the M[c]gregouris armes', and a 'Postscriptum'.[36] *DLT* is a satirical testament in sixty-three rhyme royal stanzas, spoken by the fictional counterpart of the sixteenth-century highland outlaw Duncan MacGregor (Donnchadh Làdash). From the beginning of the sixteenth century, MacGregor was hunted for his crimes throughout the central highlands. He was pursued in particular by Sir Duncan Campbell (2nd laird of Glenorchy, d. 1513) and Sir Colin Campbell (6th laird). The latter eventually executed MacGregor with his own hands in June 1552.[37]

The presence of *DLT* in MS B can thus be readily explained since it commemorates a significant event in Campbell family history and was indeed most probably written by a member of that family's household.[38] The poem might also be seen in inverse relationship to *BKA*. Commenting on its copying *upside down* at the back of MS B, Janet Hadley Williams writes, 'it could be argued that the scribe saw Duncan's story as the antithesis of King Alexander's and gave that thought physical expression'. More specifically, Duncan's worthless testament contrasts with Alexander's testament in which he attempts to order his territories and their rule before his death:

> Alexander's disposition of his considerable temporal goods is at stark vari-ance to Duncan's prefacing admission that he possesses none, and while Alexander's funeral is followed by a series of formal laments by all his men, Duncan on the contrary expects that his death will enable those over whom he held authority by fear to 'mok me now' (l. 420).[39]

Many more such parallels between *BKA* and *DLT* might be drawn. Duncan's testament can, for instance, be paralleled to the death speech of Alexander's enemy, Darius: Duncan offers himself as an example of one who has suffered

---

[35] Printed in Innes, *Black Book*, p. 299. Innes also notes (p. v) that Duncan Campbell was a keen horse-rearer.

[36] The three poems are printed in Innes, *Black Book*, pp. 151–73. All quotations here are my own transcriptions.

[37] For further information on this episode and the wider Campbell–MacGregor feud which continued throughout the sixteenth century, see Macgregor, 'Political History', Chap. 5.

[38] J. Hadley Williams, '"We Had the Ky and Thair Gat Bot the Glaikis": Catching the Echoes in *Duncan Laideus' Testament*', in *Older Scots Literature*, ed. S. Mapstone (East Linton, 2005), pp. 346–69 (353–4 and n. 37).

[39] Hadley Williams, 'Catching the Echoes', p. 351 and n. 28.

the downturn of fortune's wheel – 'My deare freindis, considder this matter weill/ And in зoure mynd exempill tak of me/ Traist not in fortune wt her fickill quheill …' (lines 274–6) – just as Darius says to Alexander, 'Bot Alexander, þow has ane fare myrroure,/ To luke to me, and think of my dollour' (lines 6826–7).

The flyleaves and spare pages of MSS A and B thus provide a lively but hitherto neglected record of *BKA*'s sixteenth-century scribes, owners and readers, whilst their many pentrials, inscriptions and – in the case of *DLT* – lengthier writings provide unique and additional witnesses of complete poems and also fragments of proverbial verse scattered elsewhere in the margins of Older Scots manuscripts and commonplace books. Although the text of *BKA* is not annotated in either MS A or MS B, the collection of inscriptions and signatures on their flyleaves reveals that Sir Duncan Campbell of Glenorchy and his household accessed these volumes with considerable frequency between the years 1581 and 1597. That Sir Duncan Campbell owned two copies of the same romance is also indicative of the importance he attached not just to this poem, but also to literature in general. In the second half of this chapter I situate Sir Duncan Campbell's ownership of *BKA* within the context of those other literary volumes in manuscript and print owned by or associated with him.[40]

Literature Owned by or Associated with Sir Duncan Campbell and the Campbells of Glenorchy

The Florimond-*fragment*

As detailed above, Alexander Levingstoun, the third scribe of MS A, was also responsible for copying the first 504 lines of the Older Scots romance *Florimond*.[41] Most probably written in the first half of the fifteenth century, this octosyllabic romance is a remarkably close translation of the Old French *Florimont* composed by Aimon de Varennes in 1188. Aimon consciously conceived of his poem as a prologue to the French Alexander cycle that tells of the heroic exploits of Alexander's ancestors.[42] Duncan Campbell may thus have commissioned a copy of the Scottish translation as a prequel to his two copies of Hay's *BKA*.

The *Florimond*-fragment was copied upside down at the back of a volume of inventories (NAS MS GD 112/22/2) produced in Duncan Campbell of Glenorchy's main households of Finlarig, Balloch and Glenorchy between

---

[40] Further information on the volumes discussed can be found in my Oxford D.Phil thesis, 'The Manuscript and Print Contexts of Older Scots Romance' (2010), pp. 102–10, 117–22.

[41] For further information and bibliography see R. Purdie, 'Medieval Romance in Scotland', in *A Companion to Medieval Scottish Poetry*, ed. P. Bawcutt and J. Hadley Williams (Cambridge, 2006), pp. 165–77 (170–1, 176).

[42] L. Harf-Lancner, 'Le *Florimont* d'Aimon de Varennes: un prologue du *Roman d'Alexandre*', *Cahiers de Civilisation médiévale* 37 (1994), 241–53.

1589/90 and 1610. Levingstoun's exemplar was either incomplete and he thus had no more text available to copy, or he was somehow interrupted and failed to return to what he had begun. The rushed and somewhat scrappy appearance of the fragment might suggest this. Alternatively, the surviving fragment may be a rough draft which Levingstoun made in preparation for a complete copy of the poem which was either lost or never produced. It is probable that a complete version of the romance did circulate in sixteenth-century Scotland, since *The Complaynt of Scotland* (c.1550) contains a reference to an episode not present in the surviving fragment, while the 1663 print of the Older Scots romance *Roswall and Lillian* cites the hero's name twice.

Lydgate's Siege of Thebes

Another romance manuscript owned by Duncan Campbell is Boston Public Library MS f. med. 94, a copy of Lydgate's *Siege of Thebes* produced sometime between 1430 and 1460 by the Carthusian monk and scribe Stephen Dodesham (d. c.1482).[43] Priscilla Bawcutt's detailed analysis of the manuscript's flyleaf annotations has revealed that it was in Scottish ownership since at least the late fifteenth century. Duncan Campbell's ownership is signalled by an inscription, accompanied by the date 1592, which appears in a blank space at the end of the poem on fol. 74r:

> This Bwik pertenis to ane Richt hono*rabi*ll
> Sir duncan Campbell of
> Glennorquhay Kny*t*.

Guido de Columna's Historia destructionis Troiae

In addition to owning romance in manuscript, the Campbells of Glenorchy also owned a printed edition of Guido de Columna's *Historia destructionis Troiae* (now NLS Inc. 25.5) produced in Strasburg in 1494. Ownership has previously been assigned to Colin Campbell, 3rd earl of Argyll,[44] but my own analysis of the print reveals that this cannot be the case. The volume's first flyleaf does contain the signature of a Colin Campbell, but an earl of Argyll is unlikely to have signed himself using this format. It seems far more likely that the signature belongs instead to a Colin Campbell of Glenorchy, most likely to Colin Campbell, 6th laird of Glenorchy and father of the book-owning Duncan. Several pieces of evidence support this. Firstly, a note by David Laing on the inside of the volume's vellum cover states that he saw the print in the Breadalbane library which housed most of the volumes discussed here and also those books acquired by the family over subsequent centuries. Laing's statement is confirmed by an inventory of books in the Breadalbane

---

[43] P. Bawcutt, 'The Boston Public Library Manuscript of John Lydgate's *Siege of Thebes*: Its Scottish Owners and Inscription', *Medium Aevum* 70 (2001), 80–94.
[44] Durkan and Ross, *Early Scottish Libraries*, p. 136.

library compiled in 1863 which lists a 'Guidoni's Historia Trojana'.[45] The print's front flyleaf also contains two shelfmarks in the same style as those on the *BKA* MSS and other Campbell-owned books discussed here. Finally, a note on the flyleaf records that the volume is 'Ex libris Colini Campbell/ ex dono domini Willelmi Ramsay'.[46] The most likely candidate for this William Ramsay is the man of that name who appears frequently throughout the surviving Breadalbane muniments during the 1540s, 1550s and 1560s. He first served in the household of John Campbell, 5th laird of Glenorchy (c.1496–1550), and then under Colin Campbell, 6th laird, as a notary public. He was presented by Colin to the parsonage of Kilmore in 1552,[47] and next moved to Colin's main base at Balloch Castle, where he continued to act as Colin's notary and also as factor for Patrick Ruthven, Colin's brother-in-law. He was chaplain of Finlarig by 1555,[48] and curate of Killin by 1557.[49] He was also installed as the first Protestant minister of Inchaiden in 1561.[50] William Ramsay thus perhaps gave his copy of Guido's *Historia* to his patron Colin Campbell sometime during the mid-sixteenth century. His ownership may explain the liturgical inscriptions on the volume's back flyleaves.

Further marginal annotations are scattered throughout the volume. The annotator (perhaps Colin Campbell or William Ramsay) was keen to highlight passages about the *Historia*'s female characters – Medea, Helen, Briseida and Polyxena – and their lovers – Jason, Paris, Troilus and Achilles. In a related vein, he draws attention to almost all of Guido's infamous anti-feminist comments. He shows an interest in marking out natural events (such as eclipses), as well as character's deaths, Paris's dream, councils, and passages about the avarice of priests and idolatry. Very similar annotations appear in CUL MS Kk.5.30, a composite Scottish manuscript containing fragments of two independent translations of Guido's *Historia*: Lydgate's *Troy Book* and the early fifteenth-century *Scottish Troy Book*.[51] Different Scottish readers thus attended to the same features and themes of Guido's *Historia* whether in translation or in its original Latin, and their responses are worthy of further study. They sit alongside Henryson's *Testament of Cresseid* as examples of the reception of the Trojan myth in fifteenth- and sixteenth-century Scotland.

Further Literary Associations

NAS MS GD 112/71/1 demonstrates that the Campbells of Glenorchy were interested in historiographical texts as well as romance. This manuscript

---

45 NAS MS GD 112/22/56, p. 146. The print is here dated 1487, but this may be a cataloguer's error.
46 Durkan and Ross, *Early Scottish Libraries*, p. 137, list two other books owned by the same William Ramsay.
47 NAS MS GD 112/51/107/(2). For a more detailed summary of Ramsay's career, see Dawson, 'Clan, kin, and Kirk', pp. 234–5. Also, MacGregor, 'Political History', p. 173.
48 NAS MS GD 112/51/89/(2).
49 NAS MS GD 112/1/103.
50 NAS MS GD 112/1/114; printed Gillies, *In Famed Breadalbane*, pp. 261–3.
51 *Barbour's Des schottischen Nationaldichters Legendensammlung: nebst den Fragmenten seines Trojanerkrieges*, ed. C. Horstman, 2 vols (Heilbronn, 1881–82), vol. II, pp. 215–308.

contains (at fols 14r–73r) a handwritten and Scotticised copy of Caxton's *Cordiale* (STC 5758) printed in 1479.[52] It was produced in the late fifteenth century by one scribe writing in a neat Scottish secretary hand.[53] The same scribe also copied the manuscript's first text (fols 1r–12v) which has hitherto been catalogued as a 'MS account of the reign of King Edward II'.[54] It is in fact a fragment of a manuscript copy of Caxton's 1480 edition of *The Chronicles of England* (STC 9991).[55] The fragment begins part way through the reign of Edward II and continues to the very start of the reign of Edward III. This period of English history was no doubt of interest to Scottish readers since it deals with the Wars of Independence between Scotland and England and the reign of King Robert Bruce.

An otherwise blank page (fol. 75v) at the back of the volume contains the following inscription, written in a 'probably fifteenth-century hand': 'Iste liber pertenit Iohannes cambell'.[56] This indicates that GD 112/71/1 is yet another Campbell-owned book, although the exact identity of the John Campbell in question remains uncertain. Another unknown member of the Campbell family also owned a second version of the prose *Brut*, an acephalous but heavily annotated copy of Julian Notary's 1515 'Cronycle of Englonde with the fruyte of times' (STC 10000), now NAS MS GD 112/71/6.

In addition to owning chronicles, the Campbells of Glenorchy can be associated with a series of psalters and books of hours. The most well-known volume is British Library Yates Thompson 13,[57] an early fourteenth-century parchment book of hours, which contains in its bas-de-page illustrations[58] scenes from *Bevis of Hampton* and *Guy of Warwick* (fols 8v–17r).[59] The

---

[52] On the dynamic relationship between manuscript and print in sixteenth-century Scotland, see D. Fox, 'Manuscripts and Prints of Scots Poetry in the Sixteenth-Century', in *Bards and Makars: Scottish Language and Literature: Medieval and Renaissance*, ed. A. J. Aitken, M. P. McDiarmid and D. S. Thomson (Glasgow, 1977), pp. 156–71.

[53] N. F. Blake notes that the volume's watermarks 'suggest a date of 1479 and certainly not later than 1485. Since Caxton's edition appeared in 1479, this copy, which was probably made in Scotland, must have been written shortly afterwards': 'Manuscript to Print', in *Book Production and Publishing in Britain 1375–1475*, ed. J. Griffiths and D. Pearsall (Cambridge, 1989; repr. 2007), pp. 403–32 (421).

[54] www.nas.gov.uk/onlineCatalogue/ (accessed 5 Aug. 2009).

[55] Caxton printed this text again in 1482 (STC 9992), but the *mise-en-page* of GD 112/71/1 appears closer to that of Caxton's 1480 edition, although it is not an exact paginary copy.

[56] Blake, 'Manuscript to Print', p. 421.

[57] M. R. James, *A Descriptive Catalogue of the Second Series of Fifty Manuscripts (Nos 51 to 100) in the Collection of Henry Yates Thompson* (Cambridge, 1902), No. 57, pp. 50–74; L. Freedman Sandler, *Gothic Manuscripts 1285–1385: A Survey of Manuscripts Illuminated in the British Isles*, ed. J. J. G. Alexander, 2 vols (London, 1986), vol. I, p. 32, (figs. 248–9); vol. II, pp. 107–9, no. 98.

[58] For analysis of these see: L. Brownrigg, 'The Taymouth Hours and the Romance of *Beves of Hampton*', *English Manuscript Studies* 1 (1989), 222–41 and J. Brantley, 'Images of the Vernacular in the Taymouth Hours', *English Manuscript Studies* 10 (2002), 85–113.

[59] Both of these romances are known to have circulated in fifteenth- and sixteenth-century Scotland. A list of romances in *The Complaynt of Scotland* includes 'beuis of southamtonn', whilst the inventory of the sixteenth-century Edinburgh printer Thomas Bassandyne contains 'ane Gy of Waruick'. *The Bannatyne Miscellany*, ed. D. Laing et al, 3 vols (Edinburgh, 1827–55), vol. II, p. 196.

manuscript was owned in the sixteenth century by an unidentified Scot who writes notes about the number of 'leifs' onto several of the manuscript's full-page illuminations.[60] A seventeenth-/eighteenth-century armorial bookplate on the inside upper cover with the title 'The Earl of Breadalbane' reveals that the manuscript was later owned by the Campbells of Glenorchy and a shelfmark on fol. 1 ('Shelf 29 number L') in the same style as those on both manuscripts of *BKA* suggests that the family perhaps acquired the manuscript as early as the late sixteenth/early seventeenth century.

A Colin Campbell, either 3rd (c.1468–1523) or 6th laird of Glenorchy, owned British Library Egerton MS 2899, a vellum Latin Psalter of c.1500 of Scottish origin which contains the names of distinctly Scottish saints, several associated with Argyllshire and Glenorchy. The following sixteenth-century inscription appears on flyleaf iii[v]: 'Liber Coline Campbell of Glenurquhay eiusdem Glenurquhay'.

The Glenorchy Psalter was sold at a Sotheby's sale of 5–7 February 1912. The same sale catalogue also lists an edition of Sleidan's *Chronicle* (1560), most probably the copy owned by Catherine Ruthven (d. 1584), wife of Colin Campbell, 6th laird of Glenorchy, and mother of Duncan Campbell, 7th laird.[61] The volume is now lost, but Innes records in his edition of *The Black Book of Taymouth* that the flyleaf read: 'This buke pertenis to Catherine Ruthven lady of Glenurquhay'.[62] Catherine's ownership of this volume parallels the unknown Issobell MacKonoschie's reading of the *BKA* MS A and suggests that female literacy was at a relatively high level within the Campbell household.

The Campbells of Glenorchy can, finally, also be associated with the early sixteenth-century Scots-Gaelic *Book of the Dean of Lismore* (*BDL*).[63] This manuscript was copied in the first half of the sixteenth century by Sir James MacGregor, Dean of Lismore (d. 1551), and his brother, Duncan Macgregor. During the fifteenth and early sixteenth centuries the MacGregors and Glenorchy Campbells were engaged in a joint programme of territorial expansion throughout Breadalbane, and it is indeed through the patronage of either the earl of Argyll or Campbell of Glenorchy that James MacGregor became the dean of Lismore. It is thus not surprising to find several poems within the *BDL* written by Duncan Campbell, 2nd laird of Glenorchy (d. 1513), which

---

60 For information on the manuscript's earlier owners, see J. Harthan, *Books of Hours and their Owners* (London, 1977), pp. 48–9; A. Rudolff Stanton, 'Isabelle of France and Her Manuscripts, 1308–58', in *Capetian Women*, ed. K. Nolan (New York and Basingstoke, 2003), pp. 225–52 (229, 242–5, pl. 10.7).

61 Sleidan's *Chronicle* (1560) was circulating in Scotland in the sixteenth century. It appears in the will of the sixteenth-century Edinburgh printer Thomas Bassandyne ('Item, ane Chronicle of Sledan'). *Bannatyne Miscellany* II, p. 200; M. A. Bald, 'Vernacular Books imported into Scotland: 1500–1625', *Scottish Historical Review* 23 (1925–26), 254–67 (262).

62 Innes, *Black Book*, p. v.

63 For the best recent discussion of this manuscript and its contexts, see M. MacGregor, 'The View from Fortingall: the worlds of the *Book of the Dean of Lismore*', *Scottish Gaelic Studies* 22 (2006), 35–85.

take as their themes the nature of women and immorality of the clergy.[64] It is also interesting to note that the *BDL* contains several poems or verses which mention Alexander the Great, including one voicing the comments made by four philosophers as they stand over Alexander's grave.[65]

In 1598, Mr Walter Bowie, notary public and tutor to Duncan Campbell of Glenorchy's children, compiled a history of the family known as *The Black Book of Taymouth* (NAS MS GD 112/78/2) in which he implicitly aligned his patron with Alexander the Great by referring to Duncan Campbell's territorial expansion as a series of conquests. He also prefaced his history with 'Ane admonitioun to the posteritie of the Hows of Glenvrquhay', which includes the following precept:

> Will thow thy honour, howss, and rent to stand,
> Conques, or keip thingis conquest to thy hand.

This implied relationship between the literary history of Alexander and the real history of a powerful Scottish family who were avid collectors of Alexander romances is both appropriate and thought provoking, suggesting as it does that Sir Duncan Campbell may have read his romance volumes for both instruction and entertainment. The taste for large single-item volumes of vernacular romance, history and theology shared by several members of the Campbell of Glenorchy family is, furthermore, unparalleled amongst fifteenth- and sixteenth-century Scottish book-owners. The family are single-handedly responsible for preserving four witnesses of Older Scots and Middle English romance, and their collection accordingly provides evidence both of the traffic of books between England and Scotland, and of Scottish interest in the epic cycles of Alexander and Thebes.[66] Sir Duncan Campbell of Glenorchy and his father Colin are, in short, two of the most significant early modern readers of medieval romance known to date.[67]

---

[64] See W. Gillies, 'Some Aspects of Campbell History', *Transactions of the Gaelic Society of Inverness* 50 (1976–78), 256–95; 'Courtly and Satiric Poems in the Book of the Dean of Lismore', *Scottish Studies* 21 (1977), 35–53; 'The Gaelic Poems of Sir Duncan Campbell of Glenorchy I, II, III', *Scottish Gaelic Studies* 13 (1979–81), 18–45, 263–88; 14 (1983), 59–82.

[65] *The Dean of Lismore's Book: A Selection of Ancient Gaelic Poetry*, ed. Rev. T. McLauchlan (Edinburgh, 1862), pp. 110–11. The *BDL* also contains two lists of the Nine Worthies that inevitably include Alexander the Great. See MacKechnie, *Catalogue of Gaelic Manuscripts*, pp. 185, 186, Nos. 171 and 201.

[66] They were also interested in documentation in general. Some 324 letters concerning the family survive, see *Clan Campbell Letters 1559–83*, ed. J. Dawson, Scottish History Society, 5th series, 10 (Edinburgh, 1997). In an effort to keep records of their transactions and bonds, Colin and Duncan also had 'bukis of bandis of manrent' made; 162 bonds of manrent were made to them between 1510 and 1611. See Wormald, *Lords and Men*, p. 101.

[67] My thanks to the following scholars who have assisted my research in preparation for this article: Priscilla Bawcutt, Jane Dawson, Martin MacGregor, Sally Mapstone, Donald McWhannel and William Sweet.

13

'Pur les francs homes amender': Clerical Authors and the Thirteenth-Century Context of Historical Romance

ROSALIND FIELD

The Anglo-Norman romances offer a welcome exception to the wide-spread anonymity of insular romance. Since Legge's seminal work,[1] these romances have been confidently associated with the milieu of the Anglo-Norman baronial class, and with places and events close to their world. Legge sees them as 'ancestral', others, such as Crane, as more generally representing the tastes and interests of the baronial class.[2] Something is known, and more persuasively speculated, about their patrons, and many of their authors are named. The argument as to whether or not these romances can be read as 'ancestral' has long focused interest on patronage, as have other approaches: the theoretical death of the author, the near-invisibility of many of these authors (although not by comparison with the Middle English versions), the interest in reception, in audience, in women in that audience, even in ownership of manuscripts – all these interests focus on the issue of *whom* these works were written *for* and prioritise the agency of the patron and audience over that of the author. The patrons are more glamorous, redolent of the colour and power of medieval lordship, and so there is a tendency to see them as setting the agenda. I should like to shift the enquiry onto whom the romances were written *by* and to re-examine the models we have of the relationship between author and patron, in order to ask whose interest is being served.

The romances under consideration here are seven narratives written between the 1170s and the second decade of the thirteenth century and a further example, *Fouke Fitzwarin*, which dates in its extant form from

---

[1] M. D. Legge, *Anglo-Norman Literature and Its Background* (Oxford, 1963).
[2] S. Crane, *Insular Romance: Politics, Faith, and Culture in Anglo-Norman and Middle English Literature* (Berkeley, 1986).

the second half of the thirteenth century.[3] The 'historical' nature of these romances provides a fruitful area for charting the growth of fictional narrative and its contribution to a sense of cultural and national identity. The two romances of Hue de Rotelande are included in this group although they do not share the English setting. Set in the Norman kingdoms of southern Italy, they provide an eccentric view of the 'ancestral' and a well-informed comedy at the expense of the fashionable romances of the matters of Britain and Rome; it may be that the Anglo-Saxon past was not available to this kind of comic treatment.

In all, the historical romances of England span three centuries and the two vernaculars of medieval England, for while the later twelfth century saw the appearance of most of the Anglo-Norman romances, the earliest Middle English versions of many of these romances date from a century later. While both these periods of productive activity have been the focus of sophisticated and wide-ranging scholarship, there is still something of a hiatus across most of the thirteenth century. To some extent this apparent hiatus is deceptive, for while the period of production is in the main concentrated on the half century around the turn of the twelfth century, the manuscript history of Anglo-Norman romance tells a story of ongoing copying through the thirteenth century and well into the fourteenth.[4] The same period also sees the beginning of translation into Middle English.[5]

The *Lai d'Haveloc*, although overshadowed by the achievement of the Middle English *Havelok the Dane*, is itself a useful example of this pattern of dissemination. The *Lai* itself dates from the turn of the twelfth century,

---

3   Thomas, *The Romance of Horn*, ed. M. K. Pope, ANTS 9–10, 12–13 (Oxford, 1955, 1964), trans. J. Weiss, *The Birth of Romance: an anthology. Four Twelfth-century Anglo-Norman Romances* (London, 1992) or *The Birth of Romance in England*, The French of England Translation Series (Tempe, 2009); Hue de Rotelande, *Ipomedon*, ed. A. J. Holden (Paris, 1979) and *Protheselaus*, ed. A. J. Holden, ANTS 47–9 (London, 1991–93); *Boeve de Haumtone*, ed. A. Stimming (Halle, 1899), trans. J. Weiss, *Boeve de Haumtone and Gui de Warewic: Two Anglo-Norman Romances*, The French of England Translation Series (Tempe, 2008); *Le Lai d'Haveloc*, ed. A. Bell (Manchester, 1925), trans. Weiss, *The Birth of Romance*; *Le Roman de Waldef*, ed. A. J. Holden (Cologny-Geneve, 1984); *Gui de Warewic*, ed. A. Ewert (Paris, 1933), trans. Weiss, *Two Anglo-Norman Romances*; *Fouke le Fitz Waryn*, ed. E. J. Hathaway et al., ANTS 26–8 (Oxford, 1975–76), trans. S. Knight and T. H. Ohlgren in *Robin Hood and Other Outlaw Tales* (Kalamazoo, 1997).

4   *The Romance of Horn* survives in five fragmentary thirteenth-century manuscripts. Hue's two romances survive together in Oxford, Bodleian Library, Rawlinson D.13 (13c) and British Library, Egerton 2515 (14c), with *Ipomedon* in three further fourteenth-century fragments and *Protheselaus* in a further thirteenth-century fragment. *Boeve* survives in two lengthy overlapping fragments – one of the thirteenth century, one of the fourteenth – and three further thirteenth-century fragments. *Waldef* survives in one manuscript of the turn of the thirteenth century. Both manuscripts of the *Lai d'Haveloc* date from the period after the composition of the Middle English *Havelok* (13c–14c). The total of surviving Anglo-Norman romances is doubled by the sixteen surviving manuscripts of *Gui* dating across the thirteenth to fourteenth centuries. *Fouke Fitzwarin* survives in one mid-fourteenth-century manuscript. For details see R. J. Dean with M. B. M. Boulton, *Anglo-Norman Literature: a Guide to Texts and Manuscripts*, ANTS Occasional Publications Series 3 (London, 1999), nos. 151–75.

5   I discuss the pattern of translation activity more fully in 'Patterns of Availability and Demand in Middle English translations "de romanz"', in *The Exploitations of Medieval Romance*, ed. L. Ashe, I. Djordjević and J. Weiss (Cambridge, 2010), pp. 73–89.

but its material comes from the earliest vernacular manifestation of the post-Conquest interest in Anglo-Saxon history, Gaimar's *Estoire des Engleis* of the 1130s. The earlier of its two surviving manuscripts dates from the turn of the thirteenth century, by which time the Havelok story was appearing in Middle English. It is this aspect of this short and comparatively simple poem that is the main subject of enquiry here – the appeal of the pre-Conquest material through the thirteenth century. The Prologue to the *Lai* is here quite explicit as to the exemplary quality of its material.

> Volunters devreit l'um oïr
> E recuntre e retenir
> Les nobles fez as anciens
> E les pruësses e les bens,
> Essamples prendre e remembrer
> Pur les francs homes amender.
> Vilainies e mesprisuns:
> Co devreit estre li sermuns
> Dunt l'um les deust chastïer
> Kar mult i ad vilain mester.

> ['Men should gladly hear, repeat and remember the noble deeds of antiquity, both the good acts and the brave, to imitate and record them for the improvement of honourable men. Bad breeding and vice – these should form the homily with which to admonish them, for the uncouth are much in need of it.' *Lai d'Haveloc*, lines 1–10][6]

It is not unusual to find this kind of prologue in twelfth-century narrative, and it is a generic feature of the *lai*, but there is a dichotomy here between the fashionable assertions of the prologue and the narrative that follows. The antiquity evoked is not that of the classical world, nor the Celtic, but that of a version of pre-Conquest England. While the condemnation of *vilainies e mesprisuns* may suggest the usual courtly didacticism, in the event the narrative that follows offers nothing of the sort: the moral issues illustrated are entirely those of rightful inheritance and good rule. It would seem to be these two factors, pre-Conquest history and the topic of good rule, that provide an explanation for the continuing interest in narratives which by the very nature of their contemporary relevance may be expected to seem outdated to a succeeding generation.

Interest in the period of production of these romances has tended, for the reasons already suggested, to focus on patrons rather than authors, and even less attention has been paid to the scribes and adaptors who kept this body of material available throughout the thirteenth century and into Middle English. So while the provenance of *The Romance of Horn* remains unclear,

---

[6] French text from *Le Lai d'Haveloc*, ed. Bell: translation from Weiss, *The Birth of Romance*.

the poem's evident connexion with the Anglo-Norman invaders of Ireland has led to a feasible association with Richard FitzGilbert, Earl of Clare, 'Strongbow'.[7] Hue de Rotelande helpfully provides an explicit context, praising his patron, Gilbert FitzBaderon of Monmouth, owner of a large library 'de latyn e de romaunz' (*Protheselaus*, line 12710). As *Boeve* provides a foundation myth for Arundel castle in Sussex, it has been connected with d'Albini earls,[8] while the strong interest in the Attleborough area of Norfolk evinced in *Waldef* suggests likely patrons from amongst the local families of the Bigods, Warennes or Mortimers.[9] *Gui de Warewic* acquires its most important patronage, that of the earls of Warwick, as it later develops into a local, even national success, but its origin seems closely aligned to either Wallingford or Oxford. Ewert's suggestion that it was written in celebration of a marriage in the D'Oilly family has been questioned.[10] *Fouke Fitzwarin* shows a strong interest in the localities of the Welsh marches and an explicit connexion with the Fitzwarin family.[11]

In the absence of the level of definite context provided only by Hue de Rotelande, locality has become the key factor in the investigation of the background and purposes of these texts, and it is a factor emphasised by the very nature of their localised narratives. However, it can serve to atomise the various texts, scattered as they evidently are around the four corners of England,[12] whereas the cultural context provided by the patrons is that of a network of family and political relationships. More could be said about this but there are good reasons for moving away from the interest in patrons that has occupied much of the discussion about these narratives. Even though something is known and more speculated about the patrons for whom these works were written, it seems clear that with perhaps the exception of the two later romances, *Gui* and *Fouke*, there is little evidence of the texts as ongoing family possessions and indeed the manuscript history suggests a widening public.

What is known about the authors of these romances can be briefly summarised. Thomas, the author of *The Romance of Horn*, presents himself as a clerical family man, not a celibate, the father of 'Gilimot' who succeeds him

---

7   See J. Weiss, 'Thomas and the Earl: Literary and Historical Contexts for *The Romance of Horn*', in *Tradition and Transformation in Medieval Romance*, ed. R. Field (Cambridge, 1999), pp. 1–14 (2–7).

8   Legge, *Anglo-Norman Literature*, p. 159; J. Weiss, 'The date of the Anglo-Norman *Boeve de Haumtone*', *Medium Aevum* 55 (1986), 237–41.

9   See R. Field, '*Waldef* and the Matter of/with England', in *Medieval Insular Romance: Translation and Innovation*, ed. J. Weiss et al. (Cambridge, 2000), pp. 25–40 (p. 37 note 26).

10 See J. Weiss, 'The Exploitation of Ideas of Pilgrimage and Sainthood in *Gui de Warewic*', in *Exploitations*, ed. Ashe et al., pp. 43–56 (pp. 54–5), and Liu, 'Romances of Continuity', pp. 150–1 in the present volume.

11 *Fouke*, ed. Hathaway et al, pp. xxvii–xxxvii.

12 This is restricted to England. Legge (*Anglo-Norman Literature*) includes amongst the Anglo-Norman romances the Scottish-set *Fergus*, but it has since been recognised as continental in both origin and circulation: see R. Zemel, *The Quest for Galiene: A Study of Guillaume le Clerc's Arthurian Romance "Fergus"* (Munster, 2006).

as poet.[13] Michael Clanchy describes him as a professional author, whose title 'mestre' identifies him as a Latinist and a schoolman; details in the romance show him to have been an accomplished musician. Laura Ashe calls him 'the English clerk, Thomas' and this follows Clanchy's interpretation of the romance's diverse regional speech patterns as a style acceptable to his audience, rather than representative of Thomas's own diction.[14]

The two romances *Ipomedon* and its sequel, *Protheselaus*, provide the strongest authorial presence, that of Hue de Rotelande, canon of Hereford cathedral, friend of the Latin clerics at the centre of Anglo-Norman court culture, most notably Walter Map. The exotic setting is offset by the intrusion of local gossip, contemporary events and personal comments. Map is humorously described as a liar (lines 7185–6), while Hue presents himself as a coarse womaniser (lines 10561–80), attributes which serve to personalise his parody of the romantic fictions of Chrétien.

Boeve de Haumtone is the work of an unnamed author who presents himself as a minstrel performer asking his audience for payment. Recent studies have shown that the author is aware of *chanson de geste* tradition and was influenced by the romances of Hue, so the naivety of self-presentation belies a well-informed literary awareness.[15] The *Roman de Waldef* is the work of a deliberately unnamed author who claims to be writing for his 'amie'.

> Ne me vuel ore pas numer/ ne le non m'amie mustrer.
> Si jo le livere puis perfere/ E a bon chief peusse trere
> Le nun m'amie e le mien/ saverai jo demustrer mult bien
>
> ['I do not wish to name myself now or reveal the name of my friend. If I can finish the book and bring it to a conclusion I can then let out the names of my friend and myself': lines 87–92]

This play with the convention of the cleric-lover is somewhat at odds with the tone of the narrative, which has little room for humour or for love, but which does show a wide knowledge of twelfth-century vernacular literature.[16] It survives in only one manuscript, with a later Latin redaction, but had sufficient currency at the time of its origin to influence *Gui de Warewic*.

There is no information about the author or audience of the *Lai d'Haveloc*. The language and geographical knowledge indicate that the author may have

---

[13] *Romance of Horn*, ed. Pope, line 5241.

[14] M. Clanchy, *From Memory to Written Record*, 2nd edn (Oxford, 1993), pp. 210–11; L. Ashe, *Fiction and History in England, 1066–1200* (Cambridge, 2007), p. 146. Pope interpreted the linguistic features to suggest that Thomas was the son of immigrants from the Loire, possibly educated in Poitiers; *Romance of Horn*, vol. II, p. 122.

[15] See M. Ailes, 'The Anglo-Norman *Boeve de Haumtone* as a *chanson de geste*', in *Sir Bevis of Hampton in Literary Tradition*, ed. J. Fellows and I. Djordjević (Cambridge, 2008), pp. 9–24 and J. Weiss, '*Mestre* and Son: The Role of Sabaoth and Terri in *Boeve de Haumtone*', in the same volume, pp. 25–36.

[16] For the literary connexions of *Waldef*, see Field, '*Waldef* and the Matter of/with England', pp. 28–30.

recently arrived from the continent, and the courtly treatment of Gaimar's story suggests the influence of the *Lais* of Marie de France.[17] The author of *Gui de Warewic* has long been assumed to be a canon of Oseney Abbey, although Judith Weiss has recently suggested the nearby St Frideswide's Priory, Oxford.[18] Either would give the author access to the books necessary for his derivative narrative and the interest in prolonging his romance through the themes of penance and conversion.

The surviving prose version of *Fouke Fitzwarin* dates from the fourteenth century but the underlying verse narrative may have originated at a time closer to the events described as taking place in the reign of John. The author is unknown but generally assumed to be attached to the Fitzwarin family whose legendary history the romance celebrates. However, inaccuracies abound in that history so the connexion may not be that close. Unusually for these romances, the literary references are to the Galfridian British traditions.

There is thus a fair amount of information about some of these authors, but it may have been taken too much at face value. Most show an awareness of contemporary developments in fiction and thus belong to a literary culture that is self-conscious, defensive and humorous. That these are authorial personae seems as likely as literal self-portraits. For there is here a pattern of assumed roles, of performance masks – the father of a line of poets, the lover-poet (that remark in *Waldef* must be a joke), the hireling minstrel, the goliardic cleric, the (rather fanciful) family chronicler. We could even include here the insomniac poet of the Middle English *Havelok the Dane*, a work which can be placed as a late example of the historical romance of the twelfth and thirteenth century rather than as the forerunner of romance in English on which it has little discernible influence.[19] In their different ways these are all self-conscious expressions of vernacularity in that they strike the range of poses available for a Latinate cleric addressing a courtly audience and they are for the most part worldly, not particularly ecclesiastical nor pious. With the exception of the author of *Gui*, these authors show little interest in doctrinal morality, repentance, confession or spiritual growth, although such topics were to become a staple of romance in English. Clerical authors they may be – but with Clanchy's wide sense of the range of 'clericus'.[20]

Above all, they lack the chivalric glamour, the sheer power of their associated patrons, and leave fewer traces. But the intertextuality evident in these romances is indicative of a network of shared concerns as well as shared material. Any attempt to understand the position of the authors in their local and literary culture has to take into account this network; the picture of the household cleric in an isolated castle clobbering together a pedestrian narrative to entertain the family in the winter evenings is not adequate. Nor

17 Weiss, *Birth of Romance*, p. xxviii.
18 Weiss, 'Ideas of Pilgrimage and Sainthood', pp. 88–91.
19 *Havelok*, ed. G. V. Smithers (Oxford, 1987), lines 2998–9.
20 Clanchy, *From Memory to Written Record*, pp. 226–30.

do these romances read as straightforward baronial propaganda, for where propaganda is targeted outwards, this is focused inwards, to provide a self-fashioning of the Anglo-Norman barony. The authors of these romances turn to the pre-Conquest history of England, or invent their own version of it, as a resource for exemplary narrative.

The work of the historians Rees Davies and John Gillingham indicates that the writing of Anglo-Saxon history is a deliberate evocation of the serious historiography of Bede and to a lesser extent the traditions derived from the Anglo-Saxon Chronicle, challenging the imaginative British history of Geoffrey of Monmouth.[21] There is realpolitik behind this challenge, a claim of England over the Celtic fringes, and it is represented in the work of Latin historians such as Henry of Huntingdon and William of Malmesbury. As with the serious Latin histories, so with the fictions of entertainment. Gaimar, who takes material from the Anglo-Saxon Chronicle, provides a source and model for these romances, as Geoffrey provides the raw material for Arthurian romances. In their different ways *Horn* and *Haveloc* evoke the period of Viking invasions, *Waldef* adopts a view of the Anglo-Saxon past evocative of Bede (who is a name in the narrative) and *Boeve* is set in the reign of a King Edgar, just as *Gui* brings in the Anglo-Saxon king Athelston. *Fouke Fitzwarin* is the exception with a narrative ranging from the coming of Brutus to the reign of John – sweeping the present moment of the other romances up into its narrative of insular history. All of this is, as Rouse's recent study has examined (although he does not apply it to these works), 'Anglo-Saxonism' – the idea of Anglo-Saxon England as an ideological statement.[22] It is also a process of 'translatio' reaching across cultural change as well as three languages. In drawing – rather freely – on Bede, these writers are translating the history of English from Latin, or indeed Old English, into French.

This history is not only unGalfridian in place and time, but also ideologically non-Arthurian.[23] There is little sense of sacred kingship, even less of the centralised figure of regal splendour, nor of the group identity of the chivalric brotherhood or for the most part of chivalric idealism. Kings in these romances are rarely admirable and the heroes of Anglo-Norman romance are more likely to challenge kingship than embody it. There are a plethora of mini-kings in *Waldef*, mostly treacherous; Edgar in *Boeve* is a wilful tyrant seizing the hero's patrimonial lands; Athelston in *Gui* needs help to defend his kingdom and, unlike his historical counterpart, is never shown leading his

---

[21] Rees Davis, 'The Matter of Britain and the Matter of England', an inaugural lecture delivered before the University of Oxford on 29 February 1996 (Oxford, 1996); J. Gillingham, 'The Contexts and Purposes of Geoffrey of Monmouth's *History of the Kings of Britain*', in his *The English in the Twelfth Century* (Woodbridge, 2000), pp. 19–40. H. Thomas describes romances such as *Waldef, Gui* and *Havelok* as 'competing with Geoffrey of Monmouth's popular work on its own turf', in his *The English and the Normans: Ethnic Hostility, Assimilation and Identity 1066–c1220* (Oxford, 2003), p. 357.

[22] R. A. Rouse, *The Idea of Anglo-Saxon England in Middle English Romance* (Cambridge, 2005).

[23] The *Lai d'Haveloc* removes Arthur from the account of Haveloc's origins; in Gaimar he plays a significant, if negative, role: see lines 407–15 in Bell's edition.

own armies whatever the threat to England; the two kings in *The Romance of Horn* display either injustice or impotence; Fouke Fitzwarin has to deal with King John – and so on. The hero of an Anglo-Norman romance challenges, opposes or rescues the king. He may come into his own kingdom – which interestingly is never that of England[24] – but only after a career of struggle which equips him with both authority and wisdom, itself a pattern that challenges available models, or examples, of kingship. All this is an integral part of the exile-and-return narrative characteristic of Anglo-Norman romance.[25] However, in the process, these narratives convey a competent and knowledgeable grasp of the procedures of good rule.

The portrait of a just ruler is reassuringly formulaic – one who achieves domestic peace and repels foreign threats.[26] In *Gui* it is expressed through the long-established insular motif of the safe roads.[27] Such portraits typically occur at the start of long romances, describing the idealised father figures whose good rule has to be restored by the hero. So the past is a place of good rule and effective justice and the present has the responsibility to restore this state of affairs. As the romances unfold, it becomes clear that good kings are those who rule through counsel – Haveloc himself (line 750) and Hunlaf in *Horn* hold a 'parlement' (line 1366); in *Ipomedon*, Meleager's *comun cunseil* takes a month to assemble (lines 2125–8); in *Protheselaus*, peace is ratified by the baronial council (line 12319); in *Waldef*, as in *Horn*, the decision to go to war is taken by a baronial council (line 3230). There are also a number of instances of baronial pressure on the heroine to marry – as in Chrétien's *Yvain*, a useful plot device to initiate a courtship crisis – but the total effect of this is an unrelenting reiteration of the ideology of consultation, a continual undercurrent of opinion in favour of baronial wisdom as a check against royal wilfulness.

The negative exempla of bad governance are equally clear-cut. The *Lai d'Haveloc* develops the scene in which Edelsi, here the evil uncle, abuses the feudal lord's power to arrange the marriage of his female ward by disparaging Argentille[28] (line 147). As is usual with the romances of persecuted queens or princesses, there are those at court who would challenge his behaviour but here they are cowed by a display of brute force, as Edelsi rides roughshod

---

[24] That Havelok becomes king of England is a major change introduced by the Middle English *Havelok*.
[25] See L. Ashe, '"Exile-and-return" and English Law: the Anglo-Saxon inheritance of insular romance', *Literature Compass* 3 (2006), 300–17 and R. Field, 'The King Over the Water: Exile-and-Return Revisited', in *Cultural Encounters in the Romance of Medieval England*, ed. C. Saunders (Cambridge, 2005), pp. 41–53.
[26] *Waldef*, lines 176–8; *Romance of Horn*, lines 505–6; *Ipomedon*, lines 52–62.
[27] *Gui*, lines 34–8. R. Rouse, 'The Peace of the Roads: Authority and *auctoritas* in Medieval Romance', in *Boundaries in Medieval Romance*, ed. N. Cartlidge (Cambridge, 2008), pp. 115–27, traces this motif back to Bede.
[28] As Bell points out in his Introduction, p. 40, the *Lai* (and the Middle English *Havelok* after it) introduces the folktale theme of the 'highest man' to add drama to Edelsi's actions; for Gaimar's audience sufficient significance would have been supplied by recent memories of Henry I's efforts to have his daughter Matilda recognised as heir.

over the ideals of consultation and good rule (lines 347–80). There is an awareness here of the weakness of the bullied court, which is absent from the Middle English with its focus on the personal situation of the hero. By deliberate contrast with the scheming villain, Haveloc himself is the simple hero who rules through the support of his barons in Denmark (line 155). As the Haveloc story demonstrates the problems of female heirs, so *Boeve* is outspoken in its depiction of the injustice endured by minors whose lands are seized by stronger usurpers – in this case the Emperor. Here the English king, Edgar, is briefly a figure who sees justice done until a personal slight turns him against the hero whom he exiles in an act of tyrannical wilfulness. There may be no new political thinking here – vernacular fiction is hardly the place for it – but there is a political awareness quite consistent with the distinction between a true king and a tyrant as developed in John of Salisbury's *Polycraticus*.[29] The only thoroughly villainous – as distinct from weak or ill-advised – king of England in these texts is the real one, King John in *Fouke Fitzwarin*; the romance is set in the reign of John and the hero is an aristocratic outlaw setting the pace for the later figure of Robin Hood.

If kings are viewed with suspicion, there are plenty of examples of strong baronial officialdom, often holding the kingdom or the fief together at times of crisis. So Horn is Hunlaf's *conestable*, the supportive baron who provides strong rule for a weak king (lines 1751–67). This is something of a motif in this romance – Hardré in Suddene and Herland in Brittany fulfil a similar role. In other romances we find Sigar, the seneschal of Denmark who restores Haveloc to his kingdom; Gui's father, the admirable seneschal of the earl of Warwick; Boeve's father, chancellor of England; the Marcher lords of the Fitzwarin family. The point seems clear enough: such men are motivated not by personal ambition (Horn may be the exception here) but by loyalty and a commitment to good governance. The wise ruler values and consults them.

The historical romances may present an idealised picture of the baronial situation, but no more so perhaps than that of the chivalric knight and faithful lover of the more courtly romances. Such exemplary history raises the question of whose interests are being served. What these romances present is not straightforward baronial self-interest, or to be more precise, self-interest is wrapped up in a larger ideological picture of the good of the land.

Work on the courtly romance has considered the relationship between *clergie* and *courtoisie* and shown how the authors embarked on a programme of education by which the warrior caste of the medieval aristocracy became moulded into the restrained, polished figure of the courtier.[30] However, as Haidu and others have noted, this relationship is complicated by the ideological differences between the authors and their audiences:

[29] John of Salisbury, *Polycraticus*, ed. M. F. Markland (New York, 1979), Book III ch.15–Book IV ch. 1.

[30] C. S. Jaeger, *The Origins of Courtliness: Civilizing Trends and the Formation of Courtly Ideals, 939–1210* (Philadelphia, 1985), pp. 234–5.

A serious defect in the argument that Arthurian romances are an idealized and reactionary self-representation by the feudal nobility is that they were not written by knights but by clerics. The cleric cannot ... be regarded as merely the knight's mouthpiece. The two inhabit a space of potential ideological conflict. In Peter Haidu's words: 'The values of the two groups are fundamentally different: we are dealing with the opposition between peace, submission, and rational self-control on the one hand, and war, anarchic turmoil, and conspicuous consumption on the other.'[31]

Yet it may be that in these insular romances the ideological gap has been bridged. There is some clerical distaste for chivalric violence and fashionable love receives short shrift, in different ways, in the romances of both Thomas and Hue de Rotelande, but the more central concerns of these texts indicate little room for disagreement. What we may have here is a rather different aspect of the influence of *clergie* on the aristocracy, a lesson not so much in *courtoisie* as in civics, less a matter of persuading the audience to be more civilised in their personal and social lives,[32] and more a matter of emphasising their wider responsibility to a concept of the realm which is in some ill-defined way larger than the possession of the monarch. So we can surmise that an author may be asked to write an 'ancestral' history, for the family or its lands, or to render the pre-Conquest past accessible – but the *sens* that derives from this *matière* may well go beyond the celebratory. This is the use of narrative to form opinion, constructing an imagined history that exemplifies questions of law and political morality.

I would suggest that the thirteenth century does provide a well-researched context for this type of clerical-baronial network and common interest, in that clerics' manipulation of the self-interest of their patrons occurs on the larger cultural and political stage of the period in the events and processes that produced Magna Carta.[33] We need to be aware of the myth, for while the Charter has become an iconic document since the medieval period, at the time it was part of an ongoing process, subject to development and adaptation. But because of its later importance, Magna Carta has been the focus of questions that concern us here, particularly issues of vernacularity, documentary publication and the relationship between the clerical and baronial.

It has long been a matter of debate amongst historians as to whether the barons or the clerics are to be credited with the Charter and its supporting

---

31 A. Putter, *Sir Gawain and the Green Knight and French Arthurian Romance* (Oxford, 1995), p. 197, citing P. Haidu, 'Le Sens historique du phénonomène stylistique: La Sémiose dissociative chez Chrétien de Troyes', *Europe* (Oct 1982), 36–47 (p. 46).

32 There is, however, a comic concern with lifestyle and courtly behaviour in Hue's romances, and some careful social observation in the contrast between the two courts, of Brittany and of Ireland, in Thomas's *Horn*.

33 For recent work on Magna Carta see J. C. Holt, *Magna Carta*, 2nd edn (Cambridge, 1992); C. Breay, *Magna Carta: Manuscripts and Myths* (London, 2002); N. Fryde, *Why Magna Carta? Angevin England Revisited*, Debates in Medieval History (Münster, 2001); D. Danziger and J. Gillingham, *1215: The Year of Magna Carta* (London, 2004).

documents. Stephen Langton, Archbishop of Canterbury, can be seen as the moving spirit, supported by a circle of well-trained clerics. This is the Langton who preached in Paris about the justification of resisting tyrants, and who adopted a rhetoric of Englishness as he challenged King John.[34] According to this school of thought, the barons of Runnymede are a greedy, self-interested group without any real grasp of the implications of what is happening. Or there is the view of Runnymede as the establishment of legal rights and freedoms by a group of high-minded barons, aided no doubt by a clerical secretariat. Recent work has argued for a more balanced relationship between the two: 'There can be no doubt that the barons were prepared to take the advice of legally schooled clerks. The notion of arrogant magnates, simply employing clerks as tools, is unlikely.'[35]

There are further questions as to the relationship between the Latin clerical culture and that of the vernacular, of the extent to which Magna Carta is itself a vernacular text. J. C. Holt is in no doubt that Magna Carta had a vital existence in the vernacular, still evident in the surviving Anglo-Norman translations: 'if Magna Carta was proclaimed at Runnymede, as it was in the shire courts and as the terms seem to require, then it must in all probability have been done in Anglo-Norman'.[36] In his opinion early thirteenth-century English is 'not a sufficiently precise tool'.[37] But Michael Clanchy disagrees (as probably would most students of Early Middle English literature), arguing that Magna Carta would have been proclaimed in both vernaculars.[38]

We know what a translation into the Anglo-Norman vernacular looks like,[39] but no English version emerged (for several centuries), because although it seems likely the Charter was proclaimed in English, it was not recorded in it: 'Unfortunately no scribe of 1215 has yet come to light who was ignorant enough of the law of the land to think that an English version of the charter was worth copying down. Writers of English were probably too well educated for that.'[40] Either way, the actual process of production is envisaged by Holt as a scene of intense, bilingual and cross-cultural activity:

> We must imagine some sort of committee sitting without the modern convenience of circulated documents. The proceedings will be oral. There is a limit to passing documents round the table. There may be too many

---

34 Hugh Thomas discusses how Stephen Langton stressed his own Englishness and how he was working in the interests of England and its people in opposing the king: 'the emphasis was moving away from loyalty to the king and towards a loyalty to land and people' (*English and Normans*, p. 336).

35 Fryde, *Why Magna Carta?*, p. 134.

36 Holt, *Magna Carta*, pp. 476–7.

37 Holt, *Magna Carta*, p. 477, note 12.

38 *From Memory to Written Record*, pp. 220–1.

39 The surviving copy, Rouen, Bibliothèque Municipale, MS Y 200, is edited by J. C. Holt, 'A Vernacular-French Text of Magna Carta, 1215', *English Historical Review* 89 (1974), 346–64. Images and transcription are also available on the CD-ROM *Introducing the Anglo-Norman Dictionary*, ed. D. Trotter (Aberystwyth and Swansea, 2007).

40 Clanchy, *From Memory to Written Record*, p. 221.

present; some will read Latin better than others; some may not read at all. Moreover, there are many, then as now, who can read well enough but cannot follow spoken Latin. So it will be best to provide a translation in the appropriate vernacular ... [this] takes us into the inner workings of the *conjuratio* of 1215, into a piece of planning in which from its very nature clerks and laymen must have shared.[41]

Fryde envisages an even livelier scene: 'a large number of people sitting round a table bellowing at clerks who valiantly included the clauses as they were agreed'.[42]

So we have a situation in which clerics and the baronage are engaged in a venture to explore the parameters of kingship, the responsibilities of aristocracy and city, the rights of free men. It is a project in which the handling of concepts and language by the clerics is at least as essential as the raw power of the barons. It is also a project that must bring the concepts of Latin legal discourse into the vernacular – and adapt from the vernacular lexical terms which belong to the world of the laity not the clerisy.[43] While it is clerical in production and the bishops were major figures in the action, Magna Carta is not particularly ecclesiastical. It is in fact a remarkably secular document, concerned after Item 1 not with the rights of the Church but with the law of the land. And of course it was condemned on publication by the Pope.

Behind these great events – and 1215 is only a moment in a long process[44] – it seems likely that those clerics operating on the smaller stage of narrative literature were also engaged in a programme of education and of opinion forming. If we place the romances into this context, we can see that this sense of urgency and importance in a joint venture is rather different from the ideological conflict between brute force and reason that Haidu finds in the tension between the courtly and the clerical. These scenes of joint, bilingual activity may be more instructive of the contexts for the production and reproduction of Anglo-Norman narrative than the projected fantasy of household minstrels or love-sick poets. Moreover, historians of Magna Carta have recognised the power of such opinion forming: 'Laymen had been assuming, discussing and applying the principles of Magna Carta long before 1215. ... The quality of Magna Carta derived not so much from their [the barons'] conscious determination as from the way their minds had been conditioned.'[45] Those historians seeking to understand the mentality of that generation might do well to consider their light reading.

[41] Holt, *Magna Carta*, p. 476.
[42] Fryde, *Why Magna Carta?*, p. 133.
[43] The English term 'utlagan', 'to outlaw', is used both in Latin, 'utlagetur', and in the Anglo-Norman translation, 'u[t]lagiez': see 'Magna Carta' on the CD-ROM *Introducing the Anglo-Norman Dictionary*, notes to fol. 84r.
[44] It harks back to the Charter of Liberties issued by Henry I at his coronation in 1100, is preceded by the Articles of the Barons, is reissued in 1216, 1217 and 1225, and copied into the first statute roll in 1297: see Breay, *Manuscripts and Myths*, pp. 44–5.
[45] Holt, *Magna Carta*, p. 296.

The very problematic qualities of Magna Carta as an iconic text support this – the parochial concerns, the sense that behind every clause there lies not a legal principle but a story, and the very voicing of some of the concerns that are already expressed in the romances. For example, the scene in *Boeve* where the king relinquishes his right to levy payment from an heir who inherited as a minor (lines 2430–6) provides a dramatic cameo relating to Item 3, just as Item 6 on the disparagement of heirs places Edelsi in the *Lai* as a tyrannical ruler. Item 39 demanding protection from exile has obvious resonance in the many tales of exiled heirs. Item 41, on the free movement of merchants, arises from a series of long-lasting grievances,[46] an awareness of which may explain the unique formulation of the 'via regia' trope in the Middle English *Havelok* (lines 51–8). Moreover, Magna Carta is itself aspirational, even romantic, in that it follows the romance trajectory of addressing grievances, restoring justice and aspiring to a state that restores and exceeds the originary golden age – that is what gives it its impact.[47]

The focus on issues of good governance, of public life, that characterises these romances goes some way to account for the sense that they do not have the concern with, or appeal to, female audiences which makes the romance genre important in the literary history of gender. For better or for worse, public affairs in medieval England were primarily a masculine area and it is quite consistent with the situation of authors and patrons proposed here that the Anglo-Norman romances should not be too concerned with emotional adventures or even spiritual crises, as are the romances of France and the later Middle English romances.

The events and concerns of the thirteenth century thus provide a context for the continuing relevance of the type of historical romance established in the last quarter of the twelfth century. In this we can recognise the agency of the clerical authors even if we rarely know more than their names. A lively clerical culture is at the heart of this – the ideas, the expression of them, the sense of history, of moving between Latin and the vernacular, their ironic or moralistic detachment from the misleading glamour of kingship – and looking to the English past for inspiration and precedent. What the evidence of the surviving romances indicates is that they saw history, in particular the history of England, as providing a legendary space for developing these ideas, for holding up a mirror in which their patrons and their families would see themselves embedded in the history of their lands and the larger realm, would see themselves engaged in defining and supporting good rule.

There is a larger issue here for the study of romance and indeed other genres. Why are we so dismissive of clerical culture? We do pay attention to named individuals, who often come across as colourful and interesting characters – Walter Map, Gerald of Wales, Hue de Rotelande – and we do find

---

46 See Holt, *Magna Carta*, pp. 290–1, 337.
47 Fryde remarks: 'Innovative and idealistic elements ... trial by peers and the right of freedom of movement ... are breathtakingly utopian' (*Why Magna Carta?*, p.135).

recognition of named, if otherwise invisible, individuals such as the author of *The Destruction of Troy*.[48] But by comparison with the interest lavished on audiences, patrons and women, the clerical writers as a group seem to suffer from the Victorian disapproval of 'monkish writers'. On the other hand, the appearance of the lay author, even Thomas Chestre, is greeted with enthusiasm, although Clanchy shows how slippery this distinction can be.[49] It is odd that academics and scholars tend to identify with the sporty types rather than the bookish ones. We should give more credit to the activities of the clerical author with secular interests.

I would suggest that we look again at our tendency to divide romances – Middle English even more than Anglo-Norman – into the popular and its 'other', the courtly.[50] There is a bookish quality about some of the Middle English anonymous romances which needs to be recognised as expanding any notion of the popular. It may be that we should have a third category – always recognising the porous boundaries between them – beside courtly and popular, that of clerical. Such a grouping does not mean ecclesiastical or pious. It does mean literate, confident of its audience and inter-textual. The authors may never be known or named but they have an authorial presence and a consciousness of the power of fiction.

The early thirteenth-century context is, I have suggested here, special and particular in its overlapping of narrative writing in both the vernaculars of medieval England and in its bringing together the interests of the knightly and the clerical groups. The ownership of England's past is shared between the patrons, with their vested interest in ancestry and lands, and the literate clerics, for whom such history provides a model and a mirror for developing the ethical values of the present.

---

[48] The author of *The Gest Historiale of the Destruction of Troy* was identified as a John Clerk of Whalley in Lancashire by T. Turville-Petre; 'The Author of *The Destruction of Troy*', *Medium Aevum* 57(1988), 264–9.

[49] On the confusion of traditional roles and the relativity of the term *litteratus*, see Clanchy, *From Memory to Written Record*, pp. 226–30.

[50] See the discussion of these poles in the Introduction to *The Spirit of Medieval English Popular Romance*, ed. A. Putter and J. Gilbert (Harlow, 2000), pp. 1–38.

INDEX

Volumes already published